The Supervision
of Pastoral Care

DATE DUE

The Supervision of Pastoral Care

Edited by
David A. Steere

WJKP
Westminster/John Knox Press
Louisville, Kentucky

Book design by Gene Harris

First edition

Published by Westminster/John Knox Press
Louisville, Kentucky

PRINTED IN THE UNITED STATES OF AMERICA

9 8 7 6 5 4 3 2 1

Library of Congress Cataloging-in-Publication Data

The Supervision of pastoral care / David A. Steere, editor. — 1st ed.
     p.   cm.
  ISBN 0-664-25074-2

   1. Pastoral psychology—Study and teaching—Supervision.
2. Pastoral counseling—Study and teaching—Supervision.
I. Steere, David A., 1931–
BV4012.S86 1989
253'.068'3—dc20   89-8970
                                                             CIP

In memory

of

George F. Bennett

pastor,

supervisor,

friend

Contents

Preface

I have always wanted a book to place in the hands of persons entering supervision in pastoral care. After watching for its appearance over two decades of teaching in the field, I decided to stop waiting. This is that book.

There were four requirements for such a text. First, it had to contain an overview of the development of supervision in the field of pastoral care. Particularly, it should provide a perspective on the rise of the clinical pastoral education movement and the extensive work that has been done in supervision there. This meant acquainting students with particular issues that emerged in the process. How do we maintain our pastoral identity while working with and learning from other professions, and how do we engage in theological integration around the concrete practice of ministry?

A second requirement was the consideration of the context in which contemporary supervisory practices developed among the professions. Whatever theory and skills we have acquired in clinical pastoral education did not emerge in a vacuum. We continually drew upon our dialogue and our relationships with persons from other professional disciplines. We cannot ignore the things they have achieved and the particular uses we are making of them.

The third requirement was that this text present a viable model for supervision capable of broad application to pastoral work that is not restricted to a partial usage in only one or two portions thereof. It must begin with the supervision of basic pastoral operations, person-to-person, and expand in one direction toward the more advanced patterns of supervision in formal settings of pastoral counseling with individuals, groups, married couples, and families. At the same time, this model must extend in the other direction into the heart of caring ministry in the local congregation, to the pastoral oversight of laypersons and the supervision of teachers and leaders in everyday parish life.

The final requirement for this book was that it prepare students to engage in the actual process of supervision themselves. Beyond a theoretical introduction, there should be practical chapters on the preparation of materials to present, the use of the supervisory hour, and the trials and vicissitudes that supervisor and student may go through to make the entire enterprise work. It would even help to have supervisors share their own experiences and tell some of their secrets to fellow supervisors, to students, and to anyone else who wants to listen in.

It was not an easy book to write. So I sought a lot of help from colleagues who supervise our students throughout the range of clinical placements in which we teach. At Louisville Presbyterian Theological Seminary where we work together, no course in pastoral care or counseling is conducted without concurrent supervised practice. This regular rhythm between theory and practice creates a dialogue within each student's mind that we hope will last a lifetime.

This book is primarily for those readers who are entering supervision in pastoral care. You may be starting in an introductory course in the field or taking the first quarter of clinical pastoral education. You may already have been in supervision for some time and are interested in making more effective use of it. You may even have supervised others for years and, like us, are still searching for greater clarity and precision. However, the principles of supervision that we will be considering and the ways in which supervision is done have a more general application. Later chapters will apply the model for supervising pastoral care to the general supervision of all phases of ministerial practice in field education. Other chapters will address its use in comprehending administrative supervision between pastor and parishioner in the local church and the supervision of teaching in the church's program of Christian education.

The term "supervision" broadly designates the process of *overseeing someone else's work.* By the time we begin to study how it's done, our minds are cluttered with images of supervisors we have encountered from all walks of life. There is the supervisor in industry who oversees production lines and gets people to do their job and meet quotas. There is the boss at work who supervises employees by assigning work loads, setting deadlines, and answering questions. There is the teacher in the schoolyard who supervises children at play during recess. Supervision at the state prison is undertaken by warden and guards to keep prisoners in line. Supervision in the military is undertaken by the "top sergeant" in the chain of command. Supervision in the arts and crafts is done by a master who shows apprentices how to perform certain tasks and watches while they learn. In similar fashion, our parents supervise, or watch over, our whole growing-up process when we are young.

In general, when you supervise me, you assume some responsibility for guiding my performance on the job, whether I work on an assembly line or in an office, whether I am selling shoes or teaching a class, whether I am upholstering a chair or doing pastoral counseling. In order to supervise me, you must have some authority in the structure of the work that is going on. In some measure, you assign and regulate my activities. You train me how to do them, and you evaluate what I accomplish, normally with some say-so about my qualifications and advancement.

When we consider professional education, the task becomes more complex. To practice medicine, law, teaching, psychology, social work, or ministry involves the integration of a wide body of theoretical knowledge around specific methods, skills, and procedures. Supervision in pastoral care, as we know it today, is the product of a convergence of efforts across these professional disciplines to train effective practitioners. Good professionals, in the better sense of the term, are people who accurately carry out something they "profess." They can say what they do and do what they say. They really "practice what they preach." On-the-job training for them is not so simple, but it is even more essential. It requires a constant rhythm of attention between conceptual understandings and concrete practice. Whatever the educational settings in which this is undertaken, whether rotations, internships, field placements, residencies, practice teaching, or clinical assignments, the key to effective learning is the quality of supervision.

It is within the interplay among these professional groups that our contemporary understandings of supervision find their origin. In chapter 1 we trace the development of supervision in pastoral care, paying special attention to the clinical pastoral education movement. Chapter 2 addresses corresponding growth in supervisory theory within the professions of psychiatry, psychology, social work, education, and family therapy. Chapter 3 introduces a model for supervision constructed from these resources for use in our clinical programs at Louisville Presbyterian Theological Seminary.

At this point, supervisors who are working within our clinical network join us to discuss key aspects of the process. In chapter 4, George Bennett describes the supervisory contract and how to prepare yourself for supervision. In chapter 5, Kathleen Davis introduces you to specific methods of working with clinical material in supervision. Mark Jensen presents ways to work with life histories from the perspective of narrative theology in chapter 6. Alexa Smith provides a summary of student responses to clinical supervision in chapter 7, which concludes our special attention to supervisory methods in clinical pastoral education.

The next four chapters amplify particular dimensions of supervision that have proved important. Darryl Tiller addresses the use of "self as instrument" in chapter 8. The supervision of pastoral counseling relationships is considered in chapter 9 by John Lentz. In chapter 10, Bruce Skaggs describes group supervision and some of the advantages of introducing a group experience into the process. And Carolyn Lindsey presents some aspects of live supervision in chapter 11.

The next three chapters address particular problems that arise in supervision. In chapter 12, Clarence Barton and Amanda Ragland discuss the task of dealing with transference and countertransference. Nancy Fontenot examines passivity and ways it can be confronted in chapter 13. Barbara Sheehan considers gender issues and the ways in which they impinge upon the supervisory process in chapter 14.

As mentioned earlier, the final three chapters apply our supervisory model to the broader tasks of ministry in the local church. Grayson Tucker, in chapter 15, applies the model to the supervision of church volunteers. Louis Weeks discusses methods of supervising teachers in a Christian education program in chapter 16. And in the final chapter, I present research in training supervisors to do this type of supervision throughout the range of ministries in a seminary field education program.

One wonders at the outset why definitive works and clear models in supervision have been so hard to come by. This is particularly true in pastoral care, where, as we shall see, we have been engaged in strong programs of clinical pastoral education since the 1920s. Among the professions, no group has developed a more thorough system for training, examining, and accrediting competent supervisors than the Association for Clinical Pastoral Education. In 1975, a number of its leaders met with representatives of the American Association of Theological

Schools in a joint task force to study supervision in theological education. Perhaps the answer, in large part, is to be found in the conclusion of this task force that, once all was said and done, they were left with the impression that their clinical consultants knew what supervision is but thought it could be adequately communicated only experientially.*

DAVID A. STEERE

---

*Charles S. Hall, "Educational Strategy with Primary Focus on Supervision: Report of a Joint ACPE-ATS Task Force," *Theological Education,* Fall 1975, pp. 68–78.

1

Clinical Supervision in Pastoral Care

David A. Steere

In 1876, a physician named George M. Beard presented a paper entitled "The Influence of the Mind in the Causation and Cure of Disease and the Potency of Definite Expectation" to the second annual meeting of the American Neurological Association in New York.[1] In it the famous neurologist maintained that disease may appear and disappear without the influence of any other agency than some kind of emotion. So new and startling was the presentation that Dr. William A. Hammond remarked that if the doctrine advanced by Beard were to be accepted, he would feel like throwing away his diploma from medical school and joining the theologians.

Quite unaware, Hammond struck a prophetic chord in prelude to a growing cooperation that was to emerge among the helping professions during the first part of our current century. Although few physicians threw away their diplomas, numbers of them were soon to join pastors in the clinical setting, concerned to treat all the needs of their patients. The result was to provide resources heretofore unavailable for the study of pastoral care. We can identify at least three major trends in what followed: (1) the rise of a holistic and developmental view of the person as an organism of uniqueness, individuality, and worth, comprising a psychosomatic whole which invited all the human sciences to a renewed interest in healing and growth; (2) a concomitant thrust toward cooperation among the helping professions, both at the operational level of praxis and at the level of theory, stimulating continual interchange of knowledge, perspective, and methodology; and (3) a growing interest in various means of studying religious experience empirically as a source of understanding the function of religion in the life process and as a source of renewing and developing theological knowledge itself.

Within this context of interprofessional cooperation, our contemporary understandings of clinical supervision in pastoral care began to take shape. There are currently two organizations that set the standards for training and supervision in pastoral care and pastoral counseling: the American Association of Pastoral Counselors (AAPC), which was founded in 1963, and the Association for Clinical Pastoral Education (ACPE), whose roots extend back to the 1920s. It was in the clinical pastoral education movement (CPE), represented by this latter organization, that the most thorough program for training, examining, and accrediting supervisors was developed among the helping professions of its time.

Clinical Training

One of the earliest expressions of interprofessional cooperation was the Emmanuel movement in Boston founded by Dr. Elwood Worcester in 1905.[2] Worcester envisioned a medically supervised, religious psychotherapy. He worked with pastors to make their counseling more scientific but also to strengthen their pastoral relationships by deepening the preeminently religious character of their counseling. Across town another physician, Richard C. Cabot, introduced medical and psychiatric social work at Massachusetts General Hospital in order to study human responses to illness and social influences that mold the character for good or ill.[3] He soon recognized that social work in all its forms did not address the patient's spiritual welfare. This recognition led him to join others in a search for meaningful ways to offer clinical training to pastors.

Beginnings

There is debate about where clinical pastoral education actually began. But it was certainly in this interface of ministry, medicine, and social work. During the summer of 1923, William S. Keller, a prominent physician, helped bring five students from Bexley Hall Episcopal Seminary into selected agencies in Cincinnati for supervision in social casework.[4] Meanwhile, Cabot stood at the center of a movement toward clinical training that was taking shape in the Boston area. Widely known as an author and an educator, Cabot is generally credited with developing the clinical pathological conference and the case method of teaching which are used universally in medical schools today.

His growing interest in the social factors surrounding human illness led him to teach in the field of religion and ethics at Harvard.

Cabot's idea was that clergy should be trained to practice theology in the same way that physicians learn to practice medicine. In 1925, he published a lecture entitled "A Plea for the Clinical Year in the Course of Theological Study." In it he urged theological students to get clinical experience outside their lecture rooms "where they could visit the sick, the insane, the prisons, and the almshouses to practice theology where it is most needed."[5] During the same period, Cabot arranged for the appointment of Anton T. Boisen as chaplain at Worcester State Hospital. In the summer of 1925, Boisen conducted in a mental hospital setting what was probably the first program of clinical pastoral education as we know it today. Four theological students were brought to the hospital as chaplain interns. They had regular contact with the patients, kept records of their observations, read in the psychology of religion, attended interdisciplinary staff meetings, and held seminars on the interrelationship between religion and mental disorders.

Living Human Documents

Boisen himself had suffered an acute psychotic episode when he was forty-four. In many respects, the program at Worcester was a result of this experience.[6] Boisen had argued with his physicians, who viewed his psychosis as being the result of cerebral damage. He was convinced that it occurred because of some disruption in his thought world. Moreover, he felt this upheaval was inherently purposive and the flood of ideas that rushed in upon him should merit careful examination. They had their origin in inner conflict and struggle. They were not unlike the mystical experiences of St. Teresa, Mme Guyon, Henry Suso, George Fox, the apostle Paul, and others. They had an organizing function, and their end was the unification of personality, not its destruction. The distinguishing feature between religious geniuses and the insane was the constructive outcome of the experience through which they passed.

Boisen's relationship with Cabot was an interesting one. Although Cabot denied to his death the existence of psychogenic factors in the origin and treatment of mental illness, he continually solicited funds for Boisen's work. Cabot had a famous lecture entitled "The Wisdom of the Body," in which he outlined the marvelous devices the body employs in maintaining and restoring health.[7] Boisen suggested once, after its delivery in

New York, that he was interested in searching for analogous processes in the human mind. Cabot shook his head emphatically and replied that he believed thoroughly in the wisdom of the body but not in that of the mind.[8]

Boisen did. He believed that empirical study of certain types of mental illness would yield new understandings of the nature of religious experience itself. The theological student should learn how to read living human documents as well as the traditional documents of the church's faith.[9] Through systematically examining the beliefs held by individuals in their own context amidst the complex entanglements of actual life, Boisen hoped to arrive at some valid generalizations regarding the meaning of the idea of God, the nature and function of religion, and the great motivational forces governing life. Theological studies needed concrete material about human life to which classroom teaching could address itself. To recognize in mental illness exaggerated forms of tendencies present in all of us was to open an avenue to understanding the normal and a means of studying the struggle of sin and salvation in bold relief.

Verbatim Records

Cabot preferred to turn his attention to how the religious resources of the pastor could be used to help patients in the general hospital setting. At Massachusetts General Hospital, he collaborated with another minister, Russell Dicks, to publish *The Art of Ministering to the Sick.* [10] It appeared in 1936, after lying in the publisher's stockroom for months until the religious editor at Macmillan discovered that it had been published in the medical department.[11] Cabot and Dicks began with the simple premise that the authoritative human need in sickness or in health is to grow. The essential task of the pastor in the sickroom is to supply an atmosphere in which growth is favored. Whatever helping acts one performs are derived from the particular needs surrounding the patient's "growing edge."

This led to the empirical study of the actual helping process itself. Toward the end of his first summer as chaplain at Massachusetts General, Dicks was summoned by Cabot for a meeting with Ida M. Cannon, chief of the Social Service Department. Cabot had been reading one of Dicks's reports. Pointing to it, he asked Miss Cannon if she had ever read anything like it. She nodded and smiled. Thereupon Cabot added, "This is the craziest thing I ever saw. Here is a man who writes down the prayers and conversations he had with a dying man. It's just crazy enough that we had better ask Mr. Dicks to stay on here for a while. We might learn something."[12]

The practice of verbatim recording, which Dicks had developed, was of immediate value in the clinical training of pastors. The exact content of what transpired between pastor and patient was written down as accurately as memory would permit. Students in training were required to submit regular verbatim records of their work with patients for supervisory evaluation. The structure of these clinical reports has remained essentially the same and is used universally in clinical pastoral education today. The vital facts about the patient were assembled, together with an impressionistic description and the pastor's reason for making the visit. The main body of the conversation was then reported in detail, as exactly as possible, citing significant movements, feelings, and changes in the relationship. Then the recorder summarized the material and estimated the patient's needs, resources, capacity, beliefs, and so forth, that should inform the processes of continuing pastoral care.[13]

Clinical Theology

Cabot and Dicks were interested in studying the actual helping process itself. Verbatim records of concrete interaction between pastors and patients became the principal instrument for conducting this research. Any concrete helping act, whether a statement, a question, a movement, a response, a feeling, or an attitude, became a fair subject for evaluation according to its effect upon the patient. The result was a different understanding of the function of theological knowledge in the caring process. Dicks often found that theological discussions with patients took on an argumentative character which in the end brought no comfort but only fatigue and disappointment.[14] The most helpful expression of the pastor's theology lay, not in the facile use of religious terms or even in clarity of belief, but in a certain quality of thought and action. The pastor's theological convictions became the frame of reference through which one opened oneself to the patient's suffering, understood it, and responded to the other's needs. Religious beliefs became the substance of what is done or acted out in the process of pastoral care, very much as the medical knowledge of the physician is employed to inform the procedures of treatment. This was the essence of clinical theology.[15] It would build a system of thought upon those things discovered in the study of God at work. Its source would be the clinical material accumulated in actual pastoral practice.

Boisen advocated that we study theology in *living human documents,* observing how the beliefs that people hold function to direct the course of their lives. Cabot and Dicks set out to develop a *clinical theology* based on the study of the actual process of God at work in concrete pastoral efforts to help people grow. These two emphases were never abandoned throughout the history of clinical pastoral education. Case studies of individuals in personal crisis continue to be a means of research into the nature of religious beliefs and their functioning. Clinical records of the actual helping process of pastoral care continue to be a source of knowledge about how belief may be enacted in relationship with others. From the beginning, such studies were regarded as a source of theological knowledge. As Seward Hiltner put it a number of years later, "The truth about how the truth operates is part of the truth itself."[16]

Supervision

During the decades that followed, clinical pastoral education grew into a movement of national proportions. Carroll A. Wise, Paul E. Johnson, Wayne E. Oates, and Seward Hiltner, by virtue of the volume of their writings and their place in theological education, became the leading spokesmen in pastoral care at midcentury and were deeply involved in it. Edward Thornton's *Professional Education for Ministry* provides the best account of the movement as a whole.[17] In 1944, its leaders met in Pittsburgh for the first National Conference of Clinical Pastoral Training. Their purpose was to reach agreement on aims and standards among the various programs. Although differences in focus and emphasis would divide its parent bodies for more than two decades, the consensus was that clinical training meant the performance of pastoral work under supervision. There were four essential requirements:

1. The work must be pastoral in nature.
2. It must be done under supervision.
3. It should be recorded.
4. These records should receive regular evaluation and criticism.[18]

A "quarter" of clinical training came to designate a three-month period under supervision, in which the student served as chaplain in a general hospital, a mental hospital, or a correctional institution. This has been expanded into a number of institutional settings, including various types of local church congregations. Today a "quarter" of CPE designates four hundred hours of supervised clinical experience in an approved training center. The four hundred hours may be done full-time over a ten-week period, or twenty-five hours a week for fifteen weeks (one semester), or sixteen hours a week for thirty weeks (two semesters).

A Reflective Discipline

Among the professions, no group has maintained more stringent standards in training and accrediting supervisors than the clinical pastoral educators. The quality of supervision came to be regarded as the key to effective clinical learning. Each of the national bodies doing clinical training organized itself around the process of preparing, examining, and certifying qualified supervisors to conduct their programs. This kind of supervision involved more than ordinary teaching ability. It called for special skills in enabling others to observe for themselves, to draw their own conclusions, to make their own applications of theory to practice, and to grow as persons in the process. Although it was not until 1967 that the Association for Clinical Pastoral Education was formed, bringing together the supervisory membership of the Council for Clinical Training, the Institute of Pastoral Care, the Southern Baptist Association for Clinical Pastoral Education, and the Lutheran Advisory Council, this common commitment to supervisory excellence united its parent bodies from the beginning.

As we have noted, the clinical pastoral educators were much more successful in doing supervision than in conceptualizing its process in any uniform way.[19] Thomas W. Klink's article "Supervision," which appeared in *Theological Education* in 1966, is one of the better statements that emerged and serves as a benchmark of the movement's continued commitment to define itself within the seminary curriculum as well as to influence it. In that article Klink defined supervision as:

1. a unique and identifiable educational procedure,
2. requiring supervisors who are both engaged in the practice of their profession and qualified to supervise,
3. assuming students as candidates who are seeking fuller qualification in the practice of their profession,
4. conducted in an institutional setting where there are functional roles in which students can negotiate a "contract for learning,"
5. maintaining roles for both supervisor and student appropriate to their particular professional identity,

6. transpiring within a wider community of professional peers associated in a common task.[20]

Whatever else was said about it, "supervision" came to designate *an extended relationship in which an experienced clinician helped trainees to reflect upon the concrete processes of their care of others in order to increase their competence in the pastoral role.* Frederick Keuther called it "the process of opening doors and encouraging the student to try new ways of dealing with patients."[21] Ernest Bruder thought the essence of supervision lay in clarifying with students how they relate to others.[22] Klink said its basic task was that of helping students examine their involvements with their patients.[23] Others described it as entering into a "partnership of growth" with students, reflecting back to them their "real being" or serving as their guide in searching for ways of individual growth and for the development of pastoral skills.[24]

Several elements in clinical supervision bear underscoring. First, clinical pastoral educators have always insisted that supervisory reflection center on *actual pastoral work* per se. Early in the movement, some supervisors permitted trainees to serve as orderlies in the general hospital setting or as attendants in a mental hospital. Common agreement soon emerged that this was a different experience from functioning in the pastoral role with all that it represents. Supervision itself needed to address the specific events of ministry under consideration theologically in terms of the kind of "ecclesial presence" involved in the chaplain's role.[25]

Second, this supervisory reflection was always focused on *concrete clinical data.* Clinical material could be presented in a number of ways:

1. *Verbatim recording* preserved the substance of a pastoral conversation either by written recall or by electrical transcription. Verbatim writing from memory still forms the core activity in most centers today. A minimum of one a week is standard.

2. *Process recording* set forth in written form the central events of an interview, stopping short of the report verbatim. Some prefer it because of its concentration on narrating the central shifts in feeling tone and the key points in the process of a relationship, particularly in advanced training programs.

3. The *case history* became standard to most programs. This constituted an intensive, in-depth study of one person and the way the present crisis fit within that person's overall life course. At least one case study per unit was a normal requirement.

4. *Dual calling,* or the practice of accompanying a student in a pastoral call, permitted the supervisor to have a firsthand

opportunity to observe clinical performance and vice versa. The live data then became a common source for mutual reflection.

5. *Role playing* in individual as well as group supervision generated live data for immediate reflection and evaluation, with the added advantage of practicing new and different approaches without the risk involved with patients.

6. *Instances of interpersonal relationships* with supervisor and peers also became productive occasions for clinical reflection. Within the give-and-take of supervision across all the relationships of a training program, the discussion of concrete events in the interaction between persons added the advantage of immediate emotional involvement in the situation at hand.

Finally, the term "supervision" came to designate a number of different forms this reflective activity could take. At the heart of the process was the one-to-one hour in which the trainee presented his or her clinical material for individual attention. At least one individual session a week is standard in most programs. But the reflective process was much broader than this. Supervisors also led *clinical seminars* in which trainees worked together in small-group discussion to address the material presented. Most programs also instituted *interdisciplinary case conferences* involving colleagues from the fields of medicine, nursing, psychiatry, social work, and psychology. And most centers conducted an *interpersonal group seminar* or an *interpersonal relations group (IPR)* to introduce trainees to basic group processes. The task of such groups was to provide a setting with peers where everyone could deal with the range of personal issues that clinical pastoral education evoked. Here there was the dual focus of reflecting upon each person's emotional responses to pastoral work and of examining the interaction and relationships that developed within the group.

Personal Growth and Professional Training

Two issues surrounding supervision stand out among those which divided its proponents during the days of the national conferences. The first had to do with its aim. Was the purpose of supervision to produce personal growth in the student? Or was it to help students develop professional skills in the pastoral role? Everyone agreed that clinical training, like all good educational processes, does and should produce personal change. But the intensity of daily encounters with deeply troubled persons forced supervisors to help students deal with their responses in these situations and to alter some of the attitudes and behaviors that inhibited their efforts to be a pastor to others. Some supervisors adopted a more *therapeutic stance* toward their task, elevating the emotional growth of the student to the position of first importance. Myron Klinkman represented this point of view:

> To my mind the accumulation of new information or the acquisition of new skills is ancillary to the chief purpose of clinical pastoral training. The primary thrust, indeed, its chief *raison d'être,* is the emotional growth of the minister or theological student.[26]

The basic objective of supervision, according to Arthur H. Becker, was

> that of reflecting for the student—in the entire range of his relationships as observed in the clinical setting—those areas of himself and his personality which have not been touched by the faith he intellectually proclaims.[27]

Joseph Knowles put it in terms of assisting the student "in becoming more aware, accepting, affirming, and transcending in his experience of selfhood and his identity as a person."[28] In centers where this focus prevailed, group sessions were frankly devoted to group therapy, and supervision became the occasion for students to work through their most apparent weaknesses in personal relationships with peers, staff, and supervisor.

Others adopted a *professional training stance,* insisting that the focus of supervision remain in the clinical study of the pastoral relationship itself. Whatever personal change may be seen as a necessary component in effective training, it is always ancillary to the basic goal of acquiring professional skills as pastors. Dayton Van Deusen insisted that the first aim in supervision

> is the student's training and education—training in know how, methods, techniques, facility in pastoral care, and in all the substantial academic and theoretical knowledge that is essential as a foundation for the practical.[29]

Within this perspective, which was largely to prevail in clinical pastoral education, goals of individual growth are always seen in terms of the capacity to function in a professional role. Charles V. Gerkin clearly expressed this stance at the Fifth National Conference in 1956:

> The atmosphere of clinical pastoral training should be "therapeutic" in that it is person-centered and not content-centered. But to give the student an open choice to make the supervisor a psychotherapist in the technical sense of that term is to change the focus of supervision from confrontation with self in role and relation-

ship to working through internal conflicts. It is my conviction that the focus of clinical pastoral education is neither psychotherapy nor teaching as such, but the student as a person in the pastoral role and relationship.[30]

Gerkin's careful weaving together of the therapeutic and the professional training stances, making the former subservient to the latter, parallels similar positions adopted in the training of psychotherapists and social workers, as we shall see in chapter 2. Good supervision does involve solid reflection in depth upon the nature of one's personal involvement with patients or clients. Both its methods and its outcome may indeed be "therapeutic." But supervision addresses issues surrounding personal change only as these issues impinge upon the trainee's capacity to function effectively in a professional role. Anything else belongs in the domain of psychotherapy proper.

Pastoral Identity

The other issue concerning supervisors lay in maintaining their pastoral identity amidst interprofessional relationships in the clinical setting. Working side by side with members of the other helping professions daily presented pastors with theories and techniques from other disciplines. How would they assimilate valuable knowledge from such fields as psychiatry, psychology, or social work and still think and work as pastors? Moreover, their clinical methods of research placed clinical pastoral educators in the position of developing new helping theories in ways that often appeared to be quite remote from their theological tradition. Inevitably this led to questions surrounding the difference between what they did and what any good psychiatrist, psychologist, or clinically trained social worker might do in similar circumstances.

This issue becomes prominent when we consider emergent theories of pastoral care and counseling. By midcentury, listening had become the normative pastoral act in most of the clinical literature. We can trace this theme back to the clinical research conducted by Russell Dicks. Among the generalizations Dicks made about the helping process based on his study of verbatim records was his theory of *creative listening.* [31] The act of listening met the needs of patients to express what was on their minds and to be understood. Listening enabled persons to voice those thoughts which were not fully formed and existed only in a shadowy limbo. By listening, the pastor assisted the patient in a process of self-creation in which something new was born.

Dicks later recalled that, to the best of his knowledge, this was the first instance of a description of listening as a method.[32]

By the 1950s the reigning theory of pastoral care was *evocative* in character and evidenced a marked affinity with a humanistic school of clinical psychology. Three of the four leading spokesmen advanced similar theories of listening. Seward Hiltner's "educative counseling," Paul Johnson's "responsive counseling," and Carroll Wise's "noncoercive counseling" (although he steadfastly refused any label for it) were all constructed along lines similar to Carl Rogers' client-centered therapy.[33] The normative helping act was that of "evoking" or "calling forth" or "leading out" resources that were internal to the person being helped. The pastor's function was to communicate understanding, to reflect and clarify the feelings expressed, and to implement consistently an attitude of acceptance oriented toward the basic worth and significance of the individual. Hans Hofmann described the work of Hiltner as attempting "to enrich pastoral counseling with the insights of Carl Rogers' psychology."[34] To this, Hiltner replied with shock: "No one who understands Rogers or me could put it that way."[35]

Hiltner, who edited the proceedings of the First National Conference on Clinical Pastoral Education, emerged as the leading voice for the clinician's *pastoral identity as theologian.* He said clearly from the beginning that the pastor could not construct a helping theory apart from the church's theology through merely importing knowledge and techniques from allied disciplines. Yet pastors could not ignore current advances made in the psychological sciences any more than they could disregard biological evidence concerning the evolution of the species a century before. Some sort of concordat was necessary that preserved the integrity of each.[36] Otherwise, the pastor would function in separate and distinct realms, suspended between thoughts and actions that are theological at one time and psychological at another.

At the same time, pastoral theologians could not remain dependent upon data from the foreign settings of therapeutic psychology with no source of understandings unique to their own experience in the practice of pastoral care. What the clinical method of study offered was a means to become a discoverer in the helping process, not merely an imitator of other professional groups.[37] Through supervision in clinical pastoral education, pastors were learning constantly to reconstruct their understanding of the faith in the light of their daily work and their systematic reflections upon it. This endeavor merited recognition as a theological discipline fully as important as the work of philosophers, historians, or biblical scholars.[38] Its task was to study empirically the concrete experience of pastoral care for such light as it might shed on the body of theological belief itself.

Dialogical Theology

Invariably, pastors in the clinical setting developed a dialogical approach to theology that interfaced their *experience* with their body of *belief.* Tendencies in this direction appeared throughout studies in the practical field. Harrison S. Elliott, for example, led an attack by religious educators upon "neo-orthodoxy" for its "authoritarian" exclusion of the current experience of the church as a legitimate source of theology, together with its denial of the relevance of scientific findings to theological understanding.[39] For Hiltner, this current experience involved both the scientific findings of the psychological disciplines among the professions and the concrete clinical data that pastors derived through systematic reflection upon their own work.

A general concern among supervisors about the character of this dialogue brought Paul Tillich to address the Fifth National Conference on Clinical Pastoral Education.[40] Tillich was a natural selection among contemporary theologians because of his use of the "method of correlation" in which the questions implied in the human situation were systematically correlated with the answers implied in the Christian message.[41] Pastoral care presupposes theology, he told the conference, but theology also presupposes pastoral care. Pastoral care helps to develop the questions to which religious symbols provide the answers. In specific acts of pastoral care, the human situation, to which the divine revelation is the answer, is seen most concretely and profoundly. Only in such correlations can religious symbols be understood and interpreted. This makes pastoral care genuine theological work.

Tillich's method of correlation had its impact on everyone. In 1962 Wayne Oates published *Protestant Pastoral Counseling* in which he sought to derive both the theory and the practice of counseling from presuppositions intrinsic to Protestant theology rather than extrinsic presuppositions from other professions which would later have to be "glued" in parallelisms to "this, that, and the other hastily remembered doctrine of theology, like a sort of 'harmony' of two different 'gospels.' "[42] Both he and Charles Stinnette questioned the wisdom of attempting to construct a "separate pastoral theology" as a discrete theory or a formal branch of theology.[43] Hiltner envisioned a more prominent role for the pastoral theologian, adopting the correlative idea only if we acknowledge that the dialogue between theology and experience is explicitly a two-way process in which truth can emerge from either source. He felt Tillich and his exponents failed to make this clear, tending to emphasize a one-way role of discovering theological answers for cultural questions.[44]

By midcentury, two principal stances were taken by those entering into the dialogue between belief and experience. The first was represented by Albert C. Outler in *Psychotherapy and the Christian Message,* proposing an alliance between the two in which the Christian employs the practical wisdom of psychotherapy while rejecting its naturalistic and humanistic presuppositions.[45] Psychotherapy could claim authority regarding the effective means of repairing and guiding human behavior, but the Christian message would be the measure of valid wisdom about the ultimate questions of existence. The result served only to increase the alienation between theory and praxis and formed a theological "marriage" analogous to the one in which the husband makes all the big decisions and the wife the small ones (our Mideastern policy vs. spending the family budget).

In contrast, David E. Roberts proposed in *Psychotherapy and a Christian View of Man* a position of fruitful interchange between psychology and theology in which "the theologian must be willing to rethink his position in connection with what these sciences are uncovering."[46] True dialogue between the two meant that the assumptions of neither were permitted to pre-empt the other. Hiltner, along with most pastoral clinicians, adopted this latter view, calling for a dialogue maintaining parity between existing beliefs and contemporary experience which did not preclude finality of authority for either.

Pastoral Theology

In *Preface to Pastoral Theology,* which appeared in 1958, Hiltner set forth the rudiments of the new discipline he envisioned. Pastoral theology was defined as "that branch of theological knowledge and inquiry that brings the shepherding perspective to bear upon all the operations and functions of the church and the minister, and then draws conclusions of a theological order from reflections on these observations."[47] The "shepherding perspective" represented the historic concern of the cure of souls—biblically, the tender, solicitous, individualized care that the shepherd in the parable exercised toward the one sheep of the hundred that was lost. Shepherding is a perspective present to some degree in everything done by pastor or church and not confined to one of the traditional "offices" of the ministry. It emerges as the dominant function in situations where human need and readiness to receive help are the primary factors.

So defined, pastoral theology, as an *operation-centered discipline,* conducts research in the pastoral dimensions of any function of church or minister. It originates with clinical studies of the on-going processes of soul care through systematic reflection on specific acts or events undertaken from the shepherding perspective. Its task is to draw *conclusions of a theological order* about the theories that govern its processes. A certain dialogue between theology and experience was present from the beginning. "In my own constructive theology," observed Hiltner, "I would move back and forth from the most concrete material I had to the most fundamental theoretical understanding of which I was capable."[48]

Hiltner believed that clinicians could maintain their pastoral identity only through subjecting their beliefs to the hard crucible of actual experience. In the practice of pastoral care, the most established doctrines from systematic theology become hypotheses to be tested. To the pastoral theologian, they are "theological questions" that are subjected to ordered reflection in clinical material, questions to which one returns with theological answers or with new theological questions. It is the starting point that separates the pastoral theologian from all other varieties of empiricists. Research is conducted from the point of view of one who is both committed to and participant in the historic task of soul care. Neutral and dispassionate observation is neither possible nor desirable.

Two general orders of theological conclusions result. First, pastoral theologians can *identify in terms of traditional theological language some of the processes with which they are dealing.* This is essentially what Russell Dicks suggested. Trends in clinical data are the source material for a clinical theology. This does not mean merely furnishing theological sanction for appropriate practices in counseling by labeling them with churchly verbiage. For example, central to Hiltner's understanding of effective pastoral care was a process of acceptance. Acceptance meant taking other persons where they were nonjudgmentally, extending unconditional positive regard and accurate empathy, evoking or "calling forth" their internal resources for dealing with their own problems. He and others related this process to doctrines of love, grace, and forgiveness in the church's formal body of theology.[49] But pastors cannot assume in advance that these expressions of formal theology deal with all the complexities and ambiguities that exist in the human situation where they are implemented. Studying the actual processes of these relationships may augment formal theological knowledge of, say, Pauline understandings of the relationship between law and grace. Even though Paul's beliefs remain normative, it is the pastoral theologian's task to explore the way they actually become operative in particular human experience, and perhaps to discover associated or related principles. Any doctrine becomes a working hypothesis that may be verified in the form of its present understanding or modified or altered through systematic reflection upon its operational significance.

A second order of theological conclusions follows upon the need for pastoral theologians to organize their findings into some type of *systematic pastoral theology.* [50] Clinical findings must be set in order in their cumulative form. The result is some sort of system, although an open one. Such a systematic pastoral theology becomes a meeting ground between formal theology and operations. Its relational structure should be adequate to encompass and give meaning to all specific instances of pastoral operations. At the same time, it may also lead to a renewed understanding of certain theological doctrines or to their correction through questioning their religious intention in the same way Luther questioned the Roman Catholic doctrine of atonement in the light of his experience. This is essentially what Anton Boisen sought in the study of living human documents. To Hiltner, pastoral theology was not ultimately different from other fields of theology in kind or content, only in methodology. Like any theological discipline, it had a second focus beyond its own unique organizing center. This lay in expressing itself through the common currencies of the faith, bringing its contribution to the village green of theological integration.[51]

The ACPE and the AAPC

As mentioned at the outset, the Association for Clinical Pastoral Education (ACPE) and the American Association of Pastoral Counselors (AAPC) are the principal standard setters for contemporary training and supervision in pastoral care and counseling. The AAPC was formed in 1963 in order to recognize and credential a rapidly expanding number of pastoral counselors. Most of its founders came out of the CPE movement and one quarter of CPE remains a requirement for membership to date. An important difference, however, was present in the situation that spawned it. Standards for the reliable training of pastoral counselors were sought among existing secular disciplines in psychotherapy. Instead of carrying the pastoral role into the interdisciplinary setting of the chaplaincy in search of a unique style of supervision, as CPE had done, the AAPC imported existing structures for training and supervision from psychiatry, psychology, and social work. Supervision from credentialed figures in these fields was required and sought. This made sense, initially, as pastoral counselors raised their expertise to levels comparable with their colleagues in the field of counseling and psychotherapy.

As the AAPC has grown over the past quarter of a century, similar efforts to establish and maintain pastoral identity can be seen. For one thing, oversight of supervision must now be assumed by a diplomate in the organization who is theologically trained. Still, the pastoral counseling movement has yet to produce the definitive work to establish its own unique approach to supervision. *The Art of Clinical Supervision: A Pastoral Counseling Perspective,* edited by Barry K. Estadt, John R. Compton, and Melvin C. Blanchette, is the best single volume. They define supervision as the primary catalyst that facilitates integration between a knowledge of counseling theory and practice and specific counseling skills.[52] An excellent job is done in constructing the "core process of supervision" from Robert Carkhuff's helping skills of attending, exploring, and personalizing.[53] Missing is some serious effort to place these methodologies in dialogue with the body of theology the authors share in common in the manner suggested by Hiltner.

Whereas the AAPC arose to credential practicing pastoral counselors, until recently the ACPE restricted itself to the sole task of training and accrediting clinical pastoral educators who could supervise students in the broader field of pastoral care. Now a new category of clinical membership has been established for individuals who have completed four quarters of training, at least two of which are advanced. At the same time, the careful training by the AAPC of diplomates and fellows at the advanced supervisory level over the past two decades has raised supervision in pastoral counseling to comparable levels of attention and examination. Together, both organizations share a growing commitment to the task of theological integration represented by the term "pastoral theology."

Practical Theology

The struggle of clinical pastoral educators to overcome the alienation between theory and practice must be seen against the backdrop of similar efforts throughout all the "practical disciplines" of theological study. From its beginning, literature in the *practical field* which encompasses all the "offices" of the ministry, such as preaching, teaching, leading worship, and church administration, suffered an estrangement between its *theological formulations* and *common practice.* [54] Principles from biblical or systematic theology were usually set forth to govern ministerial practice, followed by an abrupt shift to an unrelated discussion of *practicalia,* or the writer's distilled wisdom regarding what kind of practices, proper habits, and personal conduct existed.

At the turn of the nineteenth century, one of the keenest minds in modern theology had the vision to attack the problem. Friedrich Schleiermacher suggested a discipline of practical theology alongside philosophical and historical theology, a discipline which he envisioned as the "crown of all theological sciences," having as its task the development of a *theory of practice* in the life of the church.[55] Its job was to state the meaning of Christianity in the moment of the historical present. Schleiermacher noted that the works of his time devoted copious discussion to details and official duties of the ministry but scant attention to a workable theory of "church guidance" as it relates to the whole theological enterprise. Practical theology was (1) to develop a body of theory all its own, not simply the study of practice, but the examination of practice according to a *theory of operations* it devised, and (2) to keep this theory of *church guidance* open to the expanding experience of ministry while standing in dialogue with the church's formal body of belief. No judgment by a companion discipline was considered absolute so that practical theology could remain unchanged before the advancing boundaries of Christianity and the multiplicity of forms it can assume.

Contemporary discussions of practical theology preserve the same generative dialogue between theory and praxis envisioned by Schleiermacher.[56] Edward Farley believes practical theology can find its coherence in his concept of *ecclesial presence.* This combines (1) attention to the historical reality of the church, its mission and presence in the world, *with* (2) attention to the normative and eschatological calling of the church.[57] What emerges in the historical present is addressed by a normative ideal. The product of this dialogue is *ecclesial redemptive presence.* Practical theology must reconstitute the theology/science of the Middle Ages that discovered how all areas of knowledge contribute to understanding, guiding, and empowering ecclesial presence. Farley emphasizes a *social/political praxis* aimed at world transformation, not a praxis dominated by the clerical paradigm of "professional responsibilities" which leaves social praxis present "atomistically and sporadically."[58]

David Tracy defines the task of practical theology as making *mutually critical correlations* between what he calls "the Christian fact" with the meaning and truth of its interpretations and the meaning and truth of an interpretation of the contemporary situation.[59] A thoroughgoing praxis of social transformation is envisioned. The practical theologian will collaborate to develop models of human transformation drawing upon psychology, social science, historical studies, cultural anthropology, philosophy, ecological theories, together with religious studies and theologies. Further collaborative efforts involve developing public claims to human transformation provided by different ideals for the future. The practical theologian adopts a "hermeneutics of suspicion" for assessing these models capable of unmasking systematic distortions perpetuated by any of them. The product of all this is a disciplined reflection upon possible mutually critical correlations between secular models of moral praxis and the emancipatory thrust of Christian faith praxis.

Similar themes of dialogue and correlation guide other approaches to practical studies. Don Browning also locates the normative reflection of practical theology in the areas of ethics and moral thinking, but from a position more identified with the pastoral context of the church community.[60] He introduces five interpenetrating and nonhierarchical levels of moral thinking: a *metaphorical* level dealing with a person or a group's operative images of the ultimate context of experience; an *obligational level* involving one's criteria for determining right and wrong, duty and obligations; a *tendency-need level* focusing on human instinctual and evaluational tendencies, largely in nonmoral terms; a *contextual-predictive level* addressing common sociological, psychological, and cultural trends that condition our actions; and a *rule-role level* articulating the processes necessary for constructing a world according to the visions or possibilities opened up at higher levels. Practical theology involves mutually critical engagement at each of these five levels among (1) the central witness of the Judeo-Christian tradition, (2) the contents and perspectives of various other competing cultural interpretations of our experiences, and (3) the consultee's own personal experience and perspectives.

What all these discussions hold in common is their genuinely dialogical approach to the relationship between theory and praxis. There are differences. Debate exists as to whether we should even "lead" with theory as in the *critical mutual correlations* we have been considering or engage in making *critical practical correlations* where praxis is not simply the goal but the foundation of theory itself.[61] Practical theology with the latter view holds that only authentic forms of praxis (religious, moral, intellectual, psychic, and social) can ground an authentic doing of theology. Some, like Farley, seek to abandon the clerical paradigm in search of a *social/political praxis,* while others, like James Fowler, focus reflective activity around an *ecclesial praxis* comprised by the traditional offices of the ministry (Administration, Proclamation and Celebration, Care and Cure of Souls, Formation, and Engagement with social structures).[62] What all these models share is their resistance to any effort to subordinate praxis to theory as in "applied theology." All of them view truth as dialogical and emergent in the present. All emphasize the critical role of hermeneutics in which practical theology possesses some means to discern and correct its own systemic distortions, whether they are in the interpretation of tradition or experience. And all originate in strong commitments to a role effecting personal and/or social transformation.

Somewhere in the midst of this overarching concern to do responsible practical theology in our time, contemporary supervision in pastoral care will take its stance. The final word is not in on exactly how this theological method is undertaken in the full range of its involvement throughout life. A personal word to the reader is in order at this point. Whether you are just entering pastoral work or have been involved in ministry for years, you will soon stand at the bedside of someone who is dying, seeking to care for that person throughout that process. And you will turn to that person's loved ones, seeking to care for them in their grief as well. And you will earnestly search with supervisor and/or colleagues for the best pastoral practice to be offered in this particular situation of life and death.

All the answers are far from in. Certainly, we know a great deal. We carry with us a wealth of resurrection theology from our body of belief, narrative theological understandings of the death of Jesus and others, and the traditional hope of the Christian message. We have learned much about the process of death and dying, about the nature of "grief work" among those who mourn, and about the techniques of supportive counseling as one moves through a major crisis. We know we don't just tell people the right things to comfort them. Hope is acquired through some sort of process of mutual sharing through which one extends hope to another by being willing to enter that person's situation fully, without turning back or being overwhelmed. The wealth of things to address in this one phase of *ecclesial praxis* can become overwhelming when we consider contemporary attitudes toward the meaning of death, ministries of preparation and death education, issues surrounding the right to die, or the way we prepare ourselves to deal with the threat of our own mortality, to mention just a few.

There does not exist any common and uniform understanding throughout pastoral supervision as to exactly how we engage in this theological dialogue between theory and praxis. What we witness is an uneasy but progressive movement into such conversation involving all facets of our traditional theology with all facets of our contemporary historical experience for an understanding of truth which never has existed and probably never will exist with a capital T. Together with this is a growing understanding in the wisdom of the years that this state of affairs is not only necessary but desirable.

NOTES

1. N. D. C. Lewis, "American Psychiatry from Its Beginnings to World War II," in *American Handbook of Psychiatry* (New York: Basic Books, 1959), vol. 1, p. 8.

2. See C. J. Scherzer, "The Emmanuel Movement," *Pastoral Psychology,* Feb. 1951, pp. 27–33.

3. Several excellent summaries of Dr. Cabot's early contributions to clinical pastoral education are available: W. A. Wood, "Richard C. Cabot and Clinical Training," *The Pastor,* May 1951, pp. 14–15; R. J. Fairbanks, "Richard C. Cabot: His Contribution to Pastoral Psychology," *Pastoral Psychology,* March 1957, pp. 27–32; and idem, "The Origins of Clinical Pastoral Training," *Pastoral Psychology,* Sept. 1953, pp. 13–16.

4. For a summary of the Bexley Hall Plan and its development, see J. Fletcher, "The Development of the Clinical Training Movement of the Graduate School of Applied Religion," in *Clinical Pastoral Training,* ed. S. Hiltner (Commission on Religion and Health, Federal Council of the Churches of Christ in America, 1945), pp. 1–4.

5. R. C. Cabot, *Adventures on the Borderlands of Ethics* (New York: Harper & Brothers, 1926), p. 7.

6. See A. T. Boisen, "The Challenge to Our Seminaries," *Journal of Pastoral Care,* Spring 1951, pp. 8–12; idem, "Theological Education via the Clinic," *Religious Education,* March 1930, reprint; and idem, *The Exploration of the Inner World: A Study of Mental Disorder and Religious Experience* (New York: Willett, Clark & Co., 1936).

7. The substance of the lecture can be found in R. C. Cabot and R. L. Dicks, *The Art of Ministering to the Sick* (New York: Macmillan Co., 1936), pp. 118–131.

8. A. T. Boisen, *Out of the Depths* (New York: Harper & Brothers, 1960), pp. 175, 176.

9. A. T. Boisen, "The Period of Beginnings," *Journal of Pastoral Care*, Spring 1951, p. 15.

10. See n. 7.

11. R. L. Dicks, "The Art of Ministering to the Sick," *Pastoral Psychology*, Nov. 1952, p. 11.

12. Ibid., pp. 9–10.

13. See Cabot and Dicks, *Ministering to the Sick*, pp. 255–259.

14. Ibid., p. 18.

15. R. L. Dicks, *And Ye Visited Me* (New York: Harper & Brothers, 1939), p. 3.

16. S. Hiltner, *Preface to Pastoral Theology* (Nashville: Abingdon Press, 1958), p. 220.

17. E. E. Thornton, *Professional Education for Ministry: A History of Clinical Pastoral Education* (Nashville: Abingdon Press, 1970). See also R. C. Powell, *CPE: Fifty Years of Learning Through Supervised Encounter with Living Human Documents* (New York: Association for Clinical Pastoral Education, 1975).

18. Roland J. Fairbanks, "Standards for Full-time Clinical Training in the Light of the New England Experience," in Hiltner, *Clinical Pastoral Training*, p. 38.

19. Perhaps the best single volume on supervision in clinical pastoral education is D. Belgum, *Clinical Training for Pastoral Care* (Philadelphia: Westminster Press, 1956). Seward Hiltner's four-article series entitled "What We Get and Give in Pastoral Care," *Pastoral Psychology*, Feb. 1954, pp. 13–24; March 1954, pp. 14–25; April 1954, pp. 29–41; and Nov. 1954, pp. 21–30, represents the best available description of the actual processes of clinical pastoral supervision.

20. T. W. Klink, "Supervision," *Theological Education* 3:177–178 (1966).

21. F. Keuther, "How Are Supervisory Skills Transmitted to New Supervisors?" in *Clinical Education for the Pastoral Ministry*, ed. E. E. Bruder and M. L. Barb (Advisory Committee on Clinical Pastoral Education, 1958), p. 80.

22. E. Bruder, "Some Theological Considerations in Clinical Pastoral Education," *Journal of Pastoral Care*, Fall 1954, p. 142.

23. T. W. Klink, "How Is Supervision Carried Out?" in Bruder and Barb, *Clinical Education for the Pastoral Ministry*.

24. P. L. Swanson, "Clinical Pastoral Education in the Institute of Pastoral Care," in *Clinical Pastoral Education* (Proceedings of the Fall Conference for Chaplain Supervisors of the Institute of Pastoral Care, Framingham, Mass., Oct. 1959, mimeographed), p. 11.

25. The term "ecclesial presence" was coined by Ed Farley and is

discussed later in this chapter as it relates to the contemporary task of "practical theology."

26. M. Klinkman, "The Emotional Growth of Students in Clinical Pastoral Training," in *CPE—Supervisors' Statements: Objectives of Clinical Pastoral Training* (Proceedings of the Fall Conference of the Institute of Pastoral Care, Framingham, Mass., Oct. 1960, mimeographed), p. 61.

27. A. H. Becker, "Objectives of Clinical Pastoral Education," in *Trends in CPE: Objectives—Methods—Standards* (Advisory Committee on Clinical Pastoral Education, 1960, mimeographed), p. 96.

28. J. Knowles, "Objectives of Clinical Pastoral Education," in *Trends in CPE: Objectives—Methods—Standards,* p. 104.

29. D. Van Deusen, "Objectives of Clinical Pastoral Education," in *Trends in CPE: Objectives—Methods—Standards,* p. 100.

30. C. V. Gerkin, "Discussion," in Bruder and Barb, *Clinical Education for the Pastoral Ministry,* p. 101.

31. Cabot and Dicks, *Ministering to the Sick,* pp. 190–203.

32. R. L. Dicks, "Creative Listening and Marital Counseling," *The Pastor,* Feb. 1950, p. 17.

33. See S. Hiltner, *Pastoral Counseling* (Nashville: Abingdon-Cokesbury Press, 1949); P. E. Johnson, *Psychology of Pastoral Care* (Nashville: Abingdon-Cokesbury Press, 1953); and C. A. Wise, *Pastoral Counseling: Its Theory and Practice* (New York: Harper & Brothers, 1951).

34. H. Hofmann, ed., *Making the Ministry Relevant* (New York: Charles Scribner's Sons, 1960), p. 100.

35. S. Hiltner, "Letter to the Editor," *Pastoral Psychology,* Dec. 1960, p. 62.

36. S. Hiltner, "Pastoral Psychology in Constructive Theology," in *Religion and Human Behavior,* ed. S. Doniger (New York: Association Press, 1954), pp. 196–216.

37. S. Hiltner, "Theology and the Institutional Chaplain," *Pastoral Psychology,* Feb. 1951, p. 24.

38. S. Hiltner, "Theology and the Scientific Method," in *The Best of Pastoral Psychology,* ed. S. Doniger (New York: Pastoral Psychology Press, 1952), pp. 72–87.

39. H. S. Elliott, *Can Religious Education Be Christian?* (New York: Macmillan Co., 1940), pp. 90–139, 161, 167.

40. P. Tillich, "The Spiritual and Theological Foundations of Pastoral Care," in Bruder and Barb, *Clinical Education for the Pastoral Ministry,* pp. 1–6.

41. P. Tillich, *Systematic Theology* (Chicago: University of Chicago Press, 1951), vol. 1, p. 8.

42. W. E. Oates, *Protestant Pastoral Counseling* (Philadelphia: Westminster Press, 1962), p. 13.

43. C. Stinnette, "Some New Directions in Pastoral Theology," *Union Seminary Quarterly Review,* Special Issue, Dec. 1960, p. 98.

44. Hiltner, *Preface to Pastoral Theology,* pp. 222–223 n. 19.

45. A. C. Outler, *Psychotherapy and the Christian Message* (New York: Harper & Brothers, 1954).

46. D. E. Roberts, *Psychotherapy and a Christian View of Man* (New York: Charles Scribner's Sons, 1960).

47. Hiltner, *Preface to Pastoral Theology,* p. 20.

48. Hiltner, *Pastoral Counseling,* p. 58 n. 34.

49. See Hiltner, *Preface to Pastoral Theology,* pp. 151ff.; Wise, *Pastoral Counseling,* pp. 45ff.; and Johnson, *Psychology of Pastoral Care,* pp. 95ff.

50. Hiltner, *Preface to Pastoral Theology,* p. 220 n. 15.

51. Ibid., p. 219.

52. B. K. Estadt, J. R. Compton, and M. C. Blanchette, eds., *The Art of Clinical Supervision: A Pastoral Counseling Perspective* (Mahwah, N.J.: Paulist Press, 1987), p. 7.

53. Ibid., pp. 13–20. See R. Carkhuff, *The Art of Helping VI* (Amherst: Human Resource Development Press, 1987).

54. See D. A. Steere, "A New Pastoral Theology: A Study of Its Redefinition in the Clinical Pastoral Education Movement According to the Biblical Concept of Shepherding" (doctoral diss., Union Theological Seminary, New York, 1966), pp. 8–20, for a discussion of this problem.

55. F. Schleiermacher, *Die praktische Theologie nach den Grundsätzen der Evangelischen Kirche im Zusammenhangen dargestellt* (Berlin: G. Reimer, 1850; and idem, *Brief Outline of the Study of Theology,* trans. W. Farrer (Edinburgh: T. & T. Clark, 1850).

56. See D. S. Browning, ed., *Practical Theology: The Emerging Field in Theology, Church, and World* (San Francisco: Harper & Row, 1983).

57. E. Farley, *Ecclesial Man: A Social Phenomenology of Faith and Reality* (Philadelphia: Fortress Press, 1975); and idem, *Ecclesial Reflection: An Anatomy of Theological Method* (Philadelphia: Fortress Press, 1982).

58. E. Farley, "Theology and Practice Outside the Clerical Paradigm," in Browning, *Practical Theology,* pp. 21–41.

59. D. Tracy, "The Foundations of Practical Theology," in Browning, *Practical Theology,* pp. 62, 63.

60. D. S. Browning, *Religious Ethics and Pastoral Care* (Philadelphia: Fortress Press, 1983).

61. See, e.g., M. L. Lamb, *Solidarity with Victims: Toward a Theology of Social Transformation* (New York: Crossroad, 1982).

62. J. W. Fowler, "Practical Theology in the Shaping of Christian Lives," in Browning, *Practical Theology,* pp. 149–160.

2

Supervision Among the Helping Professions

David A. Steere

The rise of clinical supervision in pastoral care did not occur in a vacuum. At each step it was strongly influenced by the bonds of interprofessional cooperation we have been considering. We now take a closer look at this context in which the discipline of supervision found a new place of importance among the helping professions.

Actually there is nothing new about the idea of supervision. The key to professional training in the Middle Ages lay in the concept of apprenticeship that emerged in the guild system. One learned an art or a craft by apprenticing oneself to a master-craftsman who oversaw the development of skills step by step. All education for the clergy in the Middle Ages took place in such apprenticeships where a priest in training served under the oversight of a tried cleric of higher rank.[1] The chief method of teaching among the schools of the prophets that flourished in this country during colonial days was that of placing the beginning student under the supervision of an experienced minister.[2] In similar fashion, one read for medicine or law on the frontier under the tutelage of an experienced practitioner. It was only where the professional schools achieved a more formalized academic organization within the American university that supervision as a method of teaching practically disappeared.

Several factors marked the rise of interest in supervision at the turn of the century. There was the philosophy of pragmatism, where full attention fell upon historical phenomena with their antecedent conditions and consequences.[3] The standards by which concepts were analyzed and their validity determined became their practical use and value to society. Among the schools, "progressive education" dominated the scene with its emphasis on each person's own natural progression of growth through solving problems.[4] Formal understandings of developmental tasks in learning, concepts of ordered growth through regular reflection, and theories concerning progressive learning through practice began to appear in medicine, education, and psychology. Doctors were supervised in residency programs, psychiatrists in their work with particular patients, psychologists in clinical internships, teachers in practice teaching, and ministers in clinical pastoral education. As we shall see, each discipline developed its own theory of how change comes about, which in turn influenced its unique understandings of the supervisory task. The result was the rich diversity within a common practice we see throughout professional education today.

The Clinical Context

The term "clinical" literally means "at the bedside."[5] It derives from the Greek word *klinē* for the couch in the temple of Aesculapius where Greeks went to find a cure for their ills. A clinician is one who gathers data at the bedside. For physicians, clinical medicine is concerned with the actual observation and treatment of disease in patients rather than artificial experimentation or theory. At the turn of the century, a clinical year of internship became a requirement in medical education. The term was adopted by theological educators in the 1920s to designate their efforts to give seminarians clinical experience in the practice of their theology as chaplains in the hospital setting.

Soon throughout professional education the term "clinical" came to designate the application of one's discipline within the locus of its practice. Clinical psychology meant practicing psychology in the treatment of persons with emotional disorders rather than its study in the experimental setting of animal research. Educators like Robert Goldhammer adopted the term "clinical supervision" for the task of analyzing with teachers in training what took place in their classrooms.[6] To Goldhammer, the word "clinical" suggested the "close up" or "face-to-face" relationships between supervisor and teacher that permitted them to address concrete "practitional behavior."

Throughout professional literature, the word "supervision" came to have both a broad and a narrow meaning. Broadly, it designated an *oversight* of the whole educational process in the clinical setting. Supervision meant designing, administrating, and implementing the entire training program. In its narrower sense, the term came to designate a particular part of this teaching/learning process centering around *systematic reflection with trainees on the actual processes of their clinical practice.* Supervision became the core teaching method in the clinical setting and began to develop a theory all its own.

Still, uniform understandings of what constitutes effective supervision are nonexistent even within a particular professional discipline. A. K. Hess, for example, identified six distinctive models for supervision in clinical psychology during a recent study.[7] They serve to suggest some of the breadth and looseness in current supervisory practices, not just in psychology but among all the professions.

1. *Lecturer.* In the lecturer model of supervision, there is an acknowledged master who presents ideas to a group. The goal is to instruct trainess in theories and techniques. Although the method is economically efficient timewise and a great deal of excitement can be imparted by interesting presenters, the material cannot be tailored to individual needs and personal requirements for improvement in practice. Still, modification of the lecture model can prove very helpful to a clinical training program when coupled with live demonstrations, small group discussions in a workshop setting, and various modes of audience participation that enhance the experiential dimension of learning.

2. *Teacher.* In this model, the goal is to transmit specific content and selected skills to learners, normally in a small-group setting which allows for a variety of educational techniques. In addition to lecturing, the small-seminar structure, which involves interaction and discussion among participants, is more commonly used. There is opportunity for exercises involving the practice of skills with one another and the timed introduction of various methods and techniques. The teacher ordinarily possesses both experience and mastery in the field, creating a superior-to-subordinate teaching/learning relationship.

3. *Case Conference.* The case review model involves members of a staff, often with senior staff or consultants, discussing ongoing cases presented for review and suggestion. Discussions of case management and questions involving strategies and goals are permitted in a climate of free interchange, although the goals of the conference are to help participants clarify their clinical decisions and broaden their experience with different types of cases. There is a clear line of authority in which elders or senior staff members take precedence in decision making and influence over younger presenters.

4. *Collegial-Peer.* The collegial-peer model involves a cooperative discussion among those with equal role status and position

in the clinical setting. The dominant theme is one of interchange for mutual growth. The climate is normally casual, affording a great deal of support from peers and colleagues. Goals are often unstated but include getting a different view of the case and acquiring consensual validation about one's own conceptual understandings. The relationship of equals is often slightly skewed in the direction of one's becoming more senior than the other and sometimes may fluctuate according to respective expertise.

5. *Monitor.* In the contemporary scene, there is a growing role of "monitor" for the supervisor in clinical psychology. With increased sensitivity regarding the consumer and the necessity for monitoring expenditures in third-party payments, guidelines for professional review of someone's work often accompany the delivery of counseling. The monitor normally has a conservative goal to see that no harm is done. Although recommendations may be made, the major function is to safeguard treatment and avoid the novel with its potential risks. The relationship is one of an "external censor" or evaluator of a person's work in the form of regular case review. The goal of personal learning falls virtually out of sight under this type of supervision.

6. *Therapist.* Hess observes that the therapist model is by far the most common in the field of clinical psychology. Since the supervisor normally is a psychotherapist lacking an adequate understanding of a separate theory of supervision, it is not surprising that supervision itself is structured in a way similar to individual psychotherapy. The principal goal of the psychotherapy model is to help therapists grow, to free them from blind spots in their own personalities that would interfere with the acquisition of skills or inhibit their undertaking of treatment procedures in appropriate depth and intensity. Hess also observes that a lack of good training in supervision often leads superiors to resolve the ambiguities of their task by engaging the supervisee in psychotherapy. Some trust in the supervisor, or at least the perception of this person as benign, is essential. Most adherents to this approach struggle with their conflicting roles of *evaluator* and *therapist.* Hess observes that if the issue of choice on the part of the supervisee and the evaluation issue can be successfully resolved, the psychotherapy model is a powerful teaching/learning experience in personal growth.

We turn now to consider different traditions in supervision that emerged within the professional disciplines of psychiatry, psychology, social work, education, and family therapy. Attention will be given to the way each approached the supervisory task with faithfulness to the mainstream of helping theory each sought to apply in clinical practice. The result produced a variety of emphases in the format, focus, data, and aim of supervision itself.

The Psychodynamic Tradition

There are two major traditions of supervision in the field of psychiatry. First, there is the mainstream of supervision in *clinical psychiatry*. Its structure is described in the report of the 1952 Conference on Psychiatric Education held at Cornell University: general teaching rounds for senior and junior staffs, with presentation of current cases for diagnosis and therapeutic suggestions; a didactic program of weekly lectures; the acquisition of interviewing techniques and methods of nondirective psychotherapy; at least one hour a week discussing problem cases with one's counselor; careful supervision in special clinical services such as electroshock therapy; and exposure to the contributions of clinical psychologists and psychiatric nurses.[8] Although clinical assignments moved through various inpatient and outpatient services during the second and third years, the chief teaching method remained personal supervision through counseling in which residents acquired a consistent therapeutic approach that was short term, interpretive, and oriented by psychodynamic principles, although personal analysis was not required or regarded as necessary. One of the best works in this tradition is the volume by Daniel B. Schuster, John J. Sandt, and Otto F. Thaler, entitled *Clinical Supervision of the Psychiatric Resident.* [9] Although it makes use of theory and supervisory practices from several other traditions we will consider, its orientation to the general medical practice of clinical psychiatry has limited both its development of a distinct supervisory theory of its own and its influences on other professions.

Far better known is the second supervisory tradition in psychiatry, because it soon spread broadly across professional lines. It is the *psychodynamic tradition,* so termed because of its roots in psychoanalytic helping theory where the task of dealing with our unconscious motivations, or forces (dynamics) that are outside our awareness, is central to all human change. Freud considered anyone making use of the twin phenomena of resistance and transference to be doing psychoanalysis.[10] "Resistance" is the word for that mental mechanism by which we shut out of our conscious awareness traumatic or seemingly unacceptable aspects of our personal experience. We simply don't remember the painful roots of the problems we address. I make constructive changes in my life when I am helped to bring into consciousness these repressed experiences and gain insight into how they are determining my present striving. For Freud, any technique that helps one achieve this is a psychoanalytic one.

"Transference" is the term that psychoanalysts gave to the phenomenon of reexperiencing childhood emotions toward significant others with someone else in the present. In its narrowest technical definitions, transference is restricted to instances in the psychoanalytic relationship where the patient projects onto the analyst infantile feelings of libido (love, sensual attraction) and aggression (hate, primitive rage) originally experienced toward a parenting figure. Broader definitions are more common today in which the phenomenon of transference is expanded to include the whole range of human relationships with employer or spouse or friend in which we project the "face" of someone of significance from our past onto the person we interact with currently with similar effect and behavior toward that person.

If our resistance blocks conscious awareness of how earlier experiences determine our present striving, our transference behavior toward persons in the present can become a powerful source of insight into our unconscious motivation. The intensely personal relationship of psychoanalysis both required and benefited from the analysis of transference within that relationship. Of course, this meant that psychoanalysts must establish and maintain a concurrent awareness of their own reactions to and feelings about their patients, known technically as "countertransference." Learning to do psychoanalysis demanded a corresponding self-encounter in depth on the part of therapists in training to manage this countertransference.

Didactic Versus Therapeutic Emphases

To ensure this self-encounter for the therapist, supervision in the psychodynamic tradition developed an intensive, personal relationship comparable to that between therapist and patient. In the early days of psychoanalysis, a small group gathered around Freud analyzing, teaching, and supervising each other. A strong emphasis was placed on the personal analysis or "didactic analysis" of each person, which became the cornerstone of the future analyst's training. With the advent of formal standards for psychoanalytic training, a debate emerged in the 1930s concerning whether the same analyst should both analyze and supervise the student.[11] Some argued that one could supervise student analysts properly only if one knew them well through conducting their own personal analysis. Supervisory analysis, or *control analysis,* was a continuation of each candidate's own personal analysis with an emphasis upon analyzing his or her countertransference difficulties with patients. Others argued that supervision should be a *didactic* experience, focusing sole attention on how to treat the patient, separating itself completely from personal therapy.[12] The pendulum has continued to swing between these *didactic* and *therapeutic* emphases in supervision throughout the psychoanalytic movement. More often than not, it has come to rest somewhere in between.

Rudolf Ekstein and Robert Wallerstein's *The Teaching and Learning of Psychotherapy* became the classic text for supervision in the psychodynamic tradition.[13] The authors rejected a patient-centered approach, in which the therapist brings technical problems with the patient to the supervisor and is given advice. They also rejected a therapist-centered approach, which focused on the therapist's blind spots and countertransference reactions to patients. Instead, they proposed a *process-centered* emphasis on the interaction between patient, therapist, and supervisor, with a clear focus on what is happening in each relationship.

When supervision addresses the therapist/patient relationship, Ekstein and Wallerstein pointed to times when therapists ceased to respond in ways that were determined by the demonstrated needs of their patients. Instead, they acted in accord with characteristic, automatic, and inappropriate patterns within themselves of which they were largely unaware. These personal difficulties in adaptation Ekstein and Wallerstein termed *learning problems,* because they stood in the way of the student's acquisition of psychotherapeutic skills.

A similar set of difficulties appeared within the relationship between supervisor and therapist in training. Students brought their own idiosyncracies of character and mechanisms of defense into supervision itself. In spite of whatever good intentions occupied their conscious minds, they both sought and resisted learning at the same time. Each person's characteristic resistance to supervision Ekstein and Wallerstein termed *problems about learning.*

These *problems about learning* correspond to the *transference* each student displayed toward the supervisor, while the student's *learning problems* present his or her *countertransference* to patients, although Ekstein and Wallerstein preferred to restrict these terms to their classical meaning in the formal therapy relationship. These two sets of problems are always cluttering up the psychotherapeutic situation and the supervisory relationship at the same time. There is a *parallel process* at work between the two. Psychotherapists in training may give the patient in therapy what they desire from the supervisor in supervision. Or they may read into the patient elements of their own anxiety in the supervisory relationship. What students see and present from the therapeutic relationship frequently parallels comparable problems they themselves experience in supervision. It is as though the work of supervision is with a constant "metaphor" in which the patient's problem in psychotherapy may be used to express the therapist's problem in supervision and vice versa. Ekstein and Wallerstein explain that

> the dynamics of the process are analogous to psychotherapy, where the "learning block" (resistance and defense and transference, if you will) is not to be narrowly seen as the obstacle to "learning" (therapy), but the vehicle through which meaningful therapeutic progress is made. The process of supervision itself thus becomes a stepping stone back to the patient and to the content of the therapy material.[14]

This process-centered focus on the interlocking relationships of supervisor, therapist, and patient served to overcome the dichotomy between didactic and therapeutic definitions of supervision. By addressing the parallel process between a trainee's problems with the patient (*learning problems*) and a trainee's problems in supervision (*problems about learning*), issues concerning the trainee's unconscious motivation (*transference and countertransference*) could receive attention alongside a consideration of technical problems in the treatment process. This preserved, in the psychodynamic tradition of supervision, its emphasis on insight into the unconscious determinants of behavior as essential to all significant change and growth. Supervisors need not feel they have to refer any problem centering in the psychodynamics of the therapist's own personal presence to a psychotherapist outside the supervisory situation. What distinguishes supervision from therapy is its clear focus on the trainee's change and growth in the professional relationships surrounding the helping process itself.

Parallel Process

Within the psychodynamic tradition, the parallel process between what goes on in supervision and what goes on in psychotherapy came to be regarded as a universal phenomenon in all forms of treatment. Strictly speaking, the term refers to that process whereby we are able to identify in supervision certain vestiges of the relationship between the client and the supervisee and vice versa. T. Hora described the parallel process as one in which supervisees unconsciously identify with their patients and involuntarily behave in such a manner as to elicit in the supervisor the same emotions that the supervisees experienced while working with their patients.[15] H. F. Searles referred to this phenomenon as the "reflection process," in which the therapist's unconscious attempts to show the kind of behavior the patient is exhibiting with which the therapist needs the most assistance.[16] What cannot be conveyed verbally the therapist acts out with the supervisor, assuming the client's tone, manner, and behavior while reporting the case.

N. Schlessinger observed that sometimes the client will elicit a rather brief identification on the part of the supervisee.[17] At other times, a more chronic, neurotic acting out or identification may occur. If the patient's problem acted out by the therapist also happens to be a problem in the therapist's own personality, then through identification with the patient, the therapist may seek from the supervisor a vicarious resolution. Supervisees can be helped to recognize and differentiate this problem within themselves and to use the information to further their knowledge of both their own and their client's dynamics.

Ekstein and Wallerstein were among the first to acknowledge that a parallel process is going on constantly. Marjorie Doehrman, in a classic study following their work at the Menninger Clinic, underlined the two-way character of identifications throughout the relationships involved.[18] She found therapists also identifying or counteridentifying with their own supervisor and, to one degree or another, acting out the supervisor's role with them in their own relationship with their clients. In short, not only did the supervisee play "client" with the supervisor, the supervisee also played "supervisor" with the client. It proved to be of immense value to clients for the supervisor and supervisee to work through the supervisee's personal issue in supervision. Breakthroughs in the parallel situation of psychotherapy followed almost immediately. Once supervisees resolved their impasse with their supervisor, marked improvement was recorded on the part of their patients.

There are, of course, a number of variations to the supervisory practices that followed within the psychodynamic tradition. Some of the more important ones accompanied the outgrowth of group psychotherapy around midcentury. New understandings of the psychodynamics of groups led to the exploration of these dynamics as part of the supervisory process in clinical seminars, training groups, and continuous case study groups. If, in the group experience, there is a recapitulation of our formative experience in our family of origin, what richer setting for the trainee to unearth issues surrounding current problems of transference and countertransference. In most programs of training group therapists, the experience of becoming an effective member of a treatment group came to be regarded as a primary source of acquiring skills to lead one.[19] One of the chief tasks of the supervisor was to function as a group therapist to a "supergroup" of trainees.

Although it found its origins within the psychiatric community, the psychodynamic tradition influenced supervisory practices throughout the professions. Supervisors in psychology, social work, and clinical pastoral education experimented with the intensive personal relationship it required. Among psychotherapists, the hallmark of psychodynamic supervision is a continuous case presentation of the same patient week by week, following progress across the parallel process we have been considering. Systematic reflection is undertaken upon the therapeutic relationship that the trainee presents but also upon blocks and resistances to the learning process of supervision itself. Since the most important data that supervisees bring are personal data concerning their own attitudes, approaches, and feelings toward patients, process notes and personal reflection are the primary means of presenting material. Electrical recordings, both audio and video, may be helpful, but their principal use would be to stimulate immediate recall of one's internal attitudes and intentions at the point of intervention. Ekstein and Wallerstein favor a separation of supervision from administrative roles, so that full concentration can be on the therapist's personal growth in competence. Without administrative responsibility for the patient's progress, the supervisor is free to encourage maximum learning at the supervisee's own initiative and readiness and not be tempted to "treat the patient" through the supervisory process.

Social Work

Ekstein and Wallerstein acknowledge that much of their thinking was influenced by Ekstein's earlier experiences in the supervision of social work. As early as 1930, Virginia Robinson was defining social casework in terms of delivering "individual therapy" through "a treatment relationship" rather than simply dispensing goods and services by traditional "social welfare" work.[20] This involved developing a model for one-on-one supervision to teach such a process. Robinson herself drew heavily on the psychodynamic theories predominant at the time. She recognized that a meaningful supervisory relationship demanded an involvement of the student's "whole self" which in turn engendered fear, struggle, and resistance to the process. Each student's "will to learn" would be inhibited by an equally forceful "will not to learn." Part of supervision was to help students become aware of and express this resistance. Through confronting their own ambivalence in receiving help, they could discover experientially many of the fundamentals of the helping process. As we come to know the dynamics of our own struggle to use help, we also come to know our client's struggle to receive it.

Robinson stressed the similarity in the relationships between client and student on the one hand and student and supervisor on the other. Since supervision in social casework teaches a helping process, it must become a helping process itself, so workers can experience what they are learning to use with their clients. Students are helped to focus on their attitudes in the supervisory situation in order to use their personality more effectively to help clients understand and express their own. An intimate relationship exists between one's ability to be helped and one's capacity to become a helper. As students overcome their own difficulties in receiving help through supervision, they are able to give help to their clients. What the social workers described as *problems in helping* and *being helped,* Ekstein and Wallerstein discussed as *learning problems* and *problems about learning.*

Among the leading works on supervision in social work are two volumes by Virginia Robinson, one in 1936 entitled *Supervision in Social Case Work* and *The Dynamics of Supervision Under Functional Controls* in 1949.[21] Annette Garrett produced a monograph in 1954 on supervision from a psychodynamic stance in the *Smith College Studies in Social Work* which, at the time of its publication, was the best discussion in print.[22] An excellent compilation of Robinson's writings spanning four decades is found in *The Development of a Professional Self* (1978).[23] Other important works include Margaret Williamson's *Supervision: New Patterns and Processes* (1961); Charlotte Towle's *The Learner in Education for the Professions* (1954); Alfred Kadushin's *Supervision in Social Work* (1976); and *Supervision, Consultation, and Staff Training in the Helping Professions* (1977) produced by Florence Kaslow and her associates.[24]

From the beginning, clinical supervision in social casework was marked by a strong influence of psychoanalytic theory. Its aim of increasing autonomy and fostering personal growth among supervisees preserved the developmental approach to learning central to the psychodynamic tradition. At the same time, the supervisor of the caseworker assumes final authority for the client's welfare, in keeping with the policy of most social agencies where supervision is conducted, unlike the practice of separating supervision from administrative oversight of patients advocated by Ekstein and Wallerstein in the psychiatric setting. In keeping with the breadth of social casework, its supervision normally places a greater emphasis on teaching and administrative functions and must become more versatile in its scope in order to address the worker's many and diverse responsibilities. Accompanying this breadth is the need to install a wider range of supervisory models, including case consultations, tutorial groups, peer groups, and various other teams. Within a bureaucratic structure of public casework where clients are somewhat "captive," there is sometimes a greater need for monitoring and evaluating functions by the supervisor.

Clinical Psychology

The supervisory tradition in clinical psychology is heavily influenced by the scientist/practitioner model with its emphasis on careful research and stringent use of empirical data. Apart from the influence of the psychodynamic tradition we have mentioned, two discernible streams of thought can be identified. First, there are the behaviorists with their strong commitment to purity of experimental design in single variable research. Behavioral psychology did not make a marked entry into the clinical setting until midcentury. When it did, it generated no theories of supervision comparable to the ones we have been considering. Most approaches to treatment involved the accurate implementation of methods derived from research. In supervision, as in most applications of behavioral understandings, a *consultant model* was favored in which rational understandings and proper use of method and technique were discussed at the cognitive level. Only recently have members of this tradition turned their attention to developing methods of clinical supervision making use of their theories of behavioral change.

A Client-centered Approach

The other stream is the humanistic tradition, best represented in the work of Carl Rogers and his approach known as "client-centered therapy." Rogers was the first nonmedical practitioner to challenge effectively the reign of psychoanalytic helping theory. By 1939, he had rejected interpretive theory and psychoanalysis for children, advancing his concept of "relationship therapy."[25] Early on, Rogers' approach was labeled as "nondirective counseling" because of the permissiveness that characterized it in which the counselor listened, clarified what was being said without interpretation, and attempted to help people arrive at their own solution to their problems. Rogers preferred the term "client-centered therapy" to indicate that the significant activities were those of the client, not the diagnoses, interpretations, and solutions offered by the therapist to which we were accustomed in "counselor-centered" approaches.[26] Rogers offered the following thumbnail sketch:

If the counselor:

1. places a high value on the worth and capacity of the individual,
2. operates on the hypothesis that the individual is capable of self-understanding and self-direction,
3. creates an atmosphere of genuine acceptance and warmth,
4. develops a sensitive ability to perceive experience as it is seen by his client,
5. communicates to the client something of his understanding of the inner world of the client;

then the client:

1. finds it safe to explore fearful and threatening aspects of experience,
2. comes to a deeper understanding and acceptance of all aspects of himself,
3. is able to reorganize himself in the direction of his ideal,
4. finds it more satisfying to be his reorganized self,
5. discovers that he no longer needs the counselor.[27]

Supervision in the humanistic tradition soon established itself around modeling the experience it sought to teach. Client-centered therapy turned upon what came to be known as the *therapeutic conditions* of *empathetic understanding, respect,* and *genuineness.* These were the conditions that facilitate change wherever it takes place. Not only were they the curative factors in psychotherapy, both for individuals and for groups, they were also the source of creative efforts to develop therapeutic skills. To the extent that I experience and respond to these conditions as a supervisee, I become free to relate to my clients in the same way. This involves deepening my view of the human being as a person of infinite worth, unlimited resources, and a constant capacity to address and resolve life's issues. As these conditions applied equally well to patterns of interaction in groups, client-centered therapists were increasingly supervised in a group setting and trained as group therapists. In fact, these conditions apply to all human relationships. If parents create the same facilitative climate with their children, the children will become more self-directing, socialized, and mature. If teachers create such a relationship with their classes, the students will become self-initiated learners, more original, more disciplined, and less anxious. If administrators create such climates within their organizations, then their staff will become self-responsible, more cooperative, and better able to adapt to new problems.

The Scientist/Practitioner in Supervision

The humanistic tradition was faithful to the scientist/practitioner model for the psychologist through extensive research in the implementation and effectiveness of client-centered therapy. Wide use was made of electrically recorded data in supervision. Rogers felt that only with a careful study of the actual interview, preferably with a sound recording and a transcript available, was it possible to determine what purposes were actually being implemented by the therapist. At the core of supervisory reflection was the task of determining how each response to the client can congruently convey the therapist's fundamental orientation toward that individual's worth as a person. Careful one-on-one supervision buttressed by extensive research in techniques that bring effective therapeutic outcomes governs the humanistic training milieu.[28] Perhaps no other approach to psychotherapy has so carefully documented and studied its theory and methodology.

Recently, other models for supervision have appeared within clinical psychology. Again, in each case, supervision is based on assisting the therapist to acquire more of what is viewed as curative in the psychotherapy relationship. For example, supervision in *cognitive therapy* is designed to engender a higher level of cognitive functioning in the supervisee.[29] Cure in cognitive therapy is vested in increasing an individual's capacity to perceive others in the direction of greater complexity, decreasing stereotyping, and more ability to integrate discordant and inconsistent information. Successful supervision guides the trainees through exposure to people who hold a variety of worldviews, value systems, and personal constructs, developing in them the ability to integrate and synthesize these experiences in creative ways. So the goal of supervision itself is a higher level of cognitive growth. Similarly, supervision in *rational emotive therapy,* where evaluative thinking is paramount, centers its activity in approaching the therapeutic task with rational beliefs about its processes.[30] Problems arising within the supervisory relationship are managed through dispelling irrational beliefs about how it should be conducted. Such procedures, however, are not seen so much as an avenue of growth for the therapist as a rapid means to return to the principal supervisory task of teaching psychotherapists to teach their clients to reconstruct their attitudes by determining precisely how irrational beliefs lead to failure and emotional disorders.

More recently, leading proponents of the behavioral tradition have begun to broaden their approach to supervision. An application of *social learning theory* to the supervisory process by R. E. Hosford and B. Barmann is a good example.[31] They discuss the supervisor's using operant procedures such as desensitization, behavior reversal, social modeling, and self-observation with therapists in training. These behavioral techniques are employed to effect changes in behavior which the supervisor and the supervisee have determined together to be goals of the supervisory process. It appears, as Hess suggested, that supervisors of all professional schools end up conceiving of their task as practicing vital elements of therapy with their supervisees.

As in other disciplines, the actual literature on supervision itself is relatively sparse. Several texts have gained prominence in the field of "counseling psychology" and are worthy of mention. These include *Impact and Change: A Study of Counseling Relationships* and *Coping with Conflict: Supervising Counselors and Psychotherapists,* by B. L. Kell and W. J. Mueller.[32] The most comprehensive book is *Counselor Supervision: Approaches, Preparation, Practices,* completed by J. D. Boyd in 1978 and endorsed by the Association for Counselor Education in Supervision.[33] The best single volume produced by clinical psychologists is the work edited by Hess entitled *Psychotherapy Supervision: Theory, Research and Practice.*[34] In 1982, C. Loganville, E. Hardy, and Ursula Delworth wrote "Supervision: A Conceptual Model," which appeared in *The Counseling Psychologist* and represented a substantial effort to integrate into one approach existing supervisory practices across various theoretical perspectives.[35] Delworth incorporated many of the same ideas in *Supervising Counselors and Therapists* written with Cal D. Stoltenberg in 1987.[36]

The mainstream of supervision in the humanistic tradition placed its emphasis upon developing the therapist's autonomy and orientation toward the worth of persons. The predominant format was the one-on-one supervisory conference in which the supervisor modeled the therapeutic conditions of empathetic understanding, respect, and genuineness which the supervisee was being taught to implement with the client. The primary data

presented for supervision became the audio and video recording of the psychotherapeutic process where attention could be
focused on the consistent and congruent implementation, response by response, of one's orientation toward the worth of
each individual.

Education

During the first part of the century, progressive education
emerged on the American scene to dominate our approach to
teaching.[37] The type of learning that John Dewey envisioned
was "progressive" in two basic senses. First, a primary emphasis
was placed on each person's own natural progression of growth
and personal development through solving problems and
achieving goals. Second, the aim was a continuous reconstruction of experience (education has no aim beyond itself), which
made the educative process an organ of social progress rather
than a means of social conservation. By midcentury, advocates
of progressivism were engaged in debates as to whether the
goals of all learning were the "reconstruction" of society or the
"transmission" of a social culture from past generations. Those
who stood in the line of Dewey insisted that a democratic approach to education was reconstructive.

In the church a liberal wing of Christian educators reoriented
their task around the idea that education centers in the personal
needs of the child. George A. Coe of Union Theological Seminary led others in adopting the point of view that Christian
education should be "creative" rather than "transmissive," developing new attitudes and ideas instead of perpetuating a given
tradition.[38] Progressive educators often characterized their
methods as "child-centered" rather than "content-centered,"
placing a primary emphasis on the person, the person's motivation, creative powers, and initiative in the learning process.[39]
The natural affinity between "child-centered" teaching and "client-centered" therapy is readily evident in their mutual orientation toward the worth of persons and their trust in each
individual's own problem-solving capacity. Carl Rogers was a
student at Union Theological Seminary, where he was exposed
to Coe's educational philosophy and the humanistic commitments to progressivism in the theological climate there.

Like psychology, supervision in education developed its own
behavioral and humanistic streams.[40] In the behavioral stream,
scientific supervision saw its job as encouraging and conducting
research and then interpreting the findings to teachers as the
basis for improving their work. The task of the supervisor was

to discover the best procedures in the performance of particular tasks of teaching and then guide teachers to select the most effective methods. As with behavioral supervision in psychology, a *consultant* model of verbal instruction was employed in the actual practice of conducting supervisory conferences, with no attention to developing a theory governing its procedures.

The second stream is that of *democratic supervision,* which had its roots in the humanistic orientation of progressive education. Democratic supervisors attacked the old image of the supervisor as a person whose main job is to suppress individual creativity, generate fear and conformity, and squelch imaginative teachers with an established authority, whether administrative or scientific. Democratic supervision preserved the integrity of each individual teacher, protecting and upholding it at all times. Its task was primarily to release and sustain the native talent within every supervisee. Its techniques stressed warmth, friendliness, leadership as a shared responsibility, and full involvement of staff in educational planning, and contained strenuous efforts to avoid threat, insecurity, and didacticism.

As with its companion professions, supervision in the educational tradition was governed by its own theories of learning or change. The mainstream preserved the developmental approach of democratic supervision with its stress on maximum personal growth toward becoming a professionally proficient person. Its most significant expression is found in the model for *clinical supervision* advanced by Morris Cogan and Robert Goldhammer. Cogan is generally regarded as the originator, and his thinking is contained in his book *Clinical Supervision,* published in 1973.[41] Goldhammer is better known through his work *Clinical Supervision: Special Methods for the Supervision of Teachers,* which appeared in 1969 and was revised and republished in 1980 by two of his colleagues, Robert Anderson and Robert Krajewski.[42]

This model of clinical supervision called for supervisors to go into live classrooms with a carefully planned contract for observation worked out with the teacher ahead of time. Each visit for observation was followed by a well-planned conference with the teacher in which there was systematic reflection upon everything observed. An analysis of the entire teaching/learning process was conducted in which the supervisor paid attention to each supervisee's unique pattern of teaching and to the internal attitudes and ideas that were presented, together with an assessment of the students' capacity to receive these ideas and to learn from them. The aim was to increase each teacher's unique and individual capacities to express in his or her own style a more effective pattern of teaching.

Family Therapy

Since midcentury, a new tradition of supervision has emerged among marital and family therapists. This group, which cut across traditional lines separating psychiatrists, psychologists, social workers, and ministers, united to treat the family system itself rather than the individual. Believing a linear, cause-and-effect approach to understanding emotional problems to be too narrow, these therapists began working with concepts of circular causality within the family unit where psychopathology both originated and was sustained. The identified patient or the person labeled "sick" was found to provide an important role in either maintaining stability or bringing about change in that system—or both. Cure became conceived of as measures that intervened to alter constructively the way the family operated as a whole, eliminating the need for symptomatic behavior. In the process, the family therapy movement expanded to develop a new professional practice all its own. Along with it came different ways of doing supervision indigenous to the experience of working with family systems rather than individuals or groups.

Live Supervision

Within family therapy, our current methods of live supervision began to take shape. In general, the term "live supervision" describes any process by which the supervisor guides the therapist during the actual course of therapy itself. The most common way is for the supervisor to observe from behind a one-way glass while maintaining contact with the therapist throughout the session. This contact may be kept in a number of different ways. Some supervisors simply knock on the door, ask the therapist to step out, and give their comments and instructions, and then the therapist returns to resume work. Other supervisors interrupt with a buzzer, while others call in on the telephone and have conversations in the midst of treatment. Still other supervisors have intervened by putting a "bug" in the ear of the therapist, thus permitting a running commentary and step-by-step instructions at key points of the therapeutic hour. Some supervisors, on occasion, will even walk into the room, join the therapist, and work for brief periods of time on specific interventions to enhance the process.

Jay Haley believes the idea of live supervision originated with Charles Fulweiler, a psychologist in family practice at Berkeley, who began observing the interaction of families from behind a

one-way glass.[43] Fulweiler would call out particular members of
the family and coach them to break up destructive sequences,
occasionally entering the room himself to influence the pattern
of interaction between family members. Haley and his associates
at Palo Alto soon began observing their therapists in training
through a one-way glass. Then Haley moved to the Philadelphia
Child Guidance Clinic to join Salvador Minuchin in training lay
therapists. Successful mothers and fathers were selected from
families in the community who had done well in family therapy
to be trained intensively over a two-year period to do family
therapy themselves. Within this experiment, a director sat behind the one-way glass and developed live supervision as a
means of protecting the families who were being seen by inex-
perienced and untrained personnel. The notion that the supervisor could actually break into the therapeutic process and alter
its course in a more productive direction was born.

The advantages of live supervision are, of course, many.
There is the potential for delivering a much higher quality of
treatment among trainees if supervisors, with their added experience, can guide therapy in the correct direction at strategic
points. The process also eliminates the fruitless periods in reflective supervision, sitting through long segments of previously
recorded material after therapy has gone awry and the session
"lost" in an unproductive direction. With the possibility of accurate intervention and guidance from a supervisor, irrelevant and
damaging sequences of interaction may be interrupted and the
therapist experience confidence-building success early in training.

The best one-volume source on supervision from this perspective is a book edited by Rosemary Whiffen and John Byng-
Hall, *Family Therapy Supervision: Recent Developments in Practice.*[44]
There are wide variations in its use throughout family therapy.
In the structural/strategic school where issues of power and
hierarchy are seen as paramount in family functioning, the supervisor gives authoritative directives to the therapist concerning interventions and next steps in treatment. Groups behind
the one-way mirror observe and discuss, but the supervisor directs the entire process, assuming responsibility for its outcome.
Among the Milan group, who developed live supervision in
Italy, those who observe behind the window take an active part
in the treatment, writing prescriptions, rituals, and paradoxical
directives which are delivered to the family as messages from the
"team" behind the glass. Among those with stronger humanistic, less behavioral leanings who make a larger place for personal
choice among members of the family system, the team may sit

in the treatment room with the family. Instead of issuing authoritative prescriptions and strategies from behind a one-way mirror, its members openly discuss different ways of looking at
family process in a "reflective dialogue," so that supervision is
actually an open procedure conducted in the presence of the
family as part of the actual course of treatment. The family's
responses to discussions by the supervisor and team members
then constitute the next step in therapy.

Isomorphism

Initially, the experience of live supervision appears quite remote to the other traditions in supervision that we have been
considering. Such impressions, however, are misleading. The
commonalities far outweigh the differences. For one thing, most
effective programs of live supervision build upon and continue
to use traditional supervisory formats, particularly one-on-one
reflection upon previously recorded data. And similar attention
must be given to the character of the working relationships
between supervisors and supervisees. With regard to this latter
concern, the appearance of what is called "isomorphism" within
the structure of the relationships of live supervision lends cre-
dence to the notion of the universality of what was termed "parallel process" in the psychodynamic tradition.

Isomorphism is the tendency for patterns to repeat themselves at all levels of the family therapy system.[45] A particular
pattern in the parent/child relationship begins to reappear in
the relationship between therapist and parent. The same thera-
pist/parent pattern then begins to reappear in the supervisory
relationship itself. The father in the family, for example, is timid
and hesitant to assert himself in disciplining his sixteen-year-old
son. The therapist avoids recognizing this and does not confront the father or provide support toward such efforts. The
supervisor likewise has difficulty getting the therapist to "take
the bull by the horns" and insist that this relationship between
father and son be formed with an appropriate directive to express the father's authority. One and the same problem plays
itself out at each level of the system of family therapy that confronts it.

Resolution of the isomorphic issue will cascade down the
treatment hierarchy from supervisor to therapist to family members. The same parallel process is operative. As the supervisor
is successful in assisting the therapist to overcome blocks to
self-assertion, the therapist begins to succeed in helping the
father engage in appropriate disciplinary measures with his son,

who in turn stops acting out rebelliously at school. Whether we confront this parallel process within the regular rhythms of weekly reflection in the supervision of individual psychotherapy or as it reverberates throughout the different levels of the family therapy system of live supervision, the same problem reappears constantly to disestablish effective supervision and therapy until supervisor and supervisee resolve it.

To an already existing complexity of supervisory methods ranging from one-on-one reflection to group supervision where clinical material is addressed in an atmosphere that facilitates creative interchange, the family therapists contributed the practice of live supervision in which both the supervisor and a supporting group are involved in the treatment process itself. Supervision remains a reflective process. But the interval of time between reflection and return for implementation of supervisory decisions is reduced to the immediate present. Supervision has traveled full circle from Ekstein and Wallerstein's separation from the task of supervision the administrative responsibilities for treating the patient. Now everybody involved has an active and responsible role in what goes on in the treatment room.

Comparisons

Supervision as it has developed today stands at the center of an overall educational approach among the professions that moved the teaching/learning process from the remoteness of formal classrooms into clinical settings of actual practice. As an academic discipline in its own right, supervision engages in regular and systematic reflection upon that practice to ensure personal growth in professional competence. It is the locus in which theory and praxis are integrated so as to achieve their unified expression in what the professional person actually does. The following things have become evident in our discussion.

1. Effective supervision always demonstrates within its own processes the praxis it teaches. It calls for a congruence of method within its own theoretical structure that enables supervisees to experience for themselves what it is they are being taught to do with others.

2. It follows that there will always be a therapeutic dimension to supervision among the healing arts. In some cases, the supervisor actually becomes psychotherapist to trainees, as, for example, in rational emotive therapy, where therapeutic experiences with rational thinking are regarded as an essential part of the training process, or in some schools of group therapy that view becoming an effective member of a treatment group a primary

source of acquiring skills to lead one. For the most part, the theories of supervision we have been considering have followed the psychodynamic tradition in seeking some balance between didactic and therapeutic emphases. Ekstein and Wallerstein accomplished this quite effectively by admitting into the supervisory conversation any personal issue the therapist in training may have, either with patients (learning problems) or with supervisors (problems about learning). Supervision could then model psychotherapeutic techniques in dealing with the parallel process across these relationships.

3. Specific methods of supervision will tend to embody and express the particular helping theory held by the supervisor. For example, a structural/strategic family therapist behind the glass may call supervisees out of the room at a crucial moment and tell them exactly what to say to a client ("give them my voice") to alter a particular sequence or pattern in the family. Here competence is learned through receiving the power within a system to do competent things. However, client-centered supervisors with their commitments to develop each supervisee's own sense of autonomy and self-worth would shudder at the incongruency of such supervisory measures. They want reflective time to assist their therapists to think through on their own what to do, facilitated by the supervisor's empathy, respect, and genuineness. Supervisors in the psychodynamic tradition want to talk with their trainees about what is going on inside them as they respond to their patients, so as to establish awareness of their own unconscious motivations, and so on.

4. In the same way, the supervisory format and the data brought to it are dictated by the supervisor's own helping theory. Supervisors with psychodynamic understandings want time and distance from the treatment hour in order to create an intensely personal relationship where they can explore the therapist's impressions of the patient, reactions to the hour, and feelings toward the supervisor. What goes on inside the self is the primary data. Live supervision, with its commitment to intervening in an ongoing system, addresses the data as they unfold, in some instances even conducting supervisory reflection in the treatment room itself. The scientist/practitioner model of client-centered supervisors leads them to pore over prerecorded data in careful study of precisely what happened during therapy, with a mind toward evaluating each response in terms of its expression of underlying theory.

5. All supervisors wrestle with some sense of split responsibility for the personal growth of their supervisees and the welfare of the clients they treat. Only within the psychodynamic tradi-

tion, as we have seen, do we find some supervisors separating administrative oversight of patient care from the supervision of treatment, seeking maximum freedom for their trainees to experiment and learn from their experience. Supervision among social workers normally involves administrative responsibility for the client's welfare. In many forms of live supervision, the supervisors themselves assume responsibility for seeing that the treatment of the family on the other side of the glass stays on course. One wonders whether any form of supervision among the healing arts can ever be free of some tension between the desire to let supervisees learn by trial and error from their own experience and the desire to ensure the highest quality of practice the supervisory system can muster moment by moment.

6. The continual appearance of issues surrounding what was termed "parallel process" in the psychodynamic tradition strongly suggests its universality. Client-centered supervisors observe that the more the supervisor successfully implements the *therapeutic conditions* of nonpossessive warmth, genuineness, and accurate empathy with supervisees, the more the supervisees are enabled to implement them successfully with their clients. Supervisors in the social casework tradition discovered early that their efforts to help supervisees work through their own *problems receiving help* in supervision often served to provide an immediate resolution to particular *problems giving help* they faced with their clients. We have just observed how the resolution of *isomorphic problems* in the family therapy system is analogous to breakthroughs in *parallel process* between therapists and their patients following resolution of impasses with their supervisors in the psychodynamic tradition.

7. Finally, all of the theories of supervision we have considered view their task from a developmental perspective of human growth and learning. This developmental emphasis is understood in at least three distinct ways. First, the term may refer to the different training needs and levels of competence sought among more advanced trainees as opposed to supervision with beginners. Second, the term "developmental" is used to reflect sensitivity to the process of personal and cognitive changes that people undergo in learning. We will give some attention in the next chapter to particular developmental sequences in the supervisory process itself. Finally, the term is also used to suggest an emphasis on positive growth and sensitivity to age-related changes that people are undergoing. Such an emphasis considers how therapy is shaped according to the developmental needs emergent in the client. However, the issue of the developmental needs of supervisees at various stages of their lives has received

almost no attention among professional educators. Age has been clearly established as a factor related to "felt competence" among trainees.[46] Perhaps O. H. Mowrer made the most chilling observation on this issue in 1951 when he stated he would not say that graduate students in their early twenties could not have or acquire the purely personal qualifications that are prerequisites for therapeutic proficiency but the odds were against them.[47]

NOTES

1. L. J. Sherrill, *The Rise of Christian Education* (New York: Macmillan Co., 1944), pp. 249, 263.

2. M. L. Gambrell, *Ministerial Training in Eighteenth-Century New England* (New York: Columbia University Press, 1937), pp. 101–141.

3. W. James, *Pragmatism* (New York: Meridian Books, 1955).

4. J. Dewey, *Democracy in Education* (New York: Macmillan Co., 1926), pp. 28–62, 81–93.

5. D. B. Schuster, J. J. Sandt, and O. F. Thaler, *Clinical Supervision of the Psychiatric Resident* (New York: Brunner/Mazel, 1972), p. 1.

6. R. Goldhammer, *Clinical Supervision: Special Methods for the Supervision of Teachers* (New York: Holt, Rinehart, & Winston, 1969).

7. A. K. Hess, "Training Models and the Nature of Psychotherapy Supervision," in *Psychotherapy Supervision: Theory, Research and Practice,* A. K. Hess, ed. (New York: John Wiley & Sons, 1980), pp. 15–25.

8. J. C. Whitehorn and others, eds., *The Psychiatrist: His Training and Development* (Washington: American Psychiatric Association, 1953), pp. 8–11.

9. See n. 5.

10. S. Freud, "The History of the Psychoanalytic Movement," in *The Basic Writings of Sigmund Freud,* trans. and ed. A. A. Brill (New York: Random House, 1938), p. 939.

11. An excellent summary of these issues can be found in M. J. G. Doehrman, "Parallel Processes in Supervision and Psychotherapy," *Bulletin of the Menninger Clinic,* March 1976, pp. 9–104.

12. See, e.g., S. Tarachow, *An Introduction to Psychotherapy* (New York: International Universities Press, 1963).

13. R. Ekstein and R. S. Wallerstein, *The Teaching and Learning of Psychotherapy,* 2nd ed. (New York: International Universities Press, 1972).

14. Ibid., p. 216.

15. T. Hora, "Contribution to the Phenomenology of the Supervisory Process," *American Journal of Psychotherapy* 11(4):769–773 (1957).

16. H. F. Searles, "The Informational Value of the Supervisor's

Emotional Experiences," in *Collected Papers on Schizophrenia and Related Subjects,* by H. F. Searles (New York: International Universities Press, 1965), pp. 157–176.

17. N. Schlessinger, "Supervision of Psychotherapy," *Archives of General Psychiatry* 15(2):129–134 (1966).

18. Doehrman, "Parallel Processes in Supervision and Psychotherapy."

19. R. R. Dies, "Group Psychotherapy: Training in Supervision," in Hess, *Psychotherapy Supervision,* pp. 337–366.

20. V. Robinson, *A Changing Psychology in Social Work* (Chapel Hill, N.C.: University of North Carolina Press, 1930), p. 4.

21. V. Robinson, *Supervision in Social Case Work* (Chapel Hill, N.C.: University of North Carolina Press, 1936); and idem, *The Dynamics of Supervision Under Functional Controls* (Philadelphia: University of Pennsylvania Press, 1949).

22. A. M. Garrett, "Learning Through Supervision," *Smith College Studies in Social Work,* Feb. 1954, pp. 3–109.

23. V. Robinson, *The Development of a Professional Self: Teaching and Learning in Professional Helping Processes, Selected Writings, 1930–1968* (New York: AMS Press, 1978).

24. M. Williamson, *Supervision: New Patterns and Processes* (New York: Association Press, 1961); C. Towle, *The Learner in Education for the Professions: As Seen in Education for Social Work* (Chicago: University of Chicago Press, 1954); A. Kadushin, *Supervision in Social Work* (New York: Columbia University Press, 1976); and F. W. Kaslow and associates, *Supervision, Consultation, and Staff Training in the Helping Professions* (San Francisco: Jossey-Bass, 1977).

25. C. R. Rogers, *The Clinical Treatment of the Problem Child* (Boston: Houghton Mifflin Co., 1939).

26. C. R. Rogers, *Client-centered Therapy: Its Current Practice, Implications, and Theory* (New York: Houghton Mifflin Co., 1951).

27. C. R. Rogers and R. J. Becker, "A Basic Orientation for Counseling," *Pastoral Psychology,* Feb. 1950, pp. 33–34.

28. See C. R. Rogers and R. F. Dymond, eds., *Psychotherapy in Personality Change* (Chicago: University of Chicago Press, 1954), for a presentation of coordinated research studies in the client-centered approach.

29. D. H. Blocker, "Toward a Cognitive Developmental Approach to Counseling Supervision," *The Counseling Psychologist* 11(1):27–34 (1983).

30. R. L. Wessler and A. Ellis, "Supervision in Counseling: Rational Emotive Therapy," *The Counseling Psychologist* 11(1):43–49 (1983).

31. R. E. Hosford and B. Barmann, "A Social Learning Approach to Counselor Supervision," *The Counseling Psychologist* 11(1):51–58 (1983).

32. B. L. Kell and W. J. Mueller, *Impact and Change: A Study of Counsel-*

ing Relationships (New York: Appleton-Century-Crofts, 1966); and idem, *Coping with Conflict: Supervising Counselors and Psychotherapists* (Englewood Cliffs, N.J.: Prentice-Hall, 1972).

33. J. D. Boyd and others, *Counselor Supervision: Approaches, Preparation, Practices* (Muncie, Ind.: Accelerated Development, 1978).

34. See n. 7.

35. C. Loganville, E. Hardy, and U. Delworth, "Supervision: A Conceptual Model," *The Counseling Psychologist,* 10(1):3–42 (1982).

36. C. D. Stoltenberg and U. Delworth, *Supervising Counselors and Therapists: A Developmental Approach* (San Francisco: Jossey-Bass, 1987).

37. See Dewey, *Democracy in Education;* and T. Brameld, *Patterns of Educational Philosophy* (New York: World Book Co., 1950), pp. 89–208, for a summary of progressivism under the rubric of reconstructionism which developed from it.

38. G. A. Coe, *What Is Christian Education?* (New York: Charles Scribner's Sons, 1929), pp. 46–59.

39. O. H. Smith, W. O. Stanley, and J. H. Shores, *Fundamentals of Curriculum Development* (New York: Harcourt, Brace & World, 1950), pp. 548–560.

40. R. L. Mosher and D. E. Purpel, *Supervision: The Reluctant Profession* (Boston: Houghton Mifflin Co., 1972), pp. 15–17.

41. M. L. Cogan, *Clinical Supervision* (Boston: Houghton Mifflin Co., 1973).

42. Compare R. Goldhammer, R. H. Anderson, and R. J. Krajewski, *Clinical Supervision: Special Methods for the Supervision of Teachers,* 2nd ed. (New York: Holt, Rinehart & Winston, 1980).

43. R. Simon, "Behind the One-Way Mirror: An Interview with Jay Haley," *The Family Therapy Networker,* Sept.–Oct. 1982, pp. 18–25, 28, 29, 58, 59.

44. R. Whiffen and J. Byng-Hall, eds., *Family Therapy Supervision: Recent Developments in Practice* (London: Grune & Stratton, 1982).

45. E. A. Carter, "Supervisory Discussion in the Presence of the Family," in Whiffin and Byng-Hall, *Family Therapy Supervision,* pp. 69–90.

46. See J. R. Bradley and J. K. Olson, "Training Factors Influencing Felt Psychotherapeutic Competency of Psychology Trainees," *Professional Psychology* 11:930–934 (1980).

47. O. H. Mowrer, "Training in Psychotherapy," *Journal of Consulting Psychology* 15:276 (1951).

3

A Model
for Supervision

David A. Steere

We turn our attention now to constructing a viable model for supervision in pastoral care. In rudimentary form, such a model took shape by the mid-1960s when some experience of personal supervision became a requirement of all courses in pastoral care at Louisville Presbyterian Theological Seminary. Although our understandings of this model have deepened and expanded across the years, the basic principles have not changed. Whether we are reflecting upon an initial pastoral visit in the home or the twenty-third session of a formal counseling relationship, good supervision is essentially the same.

We have experimented with this model in a variety of settings and situations. It can be taught in introductory courses in pastoral care. It easily encompasses the type of supervision we do in courses on pastoral counseling with individuals and groups. It is readily applicable to the procedures of live supervision in teaching both group psychotherapy and marital and family therapy at an advanced level. And, as will be seen in chapter 17, it can be used to train pastors in a field education program to supervise their students' activities in preaching, the leading of worship, administration, Christian education, basic pastoral care, and social action.

Basic Supervisory Processes

When you enter supervision, you are forming a significant set of relationships with your supervisor, your peers, and the persons to whom you minister. Of course, your supervisor will show you how to do a number of things and will offer advice or suggestions about how to improve your work at important points. But by now it is clear that we are after much more than that. We are interested in creating a climate in which you can grow as a person. We want to develop lasting patterns of reflection and consultation. We want to teach a way of thinking and learning from your experience that will last a lifetime.

Definition

For purposes of definition, supervision is an extended relationship in which supervisor and supervisees agree to meet at regular intervals for systematic reflection upon the concrete practice of pastoral care in which supervisees are engaged in order to focus all available resources on each supervisee's personal growth in the pastoral role. The terms of this definition bear some explanation.

1. Supervision is conducted through an *extended relationship* that develops across time. It is not a one-shot affair, as consultation sometimes is. You benefit through regular engagement in its processes. There is a cumulative effect as you learn to use it, which increases over time and experience.

2. Supervision proceeds through *mutual agreement.* Its success is dependent upon both the supervisor and the supervisee committing themselves to its disciplined reflection. Your own involvement begins with establishing a series of contracts with your supervisor, which we will discuss later. Some define supervision as a continuous relationship with an organizational superior, reserving the term "consultation" for voluntary conferences among peers.[1] We do not believe the process is so restricted. For years, the clinical staff at the seminary have engaged in mutual group supervision to enhance their skills in working with students. Colleagues may agree on periods of time to fulfill the supervisory role with one another. But the commitment, once made, follows the clear lines of its discipline and is not left to happenstance moments of casual contact.

3. Supervision involves *systematic reflection* upon the *concrete practice of pastoral care.* You agree to present actual events from your pastoral care or counseling as clearly and precisely as you can. There are many ways to do this. They range from simple recall and reconstruction of what went on to the preparation of verbatim records, process notes, case studies, or audio and video tape recordings of your work. You may even present through role play or receive live supervision as your supervisor accompanies you in visitation, sits with you when you counsel, or observes from behind a one-way glass. Whatever the case,

supervision undertakes systematic reflection upon your concrete practice. When selecting a particular case to write up and bring to supervision, you may choose what we call a "golden egg," an instance where everything went the way you wanted it to. Or you may present an instance where you felt baffled, inadequate, or at a loss for a good way to respond. The latter is often the more productive situation from which to learn.

4. The supervisory conversation *focuses all available resources* upon understanding what transpired in the sample of practice presented. Of course, we will always have an eye on how it can be done better. But we are more interested in focusing the full resources of a theological education upon understanding what went on, because this lies at the center of our professional growth. We have discussed the development of these resources throughout the clinical pastoral education movement. Broadly speaking, they constitute the best conceptual understandings available to supervisor and student from the range of theological knowledge they share on the one hand and their knowledge of such human sciences as psychology, sociology, and anthropology on the other. The notion of *shared availability* between supervisor and student is crucial to the process. Both parties must possess conceptual tools, with sufficient mastery of their meaning and relevance to make them usable in concrete applications to practice.

5. These *conceptual tools* arrange themselves logically into two distinct orders: *(a)* theoretical constructs about the nature of pastoral care and the beliefs that govern it and *(b)* methodological principles having to do with specific techniques and operations that implement this care effectively. In the clinical method of study, any theory or belief about the helping process is subjected to the hard crucible of actual experience. Not only do our beliefs shape our practice but our practice reshapes our beliefs. Supervision cannot impart all the information necessary for understanding the resources it employs. It must rely on the larger educational context for this. Thus, as your conceptual resources increase with seasoned learning, experience, and use, so will the depth of your experience in supervision.

6. The aim of supervision is *personal growth in the pastoral role.* The words here are carefully chosen. As in all good education, personal growth is an important goal. You cannot engage in such close reflection upon your efforts to care for others without wrestling with personal changes in your own attitudes and behavior. Whatever these changes, supervision concentrates on your making them in your professional role as pastor. Many of the procedures in good supervision model the basic helping

processes they seek to teach. Skilled supervisors often function like good pastors and counselors. They stimulate self-awareness in their supervisees, encourage them to struggle with their internal conflicts as they work with others, and help them to make connections between what they are experiencing in the pastoral role and the way they relate to others throughout their lives. Specific techniques in good supervision are often indistinguishable from those in good counseling or psychotherapy. But their focus is always on personal development in the pastoral role, not on life in general outside professional relationships.

Three Clinical Poles

Our original model established the boundaries of supervisory reflection around three clinical poles in pastoral care. We were indebted to Seward Hiltner for suggesting them: the *pastor,* the *parishioner,* and the *relationship.* [2] The model itself, shown in Figure 3-1, was developed to describe supervision in the CPE setting.[3] It was soon applied to the full range of helping processes throughout pastoral care and counseling.

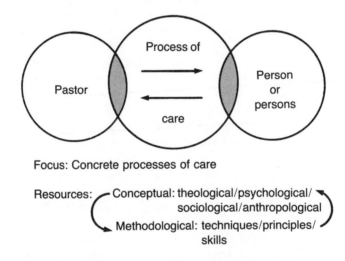

Figure 3-1. The Focus of Supervision

The focus of the supervisory conversation is clearly on the *helping relationship* itself. This is represented by the larger circle in the center which encompasses everything that goes on in a particular process of pastoral care, exchange by exchange, transaction by transaction. Whatever lies within its boundaries is germane to and admissible within supervisory reflection. Of necessity, this involves some attention to the other two clinical poles, the pastor and the person or persons receiving care.

To understand fully what happens in one of your pastoral relationships, we must know something about what goes on inside you. What attitudes, intentions, beliefs, and behaviors influence your participation? If you stand in the emergency room beside an accident victim who is dying, whatever goes on within the chemistry of your own thoughts and feelings is important data for understanding your responses. What attitudes and beliefs do you bring to this situation? How have your own life experiences affected your perceptions? What can we learn from your behavior that will be helpful in such ministry in the future?

Effective supervision will address any issue from your personal experience that this particular helping process draws within the circumference of attention. The shaded elliptical portion of the circle standing for *the pastor* that overlaps a portion of the larger circle designating *the process of care* represents that part of your personal life which impinges upon this particular pastoral event. It belongs within the boundaries of the supervisory conversation. Other matters from your personal life in general do not and would receive attention only within the domain of counseling or psychotherapy.

By the same token, it becomes necessary to concentrate attention upon the *parishioner pole* in order to understand the history, attitudes, beliefs, intentions, and behaviors of the person or persons receiving care. Only consider how much difference it would make to your ministry with the accident victim if you knew this person previously and shared something of this individual's sense of meaning and purpose in life. Otherwise, you depend solely on what general knowledge we have of personal crises, death and near-death experiences, and human responses in such circumstances. The elliptical section of the circle standing for the *person or persons receiving care* that overlaps the larger circle representing the helping process itself designates what supervision must determine about these persons in order to develop theoretical and methodological skills in extending care to them. Research in general about the character of these persons' lives and the events that make them up belongs within the domain of formal psychological, sociological, and anthropological disciplines of study, and not supervision per se.

We cannot overemphasize the importance of the circular character of learning as you develop your conceptual and methodological resources under supervision. Increasingly, you learn to say what you do and do what you say. The theoretical knowledge you profess finds immediate expression in your *professional* skill and vice versa. Each continually reshapes the other as a certain integrity grows deep within.

Structuring the Experience

There is an inescapable tension in supervision associated with what M. J. Roich described as the "up down factor."[4] Your supervisor will evaluate your work. This invariably involves some say-so about grades, advancement, and professional credentials. This authority is normally buttressed by more extensive experience and mastery of the field. The task of evaluating your performance is there from the beginning and will occupy full attention at the end. Attempts to downplay its significance or pretend it will not happen cast a pall of denial over the whole process. In good supervision, nothing in this final evaluation comes as a surprise. It is conducted in terms of clear contracts established by mutual agreement at the outset.

Supervisory Contracts

Careful discussion of the elements that go into the supervisory contract is amazingly scant throughout the professional literature. Robert Goldhammer is unusually lucid in setting forth the kind of contractual agreements that exist between observing supervisors and teachers whose classrooms are to be visited.[5] G. I. Hunter has done a good job of describing the development of particular "learning covenants" for supervisory conferences in field education, once one's goals and objectives for training in ministry have been clarified.[6] We have found Eric Berne's distinction between administrative, professional, and psychological contracts particularly helpful in considering how to structure the supervisory experience.[7]

1. *Administrative contracts* define the overall responsibilities of each supervisee. They specify regular duties, the number of hours, the schedule of meetings, the type of reports submitted, and so forth. The more precise these contracts are in terms of when, where, and how much, the better. They are normally written out in course requirements, schedules, and job descriptions. Examples: *(a)* Make pastoral visits to eleven shut-ins once each month throughout the fall. *(b)* Present five verbatim records of pastoral conversations in sufficient copies for your supervisory group for reflection during the semester.

2. *Professional contracts* have to do with particular competencies targeted for each supervisee to learn. The more that supervision can be focused on acquiring specific skills both at the theoretical

level of conceptualizing the helping process and at the clinical level of concrete practice, the better. Professional contracts need to be kept simple and definite in order to be effective. They are normally negotiated to express both the expectations of the supervisor and the particular needs of the student, with opportunities for revision as they go along. The manner in which their achievement may be accurately evaluated is of paramount importance. Examples: *(a)* Make an assessment of the spiritual resources of two hospitalized parishioners visited during the semester in terms of faith stage theory. *(b)* Develop at least three new styles of initiating conversation with persons who are unresponsive and noncommunicative.

Specific contracts for personal change become a regular part of professional contracting. Invariably, supervision unearths something about ourselves that we need to change in order to be more effective. As we become seasoned in using supervision, we readily identify recurrent patterns within ourselves that inhibit the full use of our resources in helping others. Contracts for personal change should be simple, precise, and memorable so as to keep our attention on them throughout supervision. Although these changes often carry over outside our pastoral work, the model we have presented firmly focuses the attention of supervisory conversation upon these professional relationships. I think of a current female supervisee with extensive experience in public speaking who, when threatened, tends to start talking. We came to characterize this tendency, which appeared throughout her counseling, with the adage: "When in doubt, teach." Her current change contract in supervision is "to stop teaching and respond to what the other person is saying and doing."

3. *Psychological contracts* concern the personal needs of both parties involved in supervision and how these needs will be met. We may or may not be aware of them. When formulated verbally, they express in concrete terms what I need from you and what you need from me in order for us to work effectively together. When left unexamined and unacknowledged, they often emerge to disestablish the working alliance of supervision. Effective psychological contracts follow upon candid discussion of anything getting in the way of effective teamwork in the supervisory relationship between supervisor and student or between peers. For example, as the supervisor, I found myself engaged in what seemed to be excessive questioning of the female supervisee mentioned above about her responses to various aspects of her graduate training program in pastoral counseling. She in turn seemed to remain unduly "pleasant" and "anxious."

Through discussing the character of our relationship, we unearthed the hidden contract that she was supposed to be "nice and complimentary to teacher," while I was supposed to be suspicious and mistrustful of niceness as a "symptom of superficiality and manipulation." The bind was broken by a contract at the psychological level that we regularly engage in a frank discussion of the range of feelings that developed between us as we worked together. We agreed to do so in a way that would preserve her needs for a degree of niceness and mine for a degree of candor.

Developmental Stages

Efforts to characterize the kind of learning we undergo in the clinical situation stress its confrontational nature. There is a kind of complete involvement through sustained exposure to new experiences. Previous patterns are challenged and may prove inadequate. The need to make personal changes and integrate new ways of thinking and feeling constitutes a form of personal challenge through which new levels of competence develop. The most helpful discussion of such a developmental sequence of learning in supervision is provided by C. Loganville, E. Hardy, and U. Delworth.[8] They identify three distinct stages, regardless of the particular supervisory issue that the person addresses.

1. The first stage is one of *stagnation.* It is characterized by the naive unawareness of the beginning trainee who is unlikely to realize that the issue even exists. It is marked by a false sense of security and simplistic black-and-white thinking. Supervisees at this stage may lack intensity or interest. Kurt Lewin described change by using the analogy of the "freezing" and "refreezing" of existing patterns.[9] In stage one we are "frozen" into old patterns of thought and behavior. It is characterized by narrow and rigid thought patterns, a low self-concept, strong dependency, and the notion that new learning must come from an outside source. Often supervisees think they are functioning perfectly well because of a lack of awareness of all that is involved in pastoral care. Their attitude toward the supervisor may be marked either by extreme dependence for guidance and direction or by the feeling that supervision is unnecessary and irrelevant. It is important to contracting, which is normally begun at this stage, that both supervisor and supervisee show caution in evaluating the extent to which the supervisee can grasp and understand all the areas in which development is needed.

2. Stage two is one of *confusion.* It begins with a marked shift that may come either gradually or abruptly. Its key characteristics are instability, disorganization, erratic fluctuation, disruption, and conflict. Stage two involves the unfreezing of the attitudes, emotions, and behaviors as Lewin envisioned them. This stage is troublesome because we know quite vividly that something is wrong. We may fluctuate between feelings of failure or incompetence and feelings of great expertise or ability. It becomes apparent that the golden answer is not going to come from the supervisor at all, and this stage can bring disappointment and anger. The supervisor may be regarded alternately as the magical, all-knowing figure of stage one or as an incompetent, inadequate figure who has failed to come through in stage two. It is important that both supervisor and supervisee come to regard this stage when it occurs as a sign of growth rather than impending doom.

3. Stage three is characterized by *integration.* This transition to stage three is a welcome one for both supervisor and supervisee. It also may occur gradually or abruptly and may accompany either natural events or direct supervisory intervention. It is characterized by reorganization, new cognitive understanding, flexibility, and personal security based on an awareness of our insecurities and an ongoing process of monitoring our important issues in supervision. It constitutes, in Lewin's schema, a period of "refreezing." During this stage a new worldview becomes apparent. It is composed of cognitive understandings, a sense of direction for the future, and an emergent realistic view among supervisees of themselves and their competencies. This is normally accompanied by a clear, reasonable view of the supervisor and his or her function. It is an ongoing stage of continuing growth.

One may be at any of these three stages simultaneously in supervision with the different issues one is addressing, and perhaps the most accurate picture of these three developmental stages is to see them in spiraling sequence. As any of us approach a new situation for learning, it is with a "refreezing" of what we have previously learned. We are back to stage one, regardless of all the previous growth. We move through turbulence and "unfreezing" to a "refreezing" at the next stage, and if this is to be growth and development, the spiral lasts a lifetime.

Supervisory Issues

We have been discussing these developmental stages in learning without naming any of the supervisory issues they address. Probably each supervisor could produce a different list. Again, we find the work by Loganville, Hardy, and Delworth particularly helpful.[10] Actually, it is an adaptation of A. W. Chickering's seven developmental themes in education to their conceptual model of supervision.[11] Most professional contracting at any level of training can be subsumed under one of these categories. Since it is impossible in any period of supervision to deal with them all, the list is helpful in balancing and focusing particular learning contracts against the background of one's overall professional development.

1. Issues of *competence* have to do with ability to use skills and techniques in order to carry through a particular task. Competence represents the capacity to translate our intellectual knowledge into effective action which will promote growth and change on the part of those with whom we work. Its mastery may be measured in terms of concrete behavioral outcomes with parishioners or counselees and the acquisition of specific practitioner skills we do not currently possess.

2. Issues of *emotional awareness* have to do with how effectively we use our own feelings in the task under supervision. Supervisees have a tendency to deny three particular emotional states: *(a)* feelings of frustration and anger; *(b)* feelings of inadequacy and powerlessness; and *(c)* feelings of intimacy, closeness, or sexual attraction toward someone with whom they work. Specific goals of self-awareness and the capacity to express what we are feeling take contractual shape around these issues.

3. Issues of *autonomy* have to do with developing a true sense of our own choices and decisions in a given situation. These are probably the most common issues that arise in the supervisory situation. The supervisee may have the impression that the supervisor wants control over him or her and may need to do a lot of testing in order truly to experience autonomy. Specific tasks of independent accomplishment form the grist for the contracting mill in this area.

4. Issues of *identity* for the practicing professional constitute one of the most difficult areas for supervisors to write about. These issues have to do with the capacity to develop a well-integrated theoretical identity in terms of the body of conceptual tools, both theological and psychological, with which we operate as pastors. They also involve a sense of "belongingness" within the role we have, a sense of comfort and satisfac-

tion in doing pastoral care and counseling under supervision. Contracts in this area often have to do with establishing awareness of and giving concrete expression to particular aspects of the professional functions that go with the territory.

5. Issues of *respect for individual differences* constitute a theme that runs through a number of different professional perspectives. Among clinical psychologists, those who adopt Carl Rogers' concept of unconditional positive regard make some of the clearest statements of this characteristic. It involves the ability to view other people with proper appreciation for their differences in physical appearance, background, and values. It is related to a person's ability to demonstrate empathy and caring for others. Respect for individual differences forms the basis for the capacity to relate to one another in a helpful way. Some measure of this capacity to get along with or work with others is essential to contracting in this area.

6. Issues of *purpose* and *direction* have to do with the goal-setting function in any professional discipline. These issues represent the thinking component in the work that one addresses. Contracts in this area involve the capacity to set goals in terms of concrete operational endpoints or to phrase them in terms that emphasize a process in which the parishioner or client can engage. This theme emphasizes the aspect of professional functioning in which the counselor, for example, takes firm responsibility in working toward the needed changes in attitude and behavior on the part of the client.

7. Issues of *personal motivation* to enter a particular profession may range from those labeled healthy, constructive, unselfish, or therapeutic to those at the other extreme which may be regarded as unhealthy, selfish, destructive, or neurotic. Here the issues center in what personal meaning and satisfaction we derive from engaging in a particular practice. Contracting is undertaken around one's sense of intimacy with other persons, an appropriate use of one's own power, financial gain, personal growth, intellectual growth, and altruism in the sense of feeling good about what one does. This is an area that no dimension of professional supervision should neglect, for it may have the most telling effect on the person's capacity to continue this profession across a lifetime.

8. Issues of *professional ethics* have to do with the way supervisees face the relevant issues of value and ethical propriety surrounding the practice of what they do. The capacity to think and act with integrity and ethical awareness, as well as to be conversant with some of the standards of performance required by one's professional identity, goes with this area.

Evaluation

Within this context, evaluation is a constant companion to each supervisory hour. Specific desires for the use of each individual supervisory hour may be fitted into the overall supervisory contract most relevant to what one is discussing. Regular evaluation keeps supervision sharp and on course and avoids the type of surprises and untoward endings where evaluation is suddenly a protrusive element in the relationship or a "necessary evil" at the end of everything. Of course, the goal of evaluation within this context is an accurate self-assessment and a continuation of personal evaluation and supervision across a career of professional practice. In this sense, everything that we do in supervision is in preparation for lasting patterns of consultation with coworkers that enable us to sustain personal growth in our pastoral role throughout our lifetime.

Three Reflective Dimensions

We now shift our attention to three dimensions of supervisory reflection that require continual attention. These dimensions are always present and attended to when supervision is successful. They are: (1) a dimension of *administrative oversight* which has to do with maintaining the welfare or treatment of parishioners, patients, or clients, together with whatever institutional structure supports the services that are rendered; (2) a *therapeutic dimension* of personal growth that focuses attention upon whatever insight, behavioral change, or other personal conditions need to be met by the supervisee in order to increase personal effectiveness; and (3) the dimension of a *working alliance* in the supervisory relationships themselves between supervisee, peers, and supervisor which requires periodic attention to make learning possible and the whole process work.

Each of these three dimensions can become a hook on which the supervisory process gets caught and subverted. Any one of them, if permitted to dominate the others to the point of their exclusion, will divert the supervisory conversation from its necessary task. Yet each is so vital to the process in its own time that supervision cannot continue without it. Any good supervisory session will probably involve aspects of all three. So often is this true that it gives rise to the clinical axiom: When you are stuck in one dimension, switch to another and check it out for what is needed to move through the impasse.

Administrative Oversight

As a teaching/learning process, the focus of supervision is on the competence and personal growth of the supervisee. Yet we have observed among the helping professions a constant tension between the desire to train the student and a sense of responsibility for the care of clients or patients. This inevitably involves supervision in a dimension of administrative oversight that seeks to ensure the welfare of parishioners or patients and preserve the institutional structure supporting the services that are rendered.

What distinguishes supervision from the concerns of administration in general is its aim to teach a way of thinking and acting in accord with conceptualizations of a professional role. Our model clearly focuses attention in the supervisory hour upon the concrete processes of delivering pastoral care and counseling to others. Any segment of a helping event is open to reflection and evaluation in terms of its outcome. But the aim of this reflection always goes beyond merely devising more effective strategies and methods. We are setting out to create a climate in which there can be personal growth toward lasting competence.

The process we are describing may take many turns along the way that do not immediately strengthen pastoral skills for the next helping encounter. New ways of approaching people often require periods of experimentation, trial, and error. In supervision, each of us must learn at our own pace, make our own mistakes and benefit from them, assimilate new concepts with tentative periods of incubation, and try on different methods for size with the necessary awkwardness of the novel. A good supervisor will make the conscious choice, at times, to permit us to return to a patient or counselee to struggle with our own partially formed understandings which are less than the state of the art. Often we retrace the learning process of others who have come before us, learning things for ourselves as they did. Rudolf Ekstein and Robert Wallerstein underlined the pitfalls of the supervisor of psychotherapy donning an administrative cap and attempting to treat the patient through the supervisee.[12] In supervision, it is more important that we learn to do something ourselves than that it be done as quickly and effectively as possible, say, by the supervisor's stepping in and doing it for us, which is a common pitfall in live supervision.

In tension with all these concerns for personal learning and development is this dimension of administrative oversight. For everyone there are times when administrative concerns for the care of persons or institutional well-being override personal learning. With severely depressed persons who are at risk of suicide, there are established procedures of not giving excessive nurture, obtaining clear contracts against harming themselves, and making appropriate referral, which no responsible supervisor would leave to the process of trial and error. In a correctional setting, when a chaplain supervisee lent money to one of the inmates, which is against institutional policy (and sound judgment), one of the most liberal advocates of self-discovery among the supervisory staff exercised administrative responsibility by telling the student to stop. In a neighboring institution, where residents brought a legal suit against staff and administration for malpractice in counseling, issues concerning the protection of the institution became a regular part of the supervisory conversations. As litigation increases throughout the field of health care, no supervisory program in pastoral counseling can ignore this dimension of administrative oversight in the protection of services it renders.

Where instructions, directives, and demonstrations by the supervisor are deemed an effective part of the overall learning process, there is little conflict between one's administrative and supervisory concerns. Supervisors doing live supervision in a structural/strategic approach to family therapy assume full responsibility for the course of treatment and intervene from behind the one-way glass with clear directives to supervisees about what they should do. They believe competence is learned through being empowered to act effectively rather than being left to flounder in search of one's own resources. Beginning students in pastoral care may learn much more by accompanying their supervisor on a pastoral visit or sick call, observing demonstrable procedures, than by simply being released upon people on their own recognizance.

In other situations, a subtle tension between administrative oversight and supervision follows us each step of the way. Take live supervision as a coleader in group counseling, for example. Will we learn more as supervisees if our supervisor interrupts and guides us at crucial points when we are at a loss or if our supervisor permits us to struggle a while to find our own way? How effective is our learning when our supervisor takes over and demonstrates what to do when we are stuck? And how long should our supervisor refrain from doing so in order to give us a chance to discover for ourselves, without abdicating shared responsibility in the overall course of the group treatment? Our own model makes room for all these measures at different times and places. The important thing is that neither our particular supervisory concerns for each student's growth nor our overall concerns with administrative oversight be permitted to eclipse the other.

This is frequently a delicate balance to maintain. And the same is true when we address issues of institutional welfare. Supervision is always conducted within the context of a larger system of administrative relationships constantly triangling others into its procedures. We have cited examples where our supervisor may represent the welfare of a particular patient or serve as interpreter of institutional policies at particular times and circumstances. At other times, the open nature of the supervisory relationship calls for the freedom to question and challenge existing regulations, theories, and practices. Sensitive supervisors will not permit the administrative dimension of their role to dominate it to the exclusion of such concerns.

Often exploring administrative issues serves to reveal the underlying models that govern our identity in the minds of administrators. For example, a doctoral student from our seminary proposed to his supervisor at a pastoral counseling center that he conduct a family therapy session in the home of his clients. We have recommended this practice for years, finding that a "show and tell" session at home early in treatment reveals things we would never know otherwise, swiftly and effectively. For pastoral counselors, with their tradition of visiting in persons' homes, it provides a strong means of joining the family and establishing rapport. To the administrators of the pastoral counseling center, which was located in a large regional hospital, this was an unacceptable departure from established procedures. At this point, their identity was shaped more by the medical model, which has largely abandoned house calls, than by their own historic pastoral role.

The Therapeutic Dimension

The therapeutic dimension of supervision focuses attention upon whatever insight, behavioral change, or other personal conditions need to be met by the supervisee in order to function effectively in the pastoral role. All of us encounter some *personal impasse* that gets in our way when we set out to be of help to others. Things happen to us that demand we change. Thomas Klink called these "characterologically cross-grained experiences" which he observed among students in clinical pastoral education.[13] Invariably, we get involved in relationships where our habitual mode of responding is felt to be inappropriate, but the appropriate mode of responding transgresses deeply ingrained traits of character. These experiences form critical incidents in supervision, demanding that we identify and change whatever it is that gets in the way of our professional effectiveness.

Everyone who enters supervision can count on having some personal impasse emerge, regardless of profession or background. The social workers called them *problems in helping* and *being helped,* observing that as we come to know the dynamics of our own struggle to use help, we also come to know our client's struggle to receive it. Ekstein and Wallerstein called them *learning problems,* characteristic, automatic, and inappropriate patterns that stand in the way of the student's acquisition of psychotherapeutic skills. Goldhammer referred to them as *repetitive patterns* that teachers have, sequences of behavior that negatively affect what their students learn. Wherever we seriously seek to improve professional performance, supervision will have a therapeutic dimension that works for personal change.

So you can count on your clinical experience to confront you with some characterologically cross-grained experiences. None of us can minister to the dying or the bereaved without confronting the losses we have experienced in our own life. Most of us have an internal integrity that will not permit us to ask others to deal with what we must avoid. So we are forced to come to terms with our own unresolved issues in order to face them in another. We cannot counsel a couple deeply divided over parenting their children without encountering the difficulties marking the relationships in our own marriage and family. We may get by in other settings keeping our distance through social amenities. But not here. If we are reluctant to confront other persons and consistently avoid criticism, we will prove reticent to assume authority in our pastoral work and constantly approach supervision in ways that avoid critical reflection. The same tendency will show up at home with our family and in the classroom with our teachers. Suddenly in supervision we are confronted with a long-standing pattern of behavior that requires change on our part, if we are to function effectively in the clinical setting. The particular ways in which this problem is managed distinguish supervision from counseling or psychotherapy.

The boundaries of our supervisory model clearly establish both the origin and the limits of attention to this therapeutic dimension. The origin of a personal issue in supervision is always its recurrence in the professional relationships upon which we reflect. It appears and reappears, inhibiting effective practice of our pastoral role. The therapeutic dimension of supervision addresses the presence of distortion, vulnerability, avoidance, one-sidedness, inflexibility, or any other behavior that repeatedly interferes with the supervisee's effective professional functioning. In doing so, discussion of the issues is not unnaturally restricted to the specific clinical instance at hand. Supervisees are free to generalize to the presence of similar conflicts throughout their lives, fitting their present experience into the larger mosiac of their own personal development holistically. To do so can be quite helpful to the task at hand. It is one thing for a young graduate student to discover in supervision how he failed to encourage independent thinking and autonomy on the part of a college student he visited in the hospital. It is another to become aware that one reason he did so was his sensitivity to his previous struggles with enmeshment with his own mother and his current battle with overprotectiveness in his present family life.

Good supervision will always work for personal change throughout the professional relationships it addresses in the here and now. But its attention is limited to these. It does not extend to the personal history or present family life of our graduate student. Within these limits, anything therapeutic that can be accomplished within the supervisory conversation is a responsible use of time and energy. The supervisor may model good counseling procedures in identifying and exploring the problem. Specific strategies to work through its grip in the present sphere of clinical relationships with administrators, peers, supervisor, and patients or parishioners are well within the bounds of supervisory attention. Most clinical training programs include an interpersonal relations group for students where such issues can be constructively addressed. Often such measures are sufficient to provide impetus for personal change in the professional role, especially with more seasoned clinicians who have had some previous psychotherapy. And often such changes are generalized to portions of the supervisee's personal life beyond the boundary of supervision per se.

This boundary clearly limits the extent to which the supervisory conversation can deal with issues of personal change and emotional growth. If the therapeutic dimension is permitted to eclipse the other dimensions of supervisory reflection so that each session is converted into work with personal issues, it becomes a hook that subverts the process. Again, it is a matter of maintaining a delicate balance. Just as we can become so concerned with administrative oversight in managing the process of delivering care that we forget the personal growth of the

supervisee, we can become so preoccupied with personal problems in supervision that we surrender our central focus of reflection upon concrete clinical practice. In such instances,
supervisees are referred for psychotherapy to work through
these issues outside the supervisory process where they can
receive the necessary time and attention.

In our early efforts to teach supervision here at the seminary,
we found Eric Berne's concept of psychological games helpful
in understanding unconscious collusions between supervisor
and student to avoid the hard work of supervision.[14] One prominent game we came to call "Sick." In its more pronounced
version, both parties agree that the student is so troubled, mixed
up, stressed, or confused that each supervisory hour is converted into counseling regarding these problems. Responsible
supervision addressing concrete practice is avoided. The student is "sick" and cannot be expected to perform competently.
In its more subtle forms, learning is evaded through referring
everything to one's current personal issue, excusing oneself
from substantial and critical reflection upon the work at hand.
This is a temptation for more seasoned players who would
rather appear "sick" than "stupid." Supervisors who are frustrated counselors are vulnerable.

The Working Alliance

A third dimension of supervisory reflection is the working
alliance in the supervisory relationships themselves involving
supervisee, peers, and supervisor. We borrowed the term from
Edward Bordin, who in turn borrowed it from the psychodynamic tradition where it described a quality of collaboration that
grew between analyst and patient.[15] In the working alliance of
supervision, as well as psychotherapy, Bordin points to a collaboration for change in which we can identify three aspects: (1)
mutual agreements and understandings regarding the goals
sought in the change process, (2) specific tasks for each of the
partners, and (3) the bonds between the partners necessary to
sustain the enterprise. The crucial thing for all of us to experience, however, is this bonding aspect of working together in any
cooperative endeavor. It is like the rhythmic "Heave ho!"
through which a team of persons moves a heavy object. It demands success in the building up and repair of this working
relationship. Regardless of the goal or the task at hand, the
phenomenon of shared experience, centering around feelings of
liking, caring, and trusting one another, constitutes the essential
ingredient in the change process.

Resistance. All of us can expect to encounter some substantial resistance deep within ourselves to being supervised. In chapter 2 we saw it described in various ways. Virginia Robinson observed among social workers that each trainee's best intentions to learn from supervision were accompanied by an equally forceful "will not to learn."[16] Ekstein and Wallerstein offered the most vivid description of characteristic forms of resistance they encountered among psychotherapists in training, or *problems about learning,* as they termed them.[17] Some students learned through vigorous denying, warding off the impact of supervision by reducing it to the familiar or refusing to acknowledge that any help can accrue. Others learn through submission, the too-easy manner of adopting the supervisor's offerings, leading to an imitative assumption of external trappings of content without truly effective learning. Still others react with a *mea culpa* attitude which constitutes a response with embarrassment and ready acknowledgment, magnifying one's own failings to the point of caricature and learning only by being beaten. Still others evade supervision by awarding the supervisor the task of achieving results, refusing to accept a role of responsible participation. Others have the problem of finding a problem to discuss or escape through overinvolvement by maintaining so many conflicting interests that training is obtained "on the run." Each particular resistance to supervision becomes the focus of a struggle to change one's level of professional functioning and, at the same time, a vehicle for accomplishing that change as it is worked through.

There are a number of ways to conceptualize the particular forms this resistance may take. As previously mentioned, we elected to use Eric Berne's theory of psychological games to identify a number of "supervisory games" we could observe developing between supervisors and supervisees. Some typical examples are "You're the Super," in which supervisees subtly transferred responsibility for sustaining thought and reflection to the supervisor, yielding to their superior knowledge and experience; or "Friend," in which both parties unwittingly colluded to avoid the hard work of critical evaluation under the guise of preserving friendship and collegiality. Alfred Kadushin produced a similar anthology of games in the supervision of social casework, although he is not so clear about the covert alliances that sustain them.[18] Richard Wessler and Albert Ellis conceptualized resistance in terms of "irrational beliefs" and "self-defeating philosophies" with which supervisees needlessly upset themselves. The three most common ones are: (1) "I *must* do well in supervision and be approved by my supervisor"; (2)

"My supervisor *has to* be competent and treat me fairly"; and (3) "The supervision program *must* be well arranged and effective, and I *can't stand it* if it isn't."[19]

Whatever one's perspective, some reflection upon the character of the supervisory relationship itself proves necessary to hold the working alliance to its task and maintain the cooperative bond required between persons for mutual trust. As Bordin pointed out, whatever self-defeating habits of feeling, acting, and thinking we carry into everyday life will eventually emerge to disrupt the collaboration of supervision. In the experience of building and repairing our working alliances, there are benefits beyond the obvious one of restoring an effective relationship. As these resistances are overcome, we can acquire new and more satisfying ways of responding which can, under the right circumstances, affect personal changes that generalize beyond the working alliance to other areas of our life.

Peer Relationships. Peer relationships with others in training also require periodic attention. In group supervision, issues surrounding competition, favoritism, inferiority, and superiority inevitably color interaction and influence the quality of supervisory reflection. If permitted to go unattended, they interfere increasingly with other dimensions of the task at hand. When confronted openly, they provide supervision a live laboratory of interaction where we may address how sibling relationships and family position affect contemporary functioning. Interpersonal relations groups (IPR) in clinical pastoral education provide a fertile ground for such explorations. But this is a dimension present in all seminars, case conferences, and group supervision. In the supervision of coleaders of a group or cotherapy relationships in marital and family counseling, regular reflection on the peer relationship itself is essential in order to maintain the working alliance between partners and unravel parallel processes in the system of supervisory relationships themselves which throw important light on the marital or family system addressed. As we shall see in a later chapter, group supervision provides the supervisor with important checks on his or her own tendencies toward countertransference and extends the range of supervisory functions deep into the relationships of the peer group.

Parallel Process. Still other benefits follow careful supervisory reflection upon the working alliance. I must confess that the whole idea of parallel process seemed rather preposterous to me, at first. You will recall the major theory surrounding it from our discussion in chapter 2.

1. Each one of us will tend to identify unconsciously with a person whom we counsel, without knowing it, and behave toward the supervisor in ways that show the difficulties this person posed to us, eliciting the same feelings from our supervisor that we had toward the person.

2. If the particular problem this person poses to us coincides with an issue that remains unresolved in our own life, the supervisory conversation becomes cluttered with our efforts to achieve some vicarious resolution to our own problem without confronting it, or tenaciously to resist effective strategies to deal with the problems in our client as our own difficulties blind us to their effectiveness. Progress in both the supervisory and the pastoral conversation is blocked in the same way.

3. Parallel process is a two-way street in which we not only tend to "play client or parishioner" with our supervisor but also "play supervisor" with our parishioner or client. Vestiges of one relationship are constantly appearing in the other so that we work repeatedly with the same metaphor for personal growth.

4. Resolutions in the working alliance of supervision are invariably accompanied by a parallel breakthrough in the helping process of the pastoral relationship it addresses. We experience firsthand being done with us what we need to do with the troublesome other. The same thing is true in live supervision. Resolution of an isomorphic issue between supervisor and supervisee travels down the hierarchy of treatment, empowering the supervisee to deal constructively with family members beyond the one-way glass.

As good fortune would have it, while writing this section and groping for a reasonably uncomplicated illustration of this rather complex process, I attended a conference in Chicago. To my surprise, the name Dr. John H. Boyle appeared on the bulletin board of Fourth Presbyterian Church across the street from my hotel. He was scheduled to preach on that Sunday. John, who has directed a pastoral counseling center there for over a decade, was my first supervisor in clinical pastoral education at Central State Hospital in Louisville when I was a seminary student. An afternoon of visiting with him brought back memories etched in my own personal growth almost three decades ago.

At Central State Hospital, each student was required to establish a counseling relationship with one patient on the ward where we were assigned pastoral responsibility. I selected Emma Forrest, whose file bore the diagnosis "chronic undifferentiated schizophrenic" and a history of prostitution interrupted by three previous hospitalizations.[20] I recalled being slightly irritated when John, on several occasions, pressed me to determine why I selected her. I didn't know, except her need was obviously great. One common complaint about Emma was that she behaved seductively to fellow patients, male attendants, and doctors. I decided to concentrate on reducing this behavior which she blithely denied each time I brought it up. I kept copious notes and wrote lengthy verbatims, oblivious to my fascination with details surrounding her life on the streets, her sexual history, and her longing for the "straight life." As the time for her release approached, we struggled. She still denied being seductive with others. I became concerned about her aftercare. She expressed doubts about her ability to make it on her own. John kept raising questions about how I felt toward her and how she felt toward me. I was annoyed by his persistence. Didn't he recognize a relationship of mutual trust when he saw one?

Then one day, as Emma expressed her fears of going back to the old life, she remarked she really could look quite good when she got on the outside and she would like me to see her sometime. I talked on awkwardly about referring her to a pastor in her neighborhood, sensing that we needed to talk about something else but unable to confront the feelings she had developed toward me, which she, of course, denied and presented as her need for continuing personal care. In turn, when I presented the conversation in supervision to John, I calmly represented my own involvement with Emma in terms of pure pastoral concern. In fact, it might not be a bad idea to see her once or twice during the transition. I became furious when John again confronted me with the possibility that I was denying some of the feelings I had for her. He countered by insisting that we explore what was happening between the two of us. That was simple. He confronted, I denied—the same thing that Emma did with me. Only then could I finally acknowledge there was some curiosity on my part about how she would look on the outside, that I did entertain the fleeting fantasy of meeting her. I was able to deal, for the first time, with my own involvement with Emma as a young, single seminarian struggling with how to handle my own sexual feelings and be a pastor at the same time, and experiencing considerable uneasiness about how to put the two together.

The following week I was able to discuss with Emma the undercurrent of feelings in our relationship. She too became angry at my questions surrounding her "dependence" upon me. But, as was the case with John, once this initial anger was weathered, we were able to acknowledge the existence of affection and attraction with clear limits to any acting upon it, given the character of our pastoral relationship. This in turn led to a breakthrough in our conversations about her assuming responsibility to avoid seduction in all her relationships on the outside, creating in them things she clearly chose for herself. Upon reflection, it was obvious to me that

1. I did identify unconsciously with Emma and behave toward my supervisor in ways that denied any covert seduction in our pastoral relationship, which presented him with the same difficulties I had in working with her.

2. This particular problem coincided with unresolved issues surrounding how I managed my own sexual feelings as a single male engaged in the intimate processes of pastoral care, causing me tenaciously to resist discussing these feelings either in supervision or the pastoral conversation, arresting progress in both.

3. This parallel process was a two-way street: I denied such feelings with my supervisor, becoming angry when confronted with them, and avoided confronting the same feelings in Emma, fearing her anger should I risk their discussion. We worked repeatedly with the same metaphor of denial and the fear of anger that blocked my personal growth.

4. Resolution through confrontation of my own anger and denied sexual feelings in the working alliance with John enabled me to achieve a parallel breakthrough in my pastoral conversations with Emma, leading to some resolution of the seductive dimensions of her dependence.

To round out the experience at the conceptual level, I learned a great deal about the unconscious dimensions of what we have traditionally called bondage to sin. At that time, Paul Tillich's understandings of forgiveness as God's acceptance of us in spite of our unacceptability had come to mean much to me.[21] My own process of denying sexual feelings centered around excluding from conscious awareness what I thought to be unacceptable within myself. In order to represent such forgiveness to others, a certain measure of self-acceptance became necessary beforehand. In fact, there was a distinct process of mutual self-acceptance through which I had to go with Emma which forms the basis for the freeing experience of repentance. It is just such an awareness that no one is in a position to cast stones that undergirded Jesus' statement to the woman taken in adultery: "Go and sin no more." This seemed to prove true, whether we were dealing with angry ways by which we miss the mark in loving one another, matters of infidelity concerning sexual misconduct, or any other common expression of our "bondage to sin."

Like the other two dimensions of supervisory reflection, difficulties in supervisory relationships themselves can emerge to dominate the process and subvert the focus from its central purpose. This normally happens in one of two extremes. Either no attention at all is paid to the relationships in the supervisory room and the quality of reflective work deteriorates, yielding unvoiced frustration with one another and increasingly ineffective supervisory hours, or so much attention is paid to what goes on in these relationships themselves that other dimensions of supervision fall into the background and are neglected. In such cases, supervision is being subverted from its central purpose of systematic reflection upon the practice of pastoral care. Often some attention is needed in the therapeutic dimension. By the same token, when solid reflection upon the helping process gives way to obscurity and frustration, a careful look at what is happening in the supervisory relationships themselves is more often than not the way through the impasse.

NOTES

1. See F. W. Kaslow and associates, *Supervision, Consultation, and Staff Training in the Helping Professions* (San Francisco: Jossey-Bass, 1977), p. 5.

2. S. Hiltner, "What We Get and Give in Pastoral Care: What We Give: (1)—The Scientific," *Pastoral Psychology,* April 1954, p. 31.

3. D. A. Steere, "A New Pastoral Theology: A Study of Its Redefinition in the Clinical Pastoral Education Movement According to the Biblical Concept of Shepherding" (doctoral diss., Union Theological Seminary, New York, 1966), p. 269.

4. M. J. Roich, "The Dilemma of Supervision in Dynamic Psychotherapy," in *Psychotherapy Supervision: Theory, Research and Practice,* ed. A. K. Hess (New York: John Wiley & Sons, 1980), pp. 66–67.

5. R. Goldhammer, *Clinical Supervision: Special Methods for the Supervision of Teachers* (New York: Holt, Rinehart, & Winston, 1969), pp. 60, 73–91.

6. G. I. Hunter, *Supervision and Education—Formation for Ministry* (Cambridge, Mass.: Episcopal Divinity School, 1982), pp. 23–31.

7. E. Berne, *Principles of Group Treatment* (New York: Oxford University Press, 1966), pp. 15, 16, 87–96.

8. C. Loganville, E. Hardy, and U. Delworth, "Supervision: A Conceptual Model," *The Counseling Psychologist* 10(1):17–20 (1982).

9. K. Lewin, *Resolving Social Conflicts: Selected Papers on Group Dynamics* (New York: Harper & Brothers, 1948).

10. Loganville, Hardy, and Delworth, pp. 20–26.

11. A. W. Chickering, *Education and Identity* (San Francisco: Jossey-Bass, 1969).

12. R. Ekstein and R. S. Wallerstein, *The Teaching and Learning of Psychotherapy* (New York: Basic Books, 1958).

13. T. W. Klink, "How Supervision Is Carried Out," in *Clinical Pastoral Education for the Pastoral Ministry,* ed. E. E. Bruder and M. L. Barb (Advisory Committee on Clinical Pastoral Education, 1958), p. 109.

14. See D. A. Steere, "An Experiment in Supervisory Training," *Journal of Pastoral Care,* Dec. 1969, pp. 202–217.

15. E. S. Bordin, "A Working Alliance-based Model of Supervision," *The Counseling Psychologist* 11(1):35–42 (1982).

16. V. Robinson, *A Changing Psychology in Social Work* (Chapel Hill, N.C.: University of North Carolina Press, 1930), p. 4.

17. Ekstein and Wallerstein, *The Teaching and Learning of Psychotherapy,* pp. 142–156.

18. See A. Kadushin, "Games People Play in Supervision," *Social Work,* July 1968, pp. 23–32. Compare a discussion by D. McCarty, *The Supervision of Ministry Students* (Atlanta: Southern Baptist Home Mission Board, Southern Baptist Convention, 1978), pp. 105–109.

19. R. Wessler and A. Ellis, "Supervision in Counseling: Rational Emotive Therapy," *The Counseling Psychologist* 11(1):443–449 (1982).

20. The name and salient facts have been changed to protect this person's anonymity.

21. P. Tillich, *Systematic Theology* (Chicago: University of Chicago Press, 1964), vol. 3, pp. 224–228.

4

Preparing Yourself for Supervision

George F. Bennett

You will probably prepare yourself for supervision by doing what Sherlock Holmes said he did in solving mysteries. He said he deduced. What he said was wrong. He did not practice the science of deduction. Deduction, loosely defined, means starting any task with an overall principle and working down from that. Holmes induced. Induction involves beginning with specifics (clues in the Holmes's stories) and working up with them, assembling them to reach an overall principle (the solution to the mystery).

Inductive Preparation

You will probably try to prepare yourself for supervision deductively. Most people start with a general principle, a predetermined mind-set, and attempt to work down from that. You can get into trouble that way. Consider the following.

Carl Compley started his first supervised experience deductively. His self-preparation was deciding that in supervision he would be told what to do, what to say, as well as when to do it and say it. He also believed that if he were especially good at this, he might even be told why he was told to do and say what and when.

With this self-preparation, Carl was confused, frightened, and eventually angered by his supervisor, who also worked deductively. His supervisor began with the overall principle that was summed up at the first supervisory session with the statement, "I'm not here to tell you what to do. I'm here to reflect with you about what you decide to do."

Carl was unwilling or unable to give up his prepared mind-set—that of adopting an "I'll be told" expectation. His first supervisor was equally reluctant to relinquish his preparation. He found himself repeatedly saying such things to Carl as, "I don't coddle. My supervisees either sink or swim in this sea of suffering."

Carl grew increasingly resentful at not having his expectations of supervision met. It seemed unfair to him that anyone in authority would not act the way most authorities acted. For example, Carl's personal physician, when consulted, gave opinions, advice, prescriptions, and occasionally explanations. He did not expect his auto mechanic to tell him to fix his own car. In fact, the mechanic seemed irritated when Carl tried to figure out what was wrong with the car himself.

Carl's supervisor was not being mean or difficult. She was simply following the recommendation of her certification committee that she avoid "overmothering" her students. And she was working from her overall principle that people learn for themselves, by doing and reflecting, not by being directed. The result was not very productive, because both Carl and his supervisor insisted on being deductive. Both tried to work down from previously determined principles that were mutually exclusive.

Carl's second supervisor did what Sherlock Holmes actually did, even though Holmes called it by the wrong term. This supervisor started by clarifying with Carl what expectations each of them brought to supervision and worked out a learning contract based on them. The learning contract permitted both parties to start with what was important to each of them. The supervisor agreed to share "tricks of the trade" with Carl, telling him what might be helpful to do or to say. Carl agreed to let the supervisor shift over to him increasing responsibility for thinking things through and making decisions. Establishing such learning contracts and keeping them clear is the most important preparation we make for supervision. ·

Supervisory Contracts

Effective supervision is structured around a series of contracts in each of its three dimensions that were described in chapter 3. *Administrative contracts* set forth the concrete responsibilities or duties the supervisee will assume during the training period. *Professional contracts* specify clearly the goals for personal growth sought by the supervisee during clinical reflection, giving supervision its therapeutic dimension. *Teamwork contracts,* referred to in chapter 3 as *psychological contracts,* specify what agreements need to be made to sustain the *working alliance* of supervision itself, ensuring that supervisor and student can work together effectively.

Administrative Contracts

The administrative contract contains what is expected of supervisor and supervisee in the institution or situation where they serve. In CPE, supervisees are usually assigned specific responsibilities in providing pastoral care among patients, residents, families, and staff of the hospital, the prison, the school, the counseling center, or wherever the practice takes place. Hours spent "on the wards," scheduled meetings, groups, and other expectations are set forth in writing. Appropriate communication in the administrative chain of command is clarified so that we can get the job done at the right time with the proper people in the approved manner. Boundaries of responsibility and authority are established among professionals of the same and other disciplines, because the setting often demands that chaplains work with social workers, psychologists, physicians, nurses, custodians, and other personnel.

The administrative contract is a detailed statement of the individual supervisee's area of function within the overall purpose of the institution. In a large mental hospital, every employee, student, and volunteer is advancing the treatment of those who are termed mentally ill. Some do so by prescribing medicine, some by typing letters, some by cleaning the restrooms, some by answering the telephone, and some by providing pastoral care. Each must be aware of the specific do's and don'ts of the task assigned.

In plain language, chaplains do not proselytize on one another's wards, make medical diagnoses, do social casework, distribute medicine, ignore institutional policy, speak to media representatives regarding the institution, and so forth. There may be exceptions under certain prescribed circumstances, in which case these are included in the contract. Administrative contracts can seldom be too precise, even to the point of using telephones, borrowing pencils, requesting secretaries to type verbatims, or asking janitors to jump-start the chaplain's car.

Supervisors also make clear the areas of authority and responsibility specific to their own role in the supervisory process. These include such things as schedules of training and educational events, periods for individual and group supervision, times of availability among supervisory staff, policies for evaluation of the student's work, and procedures for complaint when the student has a grievance. Professional certification as a supervisor is to ensure that the supervisor provides these things and explains them clearly at the outset of supervision.

Ordinarily, the administrative contract is prepared ahead of time and presented to the student by the supervisor. It is usually in the form of a syllabus that outlines both the official duties and the course requirements established jointly by the institution and the accrediting or certifying agency that have united to promise the specific educational experience—for example, the hospital and the Association for Clinical Pastoral Education, or the clinic and the American Association of Pastoral Counselors.

Professional Contracts

The professional contract addresses the specific things the supervisee hopes to learn within a given unit of supervisory experience. This learning contract sets forth a framework for the student's personal growth in the pastoral role during training. The following outline of its essential ingredients was developed by Paul Andrews and can serve as a sample guide for its construction:

Outline for Clinical Learning

Each student takes the initiative in deciding what she or he wants to learn. The individual forms a written proposal of goals to be pursued during the unit of CPE, the methods she or he will use to work on the goals, and the criteria and manner of evaluating progress. She or he interacts with the supervisor if further definition is needed. The outline of goals can be renegotiated as learning foci shift or become clarified. The emphases are on taking responsibility for personal learning, developing skills for formulating goals, and using feedback and consultation.

Goals need to be:

1. Realistic
2. Specific
3. Appropriate to the clinical setting and the time limits of the CPE program
4. Measurable or observable

Attention should be given to the Objectives of Basic (or Advanced) CPE. These objectives deal with professional and personal identity and the use of consultation to enhance professional competence. A few guiding questions that may be used in formulating goals include:

1. What am I motivated to learn about now?
   Where do I feel uncomfortable and want to grow?
   What interest area excites my curiosity presently?
2. What am I willing to do to reach my goal?
3. What benefit will I gain by accomplishing this goal?
4. How will I know when I have reached it?
5. What would I gain by sabotaging myself concerning this goal?
   How can I set up sabotage?
6. What goals am I avoiding or postponing for now?

An example of a learning goal is given below:

> **Goal:** Learn to play the banjo.
>
> **Process:** Secure access to a banjo.
> Establish contract with a teacher.
> Attend instruction sessions.
> Practice assignments minimum 3 times/week.
> Play new pieces or variations on my own.
>
> **Evaluation:** Play at least 3 songs by end of 6 months.
> Use teacher's feedback as well as personal
> impressions to assess skills.[1]

The supervisee's own specific learning contract is prepared and presented to the supervisor for mutual consideration and agreement. It is often quite simple and brief, yet may hold profound promise. The following is typical:

"My contract for learning during this supervised unit is to improve my listening ability. I will do this by reading *Client-centered Therapy* by Carl Rogers, by writing verbatim reports of conversations with clients and reflecting on them with my supervisor and my peers, and by evaluating them in the light of the Elias Porter's five categories described in Howard J. Clinebell's *Basic Types of Pastoral Counseling.*[2] My increased listening can be demonstrated in part by physically measuring the length (vertical) of my comments and those of the clients on the typewritten pages of the verbatim."

Teamwork Contracts

The teamwork contract establishes the working alliance through which supervision is carried out. It is composed of appropriate agreements about what is to go on between supervi-

sor and supervisee as the process begins. To be effective, however, teamwork contracts require frequent additions, corrections, and revisions throughout the period of supervision as the
needs of both parties change. I usually begin supervision by
telling the supervisee a parable about insurance agents and
hardware store clerks. Insurance agents have numerous "goodies" to sell their clients: inexpensive term insurance to give
immediate protection for a period of time and nothing else,
tax-sheltered annuities to provide income in the future when
one is in a lower tax bracket, and so on. The insurance agent
must get the client to pay attention, to show interest, and to
decide to buy if the agent is to be successful.

The hardware store clerk is different. Oh, there are plenty of
"goodies" for sale. I have seldom seen anything in a hardware
store that I didn't want. Even though I don't even know what
some things are for, they are hefty, shiny, and interesting. But
the clerk obviously gets paid by the hour whether I buy anything
or not. If I don't buy, the clerk does not have to work (unless,
of course, there is stock to be put out on the shelves, in which
case my desire to buy something is an interruption of the clerk's
job). It is I who must get the clerk's attention (forget interest)
and decision to sell me what I want.

"Excuse me," I say, intruding on the clerk's leisure.
"Yeah?"
"I need a Phillips."
"Phillips is milk of magnesia. You need a drugstore."
"Oh, I'm sorry. I meant a screwdriver."
"Aisle Nine."

I finally find Aisle 9 and at last locate what I want. I take it back
to the clerk.

"Now what?"
"Uh, I'd like to buy this one."
"Cash or charge?" with a lamenting sigh—as I said, forget in-
terest.

In my early years of supervision, I was like an insurance agent.
I just had to sell my supervisees all the "goodies" of pastoral
theology. I seldom got their interest either. Of late, I'm more of
a hardware store clerk. If they want it, they have to ask for it by
the correct name and look in the place to which I refer them.
The polite way of saying this is that my overall principle is, *The
supervisee is largely responsible for his or her own learning.*

There are other aspects to the teamwork contract. These include the mutual right to ask for "time out" when the dialogue

is going too fast or getting too intense; the mutual right to ask the other to withhold speaking until one has finished what one is saying, that is, not to interrupt; and the mutual right to point out when some part of the contract is being violated. The most important thing this teamwork involves is a mutual commitment on the part of both supervisor and supervisee to reflect regularly upon what is going on in the working alliance of their own relationship with a mind to making it as effective as it can be.

Ideally, the teamwork contract is also described in print from the supervisor's perspective and is the basis for mutual agreement in specifically refined detail. In part it may read:

"As your supervisor, I shall take seriously the written and other material you bring to supervision insofar as they are of importance to the work of this institution and your growth in the pastoral role. I shall listen carefully to what you say. I will look at the 'picture' of your life in this setting and in other ways related to our task. I shall work intensely to sense what you feel and to reflect as deeply as possible on what you think. This is not easy work and requires considerable concentration for which I have years of training. This, however, is not the most important work of supervision.

"The most important work in supervision *you do,* listening to you, looking at your self, becoming more aware of your feelings, and understanding more logically your own thoughts. The way you experience your work here, our work together, as well as your life professionally and personally in this universe, is your unique religion and practice. As we comprehend that together, you will experience greater command of and energy for that which you do and are."

Getting Ready for Supervision

Now back to Sherlock Holmes and some specific ways you can get ready for conferences with your supervisor. We are stressing what Holmes actually *did,* which was to take an inductive, rather than deductive, approach. This involves presenting clinical material that begins with specific details or clues about the larger process (or mystery) at hand. We discussed the three clinical poles for supervisory reflection in chapter 3: the pastor, the parishioner, and the helping relationship.

1. Since the focus of supervision is clearly on the *helping relationship* itself, begin there. Ask yourself: What is taking place consciously and unconsciously between yourself as pastor and the parishioner(s) or patient(s)? What effect may each have upon the other, what games might be afoot in the ongoing transac-

tions, what is conducive to and what blocks effective, affective communication, and so forth? A classic example: What is going on between a chaplain and a patient when the chaplain asks, "Is there anything you would ask of me as a chaplain?" and the patient responds, "You can pray, if you want to." A chapter of this book could be devoted to this example alone. What is going on between patient and supervisee?

The sharing of operational procedures based on the supervisor's experience and study constitutes an important part of reflection upon this first clinical pole. The supervisee can expect to be informed, not left to flounder, in situations where there are proven practices that can enhance the work. "What do I say when I don't know what to say to someone who is suffering?" is a common and reasonable question a supervisee may ask. The suggestion to tell the person you don't know what to say, and let the person respond is a solid, time-tested, and reliable bit of professional advice. Almost always the response conveys a sense that the suffering person feels understood, has a partner in pain, and is no longer alone in it.

2. The second critical pole for reflection is that of the *person or persons receiving care*. Ask yourself what is actually going on in the mind, the emotions, the physical and the spiritual life of those to whom you minister. Make an effort to report in detail what fears, needs, wants, angers, hopes, longings, strengths, weaknesses, and so forth, the patient or client has experienced, is experiencing, or may experience. Let yourself listen carefully to what beliefs, both explicit and implicit, are being expressed about self, others, and the nature of life itself. Carefully register your own responses to whatever the other person says or does. Make an assessment of this individual's personal and spiritual resources.

3. *Your own inner world as a pastor* is equally important. This is the third pole for clinical reflection. The more we know about ourselves, the more effective we are as pastors. All the details of the personal history that we bring to the present—old tapes that replay in our minds, sights, sounds, and situations that play upon our present experience when they remind us of similar events in our formative years—combine to shape the task at hand. We also know that current circumstances away from the clinical setting can have their influence. Are you having symptoms like those of the patient? Have you done something recently, or undergone some experience, that distracts or distorts perceptions? Do you have financial problems, family frictions, an impending deadline, or some powerful success to celebrate? Such matters influence your thought, feeling, and behavior in

the pastoral role. What is going on in your own life? Don't hesitate to report these things as part of the clinical material for supervision.

I must acknowledge that I have contradicted myself through encouraging you to prepare yourself for supervision by being *inductive,* starting with nothing and working with what comes your way. For that in itself is deductive, starting with an overall principle from which to work down. Suggesting that you merely change your overall premise for approaching supervision (and life) without the therapeutic dimension of personal change that it provides would place a handful of words against your total life preparation for supervision, a most unequal contest.

Rather, I urge you to clarify what your overall premises are as you approach supervision—no overhauling of your overalls! Recognize them. Reclarify them and those of your supervisor, with your supervisor, at the outset and throughout. That is the way to prepare yourself for supervision.

NOTES

1. Unpublished guide for developing learning contracts. Paul Andrews is director of Consultation and Education Associates in Louisville, Ky.

2. C. R. Rogers, *Client-centered Therapy: Its Current Practice, Implications, and Theory* (New York: Houghton Mifflin Co., 1951); and H. J. Clinebell, *Basic Types of Pastoral Counseling* (Nashville: Abingdon Press, 1966).

5

Working with Clinical Materials
Kathleen Ogden Davis

Clinical material is the essential substance for learning from one's experience in ministry through engagement with a qualified supervisor. The trainee can invite the supervisor to accompany him or her on a pastoral visit and then engage in dialogue for understanding and evaluation at the conclusion of the visit. In that situation, the supervisor has the opportunity to observe the ministry firsthand without its having first been filtered through the trainee's own perceptions, insights, and viewpoints. While a visit made by supervisor and trainee together offers some unique advantages, the presence of the supervisor inevitably affects the dynamics of interaction between the trainee and the person(s) visited. Other authors in this book will address the possibilities inherent in such immediate, on-the-spot supervision. This chapter focuses on the trainee's reporting of the clinical material (the pastoral experience) in supervision separated in time from the experience itself.

Options for Reporting Clinical Material

A variety of formats are well suited for the presentation of clinical experiences. Medicine, social work, and other professions value clinical education as highly as pastoral ministry and utilize some of these means for reporting and learning. Audio or video recordings may be made with the permission of both the trainee and the persons who are the subject of the trainee's ministry. Clinical material can also be reported by narrative accounts (stories), process notes (contemporary accounts of a series of visits), incident reports (reports of visits significant for some purpose in the pastoral relationship), and case histories (somewhat detailed narratives of the person's previous history, presenting issues and initiation of a pastoral care plan with an assessment of the effectiveness of the pastoral relationship). A trainee may present a series of reports based on a recurring theme, such as when to pray and how to respond to tears. Clinical material can be forcefully reported in an artistic format: music, art, drama, poetry. The verbatim account is the time-honored tradition within clinical pastoral education, although any of the means for reporting clinical material have been and are utilized in training programs for ministry.

The Verbatim Account

The verbatim account requires the trainee's close attention during the visit that is to be reported. Soon after, the trainee reproduces the visit in dialogue form, according to memory. This chapter addresses the verbatim format and the ways to make use of it in supervision. My own experience and training as both student and supervisor have included the use of verbatim accounts to present and discover theological issues in pastoral visits. As I struggled to define myself as a minister, I found the verbatim a worthwhile tool which contributed to my learning to be a pastor. It gave me a method for applying my seminary education to the practice of pastoral care.

Most church traditions consider formal academic preparation helpful for ministry. Many see it as an essential requirement for an informed and responsible ministry. A growing number of church groups require or recommend supervised clinical training also for acceptance into ordained ministry. The way in which a minister incorporates and integrates the "dry bones" of doctrinal, systematic, and biblical theology into the sense of self and engages life theologically in the moment of encounter with living persons becomes the gist of verbatim material. Bridging the gap between the study of theology and the experience of theology is at the core of supervised clinical pastoral education. One minister describes his own experience in training:

> I'll never forget the difference in the learning process between the theological classroom at the seminary and the theological clinic at the hospital. Doctrines which were of academic interest in the classroom became living and breathing issues at the bedside, in the emergency room, and in the morgue.[1]

The peculiar pastoral role of the minister lies in his or her ability to understand and interpret theologically the events of life: growth, passages, work (calling), marriage, birth, aging, illness, and death. Discerning meaning and purpose in the ordinary and the routine, as well as in the drama of crisis times, is the task of the pastoral theologian. The observation, listening, and purposeful reflection reported in a verbatim account often provide access to meaningfulness communicated even in apparently aimless conversations. As a former student of the late Anton Boisen remembered, "By careful imaginative listening I began to perceive the inner meanings of confused words and garbled symbols, and that erratic behavior, pointless to others, was seldom pointless to the patient."[2]

Constructing the Verbatim

My experience and training have been in the pastoral care departments of general hospital and physical rehabilitation settings. The guide for constructing a verbatim report is presented from within this context. Different settings, such as correctional institutions, mental hospitals, and outpatient centers, may require adjustments in this format to fit the unique situations that may exist in those facilities. The verbatim can be divided into three major sections: introduction, body, and evaluation.

Introduction (Context of the Visit)

The trainee reports any relevant information learned prior to the visit: age, sex, race, church membership, family, and reason for admission to the hospital. The chart may reveal significant events during the hospital stay, such as surgery, relapses, serious depression or suicidal thoughts, family conflicts. The introduction should describe, in summary, previous visits, if any.

The trainee would want to include any issues or concerns raised in prior conversations and the progress of the pastoral relationship. For instance, a patient may have spoken of a troubled marriage, worries about a child, anxiety over upcoming tests, grief and sorrow over certain deaths, fear of becoming a burden to the family, guilt over past events, regrets in regard to opportunities not taken. The patient may have mentioned dreams and hopes for the future, reliance on God's care, or anger about his or her illness.

It is helpful for trainees to begin the verbatim with some comment about the purpose of the visit. Entering the patient's room with a reason in mind enables the trainee to focus deliberately on how he or she intends to be helpful. Referral by a hospital staff member for a particular reason may provide the impetus for the visit. The visit may be one made in the process of continuing pastoral care with attention to issues already discovered. A first visit initiated by the trainee may have several purposes: introduction, orientation to chaplaincy services available, and formation of a pastoral relationship.

The recording of observations made upon entering the patient's room, or whatever the location of the visit, may be important. Is the person alone, or are visitors, other patients, or staff present? Is the patient dressed in a hospital gown, regular nightclothes, or street wear? Do cards and flowers fill the room, or are there no indications that the patient is part of a supportive community? Is the person in bed or on a chair, lying flat or sitting up, playing cards, watching television, reading, writing, or staring out of the window? Is the patient thin and gaunt, obese, resting comfortably, or restless and agitated? Are there intravenous needles and tubes, monitors, or other medical and technical paraphernalia about the room? Does the person appear to be worried, upset, sad, or peaceful? Careful observation of the context for this patient can inform the direction for this particular visit.

Body (Content of the Visit)

It is here that the trainee reproduces the conversation from memory, in full or in part. Because the beginning of the visit often sets the tone and contains significant information for the pastoral relationship, the trainee should carefully recall all introductory remarks. For much the same reason, the closing of the visit needs to be reported with some attention to detail. If the visit was a lengthy one, parts may be summarized before resuming the more detailed recall of the conversation. It is helpful to report prayers in entirety, while the scriptures that were read may be cited by chapter and verse number.

Movements, positions, and other bodily behaviors or gestures are often revealing and should be observed and reported. Whether the trainee sat across the room, stood beside the patient, or pulled up a chair to talk at eye level may indicate the trainee's degree of comfort or discomfort with the patient. If the person being visited reaches for the trainee's hand or if the trainee touches the person during prayer, these actions may raise issues of acceptance, intimacy, or invasion of privacy.

Tears, welling up or spilling over, by the trainee or the person being visited, deserve attention, as do laughter and trembling. Changes in demeanor, such as puzzlement, sadness, or wistfulness, may help in understanding what occurred during this visit.

Whether the body posture was relaxed or rigid, whether the voice tone contained indications of anger, whining, or impatience, may be important to learning from this visit.

The pastoral trainee's feelings and internal thoughts, questions and reflections contemporary with the visit, can help to explain the directions taken in the conversation or what was avoided and left unsaid. These also may reflect the trainee's own process for responding to emotion, internal conflict, and stress. For instance, if a patient does or says something that the trainee interprets as rejection, a trainee who is deeply hurt by the perceived rejection may quickly end the conversation in order to flee to safety. These and other remarks that are explanatory in nature rather than a verbatim record of the actual dialogue should be placed in parentheses or distinguished by some other means from the actual conversation.

Despite a faulty memory that falls short of mechanical accuracy, the trainee's own recall in retelling the visit reveals what he or she has deemed significant (and insignificant). While the account will not be exhaustive, the trainee has chosen what to share with the supervisor by selectively committing that memory to writing. The importance of what is reported in the verbatim is generally not undermined by the trainee's claim of error or omission, despite attempts to do so.

Evaluation (Learnings About the Patient, the Trainee, and the Helping Process)

The evaluation is vital. Without it, the verbatim serves only as a test of the trainee's ability to recall a conversation. The degree to which the trainee takes responsibility to examine and reflect upon the pastoral visit for his or her own learning is demonstrated in this final part of the verbatim format.

Length of visit. It is helpful to record the approximate length of the visit. If the patient invited the trainee into a more significant discussion and the trainee made an excuse or quickly ended with prayer, such a response is telling. Lengthy visits with no apparent purpose may relate to the trainee's reluctance to claim a pastoral identity.

Purpose of visit. The trainee may evaluate whether the initial purpose and intent of the visit was achieved, and in what manner. If the intent changed during the visit, then the reasons for the change should be noted. The revised purpose of the visit is itself subject to appraisal as to how it was addressed.

Psychological and theological assessment. Here, the trainee explores his or her own feelings and other internal processes during the visit in the light of how they affected the course of the pastoral conversation. It is illuminating to discuss the psychological dynamics occurring with both the trainee and the person visited to determine their impact on the visit and on the trainee. Examples include distrust of the pastoral trainee and the way in which he or she handled the trust issue in the pastoral relationship. Other issues may surface, such as intimacy, acceptance, rejection, transference, identification, low self-esteem, anger, and seductiveness. Theological issues raised directly or implicitly should be named and described and the pastoral response to them examined. Theological issues may include guilt and the need for confession, repentance, and forgiveness. Other theological issues might focus on grace, redemption, acceptance, reconciliation, and healing.

Identification of pastoral strengths and weaknesses. In this section, the trainee needs to claim specific pastoral strengths evident in the visit, as well as weaknesses, limitations, and areas in which growth is needed. A trainee whose strength lies in the ability to gain confidence and trust has the opportunity to discover this strength when the evaluation shows that the patient moved the conversation to a deeper, more meaningful level. Another trainee may learn that her prayers are specific, intimate, and even profound, while her growing edge lies in the application of these qualities to her pastoral conversation. Still another may find that he repeatedly identifies his own unresolved personal and theological issues, such as loneliness or anger, in patients whose own issues may be quite different.

Future Plans. Finally, future plans for ministry with this patient should be made, with specific pastoral recommendations. The evaluation should inform the trainee's prospective ministry with this patient. Issues raised in this visit can shape the direction of future visits when the trainee takes the time to reflect on the best ways to be helpful in this situation.

A Verbatim Account

It might be useful at this point to look at an actual verbatim. This is a verbatim report written during my own basic training under the supervision of Isaac Njuguna Kuria, director of Chaplaincy Services at Humana Hospital University of Louisville (then University/Louisville General Hospital) in Louisville,

Kentucky. It is not meant as a model verbatim but a sample to demonstrate the technique. P refers to the patient; C to me, the chaplain; W is the patient's wife; and D is the doctor.

> *Introduction.* Late one evening, when I was the only chaplain on duty, I was paged to the oncology unit. When I arrived there, a nurse told me that this patient's wife had just told him their daughter died in another hospital. The nurse was concerned about how they were coping and had asked if they were willing to see a chaplain, and they were. When I entered, the patient was in bed, a thin, frail black man. His wife, a small, worried-looking woman, was seated near the foot of his bed. Both of them had meal trays, but they were only dabbling at the food, as if dazed.
>
> They barely noticed my entry. I sensed they were confused and at a loss for direction, so I stepped near the patient and told him why I was here. I felt I needed to take the initiative.

C1: Hello. I'm Kathleen Davis, the chaplain. Your nurse just told me that your daughter died.

P1: Yes. I feel sick. Would you ask the nurse to call the doctor for me?

C2: Sure. (*I went out for a moment to ask the nurse to page his doctor.*) She's going to call him. How are you feeling?

P2: Oh, I'm having cramps and nausea.

C3: (*I touched his shoulder.*) This is a pretty terrible thing to happen. It's really okay to cry at a time like this. (*Then he broke loose in tears.*)

P3: She was so sick, she had so much pain. I knew it was coming. She told me, "Daddy, I'm so tired I'd just like to sleep and not wake up anymore."

C4: What happened?

P4: She had brain cancer. I've got cancer too. And she left three little children. Oh, I'm going to miss her so.

C5: Would you like to pray?

P5: Yes, please. (*His wife nodded, and I touched both of them.*)

C6: Lord, we come to you in great need. These two people have lost their daughter, still a young girl. We don't know why, and we don't really understand. But they have lost their daughter, whom they deeply love. For them we ask your strength and your hope that they may be able to let you carry some of their burden and lean on you as they grieve.

We pray for her young children, that you will comfort them as they mourn and that you will guide them as they grow, that they might remember their mother and her love for them as she watches over them from her home with you. Father, we come to you in the name of your Son, Jesus, because he knows the hurt and the loneliness we feel. He lost people close to him, and he wept tears for those he loved.

Lord, we know you've taken her away from pain and away from suffering. We believe that she's secure with you and in peace at last, resting in your arms. Still, Lord, it's hard for us here and we cry for ourselves now, but we know that one day we'll join her in the place you've prepared, a place not made by human hands, a place where there'll be no more crying, a place where you'll wipe away every tear, and there'll be no more dying.

We thank you for your sure promises and your love and presence here with us now, in the name of our Lord Jesus Christ, who is able to keep us from all harm. Amen. *(All three of us wept during the prayer.)*

P6:   Won't that be some day! No more crying. No more dying. And I'll be with my little girl again. She's not gone forever. It won't be long, and I'll see her again, and she won't have any more pain, no more needles, no, Lord. She'll have a new body.

W1:   She died yesterday at another hospital, but I didn't tell him then. He had all these tests to take yesterday.

P7:   You did right. I probably couldn't have made it through those tests if I'd known about her then. *(At this point a young resident entered the room, and the patient asked for medication.)*

D1:   We don't have any painkillers for the kind of pain you have. *(He sat down to talk with the patient about his daughter. I was concerned about the wife, so I turned to her.)*

C7:   This must be terribly hard for you with your husband in the hospital, too. *(She said nothing but pulled a picture of her daughter from her purse and handed it to me.)* Oh, she was a lovely girl. She must have been very special to you.

W2:   She lost all her hair with the cancer.

C8:   That must have been very difficult, watching her suffer.

W3:   She was only thirty-one. *(I touched her hand, and she held mine as we sat silently together.)*

P8:   Well, I'm going to wear the pants in this family! I always have, and I can't stop now. I've got three babies to raise, and I'm going to raise them like I raised their mother. She wanted me to. She told me. "Daddy, I want you to raise my kids just like you did me." We used to have wonderful times, you know, family picnics and all. Now her mother's had a stroke, but I'm going to raise those kids.

D2:   You don't have to do it all at once. There'll be time for that. But you don't have to put on your pants and be the strength of your family right now. There's still time now for you to cry and to grieve.

P9: Oh, I see what you're saying. I was trying to do it all at once. I guess you're right. I'm trying to rush everything. But each thing has to take some time. *(The doctor said good-bye and started to leave. I stayed a few moments more, just touching both the patient and his wife.)*

C9: I think I should go now too. I feel you and your wife need some time alone together to talk about your daughter, to share your memories of her and to cry together and comfort each other. If you feel like talking later, just have the nurse call me. God bless you both, and you'll be in my prayers.

P10: Thank you for coming.

EVALUATION. I think this visit helped the patient to find acceptance for his grief and his tears. At that point I think he needed a third party to facilitate this process. His wife was trying to be his strength, and her stoic stance was impeding his grief. Perhaps she had grieved a lot the day before. Possibly she was thinking about his death. I wasn't really able to get her to share much with me.

The visit lasted about half an hour. Initially, the patient seemed very sick and expressed what I thought was a desire to die soon (P6). Later, as he began to think about his three grandchildren, he visibly became more energetic and seemed to have a purpose for living. If his cancer is at all subject to psychological influences, his chances of surviving may be greater now.

Theologically, the patient expressed firm convictions about God and afterlife which seemed to comfort and assure him. Particularly during the prayer, I felt an overwhelming sorrow. This was the third time in a week that a girl younger than I had died of a terrible disease. My grief over the other two whom I knew, my grief over my own mortality, and my own terror of losing a daughter seemed too much. I felt that I shared their pain and their grief, and the prayer was my prayer for me as much as for them. I also felt hurt and confusion about death swooping down so unfairly and taking away people with so many dreams yet unfulfilled.

The Supervisory Conversation

This is a recount from memory of that portion of my next meeting with my supervisor that revolved around this particular verbatim. In that session, my supervisor noted the directness of my initial statement at C1 and asked me what was going on that I got to the point so quickly. My response was that since the nurse informed me she had advised the patient that she was calling the chaplain, I was confused when I arrived as the patient and his wife were doing their best to act normally. Since he knew why I was there, I thought it would be easier to get to the point. I *now* understand that straightforwardness is very much a part of my own pastoral style, and, while I value that aspect, I need to avoid being too brusque.

My supervisor accepted my explanation but then directed my attention to the abrupt manner in which I asked to pray. I agreed that, as I reflected now on this visit, it did seem that I prayed rather suddenly, but again, I didn't think that was terribly significant. He then gently pushed me to discuss my feelings during that visit. During this supervision and afterward, I became more aware of how I felt and how my feelings impacted that visit. This is the supervisory conversation that took place.

C1: Well, I was a little anxious, maybe a little surprised. When I walked in, I expected to find everyone upset and crying. Instead, he and his wife were calmly picking at their dinner as if nothing was wrong.

S1: Did you not want to go see this patient?

C2: Well, no. But I was the chaplain on duty, so I had to go. I did want to get it over with.

S2: Did that have anything to do with the other deaths you experienced before being called to see this man?

C3: It could be. I felt like I had more than my share that week. Grief seemed to be unending, and I was tired of it and wanted to be done with it.

S3: Did you feel you had any comfort or assurance to bring them?

C4: No . . . I felt drained and comfortless. None of these deaths made any sense. I felt overwhelmed by the tragedy of young lives cut short. That's probably why I prayed so quickly. I was at a loss how to deal with death. Since I felt I had no one to comfort me except God, then God was their only hope, too.

S4: It was a moving prayer. You seemed to be in touch with their feelings.

C5: The prayer felt right at the time.

S5: These people seemed very willing to allow you to enter this time of grief with them.

C6: Yes, I found them to be pretty open.

S6: Were you open with them?

C7: *(This question seemed to cut right through me, and instantly I knew I wasn't.)* I thought I was, because I cried. But now I think maybe I was afraid of all the feelings I had with them, so I moved into prayer, where that kind of intimacy feels more comfortable for me. Now, I wonder, did I cut them off and try to stop their grief process once I got it started?

S7: What do you think?

C8: I might have. In my prayer, I moved into hope for a new and better life, which may have communicated that death was fairly insignificant. Maybe that's why the patient began talking of taking charge in the family—that puts him in more control—it's orderly, instead of disorderly, like death.

Learnings About Myself

During this supervisory meeting, and since then as I have reflected on it and on the verbatim of this visit, I realized that I was sadly unaware of my own feelings when I walked into that room. I had tried to steel myself against more pain and grief but not very successfully. I was confused and disheartened, and I floundered in my own feelings of helplessness. Spiritually, I had neither sought nor found any earthly comfort and didn't believe I could provide that for these people. My prayer was my desperate flight to God, seeking consolation in promises of an ultimate goodness in tomorrow.

My supervisor ministered to me in my grief and helped me to take time to grieve. This was the beginning for me of learning how to let others in on my feelings so they could comfort me. After this visit, I made no plans to follow up on this family but referred them to the chaplain regularly assigned to their unit. Since then, I have come to understand this as one way I have avoided my own feelings of grief. Now I know enough about grief and about myself that I would plan to attend the funeral home or the funeral itself, or schedule another visit so that I can express my grief with them and put some closure on it.

Learnings About This Family

As I thought more about the visit, I became acutely aware of how thin and emaciated the patient appeared. I suspect that all of us in the room had this man's impending death in our consciousness at some level. The patient's statement at P6 that "it won't be long" before he joins his daughter is a conscious admission. His wife's apparent stoicism was probably her way of shielding herself against the vulnerability of death (his death, their daughter's, and possibly her own, since she had suffered a stroke herself). I am sure she was worried about the future and the raising of their grandchildren. My own difficulty with grief kept me from ministering to this concern.

Learnings About the Helping Process

The abruptness of my initial statement was perhaps experienced as intrusive. It would have been preferable to use a gentler approach and let them tell me all they needed to tell me. Through observation and reflection upon this visit and other visits, I have discovered the power of touch in the release of pent-up tears and emotions. The patient's body became less rigid and more relaxed as his tears flowed. Touch is an intimate gesture of caring which may help to permeate the "walls" we erect for strangers.

While I affirm my prayer as heartfelt and sincere, I can now recognize that the timing met my needs more than it did theirs. I rushed to dump all my grief and theirs in God's lap, perhaps its rightful resting place ultimately, but not then. The prayer may have contributed to the patient's "bounciness" of emotions and attitudes, as he moved from a wish for death to a courageous spirit of "I'll do it all." Because I did not permit myself to be still long enough to experience fully the deep sadness and pain in his life, he may have found it harder to stay in that painful place as well.

Theological Conclusions

Several theological learnings can be gleaned from the discoveries of this visit. One is that no real healing can begin to occur until the pain inflicted is permitted to be felt and suffered through. The cross always comes before the resurrection, and there do not appear to be any shortcuts to hurry through the pain in order to arrive at a glorious resurrection. Instead, grief that is unresolved and unattended becomes an unending dull pain that can become overwhelming when a new cause for grief develops. The way in which I had avoided my own grief and struggled to be strong is a case in point, since all that grief came rushing in on me as I listened to this family's story of death. Sensitivity to the right time, the *kairos* of any event, is the task of ministry. Insensitive to myself and the time I needed to allow myself to grieve, I found it difficult to give this family the time they needed.

Another theological implication is that, while our hopes and visions soar to another life that is eternal when we are faced with the mortality of our human nature, our existence is still rooted in the heartbreaking world in which all living things must die. The vision can provide us with hope in the present, but therein lies the potential illusion of immortality which can lure us to deny the painful reality in which we presently find ourselves. This family's reality was a tragic one: two aging, weakened individuals grieving the loss of their daughter and the loss of their own health at the same time that their situation demanded investment in their grandchildren's lives, now and in the near future.

They were living in the time that "is," and, with my assistance, looking toward a time that "will be" but is "not yet." Rather than looking at the one and ignoring the other, the minister must help them keep both in sight while living in the tension-filled ambivalence of hope and despair. As I tried to flee from this myself, I did them no service. The saving grace may be that both they and I needed a moment's respite from life's tearful journey: a reminder that death does not have the final word.

Diversity of Models for Use of Clinical Material

Presenting the verbatim material to the supervisor is only the beginning in learning how to use the clinical report with supervision. The trainee or the supervisor may have conceptual or practical concerns arising from the clinical material. These may relate to psychological, social, theological, pastoral, or personal issues. The manner in which the supervisor addresses these issues with the trainee and the emphasis given them will differ according to the trainee's and the supervisor's interests, knowledge, and skills. While the wide variety of styles available is beyond the scope of this chapter, an illustration may be helpful.

A trainee I supervised seemed quite unaware of the way in which he had controlled the conversation and distanced himself from the patient's concerns and feelings. I invited him to read the part of the patient aloud with me, while I read his part of the dialogue. As we switched roles, the feelings and messages communicated in that pastoral visit were re-created. With the benefit of that mini-drama, the trainee became aware of the effect he had on this patient. As a result, he then was willing to seek further understanding of himself as well as to explore alternative pastoral styles.

Caveat Against the Illusion That All Has Been Learned

In *The Wounded Healer,* Henri Nouwen urges an awareness that everyone is a complex being. He warns against the temptation to believe that any human being can be completely understood: "The mystery of one man is too immense and too profound to be explained by another man."[3] Nouwen was writing about a verbatim of a visit between a theological student and a lonely old man. That caution is always necessary for persons rich with the wisdom of concepts, theories, structures, and systems eagerly awaiting application.

While the search for understanding is imperative if theological training is to be taken seriously, the meanings of one person's life are so rich, deep, and varied that neither one excellent verbatim nor an intense and thorough supervisory session should be expected to eliminate the mystery. If it does, in all likelihood the process has terminated prematurely with self-satisfying and faulty conclusions.

Personal and Professional Growth

Most trainees will learn much about themselves by sharing their clinical work with a supervisor in this manner. Issues of individuation, differentiation, defense mechanisms, withdrawal behavior, vulnerability, warmth, openness, personal family history—all may be presented in verbatim material, knowingly or unknowingly. The trainee's and the supervisor's efforts are focused on discovering the obvious as well as the concealed, exploring the unconscious as well as the conscious. This self-awareness often facilitates personal along with professional learning and growth.

Fears shared with another may take on a sacramental significance. Grace may have been extended to another without having been named. Sin and guilt may have been deemed inconsequential through a premature pronouncement of forgiveness. The trainee's own experience of the absence of God in her life may be revealed in her reluctance to pray.

I hope it is clear that one does not take a variety of possible meanings and toss them indiscriminately onto the trainee and/ or the person visited. Instead, both the trainee and the supervisor seek to listen, think, and feel carefully and clearly enough that, together, they might discern the Spirit moving in the pastoral encounter and in the supervisory session.

Use of Verbatim Beyond Training

If the self-evaluation process of a verbatim is learned with any mastery, the trainee can use it for future ministry, with or without the aid of a supervisor. When a pastoral visit has left the minister confused, puzzled, upset, or even thoroughly pleased, writing it in the verbatim format will often help in knowing and understanding what transpired. Discovering what went wrong and why is only one side of the process. The other, equally important, is determining what one did to minister effectively so that such gifts can be claimed as part of the professional repertoire of skills.

The verbatim process permits a trainee to ascertain strengths and weaknesses in ministry. It is a stumbling block only to those who practice "seat of the pants" pastoral care, choosing from a limited and repetitive formula. Such folks are often unaware that any choice or decision was even made—"it felt right"; "the right words just came out of my mouth"; "our personalities just didn't work together." Through observation, reflection, and evaluation, one's own pastoral style can not only be recognized but enhanced and developed. A responsible ministry of pastoral care that is theologically sound and consistent, as well as personally effective, is the prize to be sought.

NOTES

1. C. R. Woodruff, "Theological Reflections in the Supervisory Process," *Journal of Pastoral Care* 34(3):198.

2. J. L. Cedarleaf, "Listening Revisited," *Journal of Pastoral Care* 38(4):311.

3. H. J. M. Nouwen, *The Wounded Healer* (Garden City, N.Y.: Doubleday & Co., Image Books, 1972), pp. 62–63.

6

Life Histories and Narrative Theology

Mark Jensen

Every day, pastors have people call them and ask to talk. In the pastor's office, in parishioners' homes, in grocery store aisles, ministers are told stories of wonder, sorrow, shame, and joy. One of the prototypical postures of Protestant pastoral care is that of pastor listening to a burdened parishioner. With what kind of ears do we hear those stories? How do we pan for spiritual gold in the stream of words with which we are greeted? Can we articulate principles by which we interpret these tales of life journey which are entrusted to our care? One dimension of supervision focuses on learning uniquely pastoral principles for interpreting the life stories of our parishioners.

Pastor: Interpreter of Texts

There is another typical posture of the Protestant minister that has to do with interpretation. It involves the minister opening the sacred texts in the presence of the people. The preacher is asked to read and interpret the texts of scripture for the life of the congregation. What do interpreting texts and listening to the stories of parishioners have to do with each other? Are pastoral care and preaching completely separate tasks requiring separate skills? The central focus of this chapter will be on utilizing the life stories of parishioners. In the latter part of the chapter, I will discuss some important continuities between these tasks of interpretation.

Anton Boisen captured the imagination of many in the theological world with his plea that we give attention to the "living human document." By that metaphor, he hoped to effect some change in theological education. He hoped to focus as much careful attention on the concrete plights of people in crisis as was normally focused on the documents of the church. His autobiography is a stirring testimony that his life story and his theological convictions yearned for integration, and he sought to find ways to train pastors to meet their parishioners with similar struggles. The method that Boisen and others, most notably Richard Cabot, pioneered in theological education is called the clinical method. It holds that what we see in our concrete experiences of ministry needs to be in dialogue with the assumptions about persons and ministry we bring to the ministry situation. The dialogue helps both our theory and our ministry. Some of the primary data that are grist for theological reflection are the unique life stories of the persons to whom we minister.

The Life Story: A Tool in Ministry

Mrs. R, whose husband was seriously ill (terminally ill, said the doctors), was talking to the chaplain in the hall. "I just can't pray," she said through tears. "I've always been able to pray, and now I can't. My prayers don't get any higher than the ceiling." She has come to the chaplain with a religious problem. In addition to the stress of a dying husband, she feels guilt for not being able to pray and deprived of the comfort of this religious resource. What is the chaplain to do? To be sure, there is no single, "right" course of action.

"Difficulty with prayer" and "dying spouse" are not simple pastoral assessments that lead to universally agreed upon prescriptions for action. What individualizes both assessment and pastoral intervention is the particularity of the parishioner's history and situation. Fortunately, the chaplain had had several previous conversations with this woman and her husband and had been able to learn some of their history. Despite the doctors' word that Mr. R's disease was in an end stage, Mr. R had continued to proclaim that he would soon be the recipient of a miracle. Mrs. R was not so sure. "I think he will get his healing in heaven," she had said. She had wondered whether her faith was weak, since she was not convinced that a miracle would soon make him better. Further conversations with Mrs. R revealed some other crucial events in her history. Her father had died as a young man with cancer. Later a brother to whom she was close had died. Finally, her first husband had died when they had been married only a short time. Do these events in her history and her current problem with prayer have anything to do with one another? Surely they do. Mrs. R may feel "cursed" by God in the wake of these griefs. She has probably felt abandoned by these important men, and in anticipating another grief, she may feel abandoned by God. If in some way Mrs. R has learned to feel responsible for these deaths (however unrealistic that may be), her sense of guilt may leave her feeling unworthy to bring her concerns to God. She has already intimated that she feels less than faithful for her doubts about a miraculous cure. Some understanding of her history may facilitate a more complete understanding of her current dilemma. Through that understanding, pastoral care can now move from generalized nurture to careful and individualized pastoral assessment and care.

People like Mrs. R often come to us when they are in crisis. A crisis occurs when relatively enduring patterns of living are disrupted. Anxiety rises to levels that feel unmanageable and persons in crisis often feel out of control. We can learn crisis intervention skills—indeed, we need them to get through any week in ministry. We need more, though, to carry us through the long haul of ministering to people over an extended period of time. What is missing in brief, crisis-oriented encounters is a context for the present crisis and a vision for continuing ministry and growth. Is this the first time such a crisis has ever happened in the life of this person or family? What did other crises mean in their life? What happened before things got so bad? Where had the journey taken people before they found themselves in our presence having this pastoral conversation? We need to know the answers to these and other questions if our ministry to persons in and out of crisis is to be whole.

Some of a parishioner's history usually emerges in even the briefest of crisis ministries. Often what we know of someone's story is piecemeal, imagistic, or even secondhand. Sometimes this is enough for the urgency of the moment. Why, then, concern ourselves with any more? Why would we seek to know more about a person's story as we minister to her or him?

A pastor does not explore the life history of a person in the same way a clinical pathologist would explore the natural history of a disease. While we may be moving toward a pastoral "diagnosis," we are not in search of some single, historical *cause* for the current malady. Instead, we are looking for a *context* for our understanding and the understanding of the person who has come to us. Even a brief focus of inquiry on a parishioner's history may help the current distress seem less ultimate. It may be that this person can immediately recall another time when life seemed similarly out of control. Such memories can relieve some of the pressure of the anxiety of the moment. They can provide needed distance from the seemingly overwhelming pressure of the moment. Pastor and parishioner may learn that the current crisis is a repetition of crises that have occurred before, and it may be time to ask deeper questions about how the parishioner contributes to the cycle. Finding a context for the current crisis helps provide distance and discernment.

John, age twenty-three, came to see his pastor during the Advent season. He complained that he simply did not feel close to God. Joy, he said, was not part of his current experience, and he thought it should be. Indeed, he found himself angry at the celebrative hymns and decorations. As John continued to talk, some of the following emerged. John's grandmother had died during this season a year ago—a grandmother with whom his family had always celebrated Christmas. Further, John had been jilted by his girlfriend during the summer, a woman some years older than he, with whom he had maintained a secretive relationship. Additionally, there was currently a good deal of tension between John and his father and stepmother, with whom John had lived until a year ago. John had been very involved in a Christian student organization in college and had developed a deep religious faith and devotional practice. Now it no longer held the same meaning for him.

A pastoral assessment must include all of these elements. John's pastor encouraged him to remain honest in his feelings toward God. He suggested that his image of God might be changing, perhaps deepening his college experience of warmth and enthusiasm. He also pointed out that John had some unresolved griefs that needed attention. He referred him for pastoral counseling and promised to stay in touch. He gave John *The Cloud of Unknowing* by Saint John of the Cross, which describes the darker elements of the spiritual journey, and promised to remember John in his own intercessory prayer disciplines.

When pastor and parishioner move to place a current life situation in a larger context, they are also moving toward exploring the *meaning* of this event in the life of the parishioner. Put theologically, the minister challenges the parishioner to interpret this event in the light of what he or she holds sacred. The pastor invites interpretation of this and other events of the parishioner's history, in the light of the conviction that the Divine is active in the affairs of the particular and mundane. This event may shatter inadequate myths by which one has lived. It may confirm convictions felt earlier but forgotten in recent years. It may serve as a parable that challenges particular directions in one's life. It may be another act in a continuing drama that needs attention.

The context of the pastoral relationship itself will determine how extensive is the history that is elicited. In pastoral care relationships, which are often briefer and at the initiative of the pastor, the history gathered may remain sketchy and anecdotal. The formal counseling relationship may be structured from the outset toward a more extensive exploration of a parishioner's history. In either case, the minister will want to be aware of the potential of one's life story as a resource for meaning.

Assuming that pastoral care and counseling will require us to be sensitive to the particular stories of our parishioners, we still need to address the issue of the kind of history it is we are eliciting. What kind of history do we want people to explore? One approach is to get a more or less "symptomatic" history. Persons come to us with a complaint about their life situation, and we find out how long it has hurt. There are various histories and subhistories we learn from psychiatry and psychotherapy: work history, sexual history, marital history, family history. Pastoral literature has taught us to take more explicitly religious histories. James Fowler has integrated developmental, structural, and religious perspectives in his theory and interview method. These particular histories seek a unity in a perspective that is distinctively *pastoral.* As Seward Hiltner taught us, the pastoral perspective colors all that we see and do. Hiltner's guiding image for pastoral practice and perspective was the shepherd. This image, as well as others, is grounded in the sacred stories around which the community of faith gathers.

At least two tensions abide in a pastoral approach to life story. The first tension is between "objective" history and "subjective" history. The goal of a completely objective history is an illusory notion, perhaps not even desirable if ever attainable. The pastor is not a detective looking for facts or clues with which to solve a case. The task of pastoral diagnosis or assessment is not something the pastor does in isolation from the parishioner, once given the right data. Pastoral assessment is a dialogue seeking mutuality. Together, pastor and parishioner are seeking to agree on areas of spiritual health and distress, on events of wounding and blessing, on themes of sin and forgiveness. Yet, by the process of this dialogue, the pastor invites parishioners to bring their subjective history into community, where it can be shared with the story of the larger community. Conformity is not the goal. The mutual enrichment of person and community is the goal. As a "private" history comes into the light of caring community, it can lose some of the power of its pain and discover its potential for wholeness.

Another tension in exploring a parishioner's history lies between seeking an explicitly religious history and knowing that all history is religious history. The minister represents the sacred dimension of life and attends to the explicitly religious experiences and distresses of the parishioner. The sensitive pastor will discover in giving attention to explicitly religious experiences a wealth of untapped resources. We live in a culture that does not have permission to discuss religious experience. As a result, powerful religious experiences often go without the caring attention they need in order to be integrated into a person's life. At the same time, the pastor recognizes the revelatory potential of all of a person's history, and models for the parishioner a sensitivity to the transcendent and the tragic themes in a history that seems mundane, "secular," or profane. The privatism of American culture's attitude toward religion fragments our experience. The pastor can encourage attention to the interior life and the cultivation of experiences with the sacred. At the same time, the pastor can challenge the false separation between what is secular and what is sacred.

Part of our challenge is to understand the importance of life history as a way of understanding persons in our care. Another, practical challenge is simply learning how to get that valuable data in front of us. How do we elicit the kind of history that gives us a context for understanding and ministering to people?

Eliciting the Life Story

The methods in any act of pastoral ministry need to be suited to the situation and to the goal of that ministry. Further, they need to be integrated into and flow out of the person of the pastor. It would be inappropriate for a chaplain who is making random initial visits on a hospital ward to begin by asking detailed questions regarding a person's history. Not only would it be psychologically intrusive, it would not be in keeping with the purposes of an initial visit where one is an uninvited guest. That kind of careful inquiry awaits the formation of some kind of agreement about the nature and purpose of the pastoral conversation.

In a context of pastoral care, initiative often rests largely with the pastor, especially early in the caring relationship. If a patient or parishioner displays some interest in receiving pastoral care, one of the ways of building relationship and sharing initiative is to elicit brief histories that relate directly to the crisis. "What has brought you to the hospital?" "What has it been like . . . [to be. pregnant, to find out you have cancer, to think of facing surgery, to imagine changing jobs]?" Questions like these allow much latitude for parishioners to share as much or as little as they need. It allows them to begin (or to continue) conceptualizing and symbolizing this event in the context of their larger story, and to do it in relationship. In finding and sharing the images that capture for them the meaning of the crisis event, they begin to move toward integration of events that can seem disconnected and overpowering.

One of the ways to elicit history and begin the search for resources to cope with crisis is to ask the person whether anything like this has ever happened before. Such a question begins to relate now to then, the strange to the familiar, furthering the process of integration. In the process of discovering how this crisis is like others through which the person has grown, hope is instilled into the present. When the pastor examines the ways in which the present crisis is similar to and different from other chapters in a person's history, the most pressing agendas for growth and pastoral attention can come into focus.

Questions and interview techniques that engage the imagination of the parishioner bring to the surface the potential for symbolization of the actual and the hoped for. James Hillman states that story awareness is in itself therapeutic.[1] Engaging the imagination in the service of healing raises parishioners' awareness of their stories. By attending to our history, we realize our status as cocreators, not merely passive recipients or victims of our history.

Sometimes a pastor's awareness of the life story of a parishioner comes as a result of a long relationship through times of crisis and equilibrium. This shared history becomes a primary resource at the disposal of both. The pastor can recall what he or she knows of a parishioner's history and share images about the current event out of that context. The parishioner can confirm or correct the pastor's observation. In the instance of the pastoral relationship that has extended over a long time, memory becomes a primary resource in the service of hope.

The Life History in Ministry Supervision

Recall the model for supervision advanced in chapter 3. Reflection upon a parishioner's life history is focused on the third, clinical pole, that of the person or persons receiving pastoral care. Exploring and drawing upon a person's life history in ministry to him or her falls most clearly in this pole of the supervisory field. As we will see below, issues of life story do not always limit themselves to this pole, even if they originate there. The effective minister also needs to have some understanding of his or her own life story and the way it affects his or her care of souls.

When the pastor or the pastoral counselor explores with a person that person's life history, the presenting crisis comes into clearer focus. We see the antecedents of the present crisis and its echoes in the other dimensions of a person's life. What John and Mrs. R presented came into clearer focus as the minister understood and explored with them their histories. Their questions were no less theological ones when looked at in this way. Rather, the depth of their spiritual distress came to life. Pastoral care must not reduce their spiritual difficulties to "mere" psychological categories with historical "causes." Neither should pastoral care spiritualize the concrete relational and intrapsychic dimensions of their distress.

A number of tools and methods exist for exploring life stories in the context of ministry. Some focus more on intergenerational dynamics, with most attention to the structure of the family of origin. Some look more closely at developmental milestones and individual experiences of them. Others focus more explicitly on religious memories and experiences. What they have in common is that they provide some structure for ordering a large amount of data. Administered mechanically, they will be a barrier to relationship, even if they help to gather data. Experimentation with one or several in the context of supervision can help the pastor find and utilize his or her own natural style of pastoral conversation. It is essential to remember that whatever method one uses to explore history, the context of this exploration is the pastoral *relationship.* Exploring life stories becomes a part of the art of pastoral ministry, evolving within the pastoral relationship. (One approach is outlined in the appendix to this chapter.)

Wayne Oates describes what he calls a "thematic approach" to pastoral diagnosis. He explores life history around the rubrics "the way things were," "the way things are," and "the way things can change."[2] Edgar Draper developed the Religious Ideation Questionnaire (RIQ), which Dan McKeever explored as a tool for pastoral assessment.[3] James Fowler and his associates have developed and are continuing to research the implications of Fowler's Faith Development Interview as a model for exploring life stories.[4]

A number of methods also exist for using the life history in individual and group supervision. One of the most common is the case conference. In a group case conference the spheres of the supervisory relationship and the supervisee's peer relationship are also activated in the learning process. Students present, instead of a simple verbatim, a verbatim placed in the context of a rather thorough history, as the student has been able to gather it in the pastoral relationship. Another method is for the student to present a history of his or her relationship with a parishioner (extending over a number of pastoral encounters) alongside the parishioner's life history. This kind of study allows us to see if and how the themes of a parishioner's life history are being replicated in the current crisis and pastoral relationship.

Sometimes the life history of a parishioner will parallel that of the minister in ways that produce anxiety or conflict for the minister. Here attention shifts to the pastoral pole which now becomes the focus in supervisory conversations. Pastor and supervisor may need to give explicit attention to themes in this sphere that impinge upon the care given to parishioners. Linda found herself ministering to a woman in an intensive care unit who had a problem with substance abuse. Linda's mother had abused alcohol for years, and Linda found herself paralyzed in ministry to this patient. She needed to turn aside and name what was unexamined and unfinished in her own life story as she continued in ministry to this woman. Were she simply to react to her as she had to her mother, she would have seen clearly neither her own story nor that of the patient, who was different from her mother in important ways. These parallels can be named and examined or referred for therapeutic work. Particular themes of grief or abandonment or abuse may provoke anxiety in the minister who has these themes as parts of his or her own history. Supervision helps the minister to learn to walk between the perils of overidentification and detached aloofness. Ministry in depth will always raise themes for the sensitive and reflective minister that are in need of attention in his or her own story. Recognizing these themes and remaining responsible in pastoral relationship are the goals of supervision that looks at life stories of parishioner and pastor.

Narrative: A Form Uniting Clinical and Theological Reflection

I suggested at the outset that the pastor's role as interpreter of scripture and interpreter of life story (neither done ex cathedra) have some basic similarities. Both are theological tasks. Both move from primary data (events of life story, texts of scripture) to some theoretical aids (theological and psychological assumptions, historical-critical tools) to some interpretive suggestions. Such is the method of clinical education and of pastoral theology.

Not only is the method of interpretation similar, scriptural texts and life stories have a similar form: *narrative.* To be sure, the texts of scripture are of many genres (as are our stories of self), but scripture is fundamentally narrative of divine and human encounter. When the writers of scripture set out to describe their experiences with and understandings of God, they did not write a systematic theology. They wrote poems, songs, and accounts of what they had seen and heard. When we set out to describe what is sacred and profane, we tell stories of our experience. Doctrine and systematic generalizations arise only *after* the formative stories have been told.

Stephen Crites wrote a now-classic essay in 1971 entitled "The Narrative Quality of Experience."[5] He argued that our experience is inherently temporal in form and in memory. When we recollect that experience to communicate it to others, the form we inevitably use is narrative: we tell a story. It is a distinctly human characteristic that we have a self-conscious history we can share in the form of a narrative. Not only do we use stories to represent the past, we "live in" stories that inform our understanding of our present and our future. The Christian community gathers around a set of sacred stories that lend meaning to past, present, and future time. Early Christian preaching was essentially telling the story of Jesus, asserting that the life of this one had changed the meaning of history.

Streams of interest in both philosophical theology and biblical criticism have converged to produce a flood of literature in "narratology." "Narrative theology" is a phrase that describes a wide range of studies in biblical and theological areas. Following Crites's insight, scholars have continued to examine the implications of this fundamental form of experience for the way we interpret scripture and construct theology. Pastoral care literature is beginning to make applications for pastoral theology and practice.[6] It appears that Boisen's metaphor "living human document" is alive and well. Like the best metaphors, it is continuing to shed light in ways not apparent even to its author. The field of "narrative theology" is expanding more rapidly than the best of readers can comprehend, and a summary is impossible. Among the most promising elements of the entire movement is that it is interdisciplinary. Pastoral ministry and pastoral theology at their best are always interdisciplinary. How is it helpful for our task of understanding life stories in ministry and supervision?

Stanley Hauerwas has rendered a definition of narrative that gives us a clue: narrative is "nothing less than the connected descriptions of actions and sufferings which move to a point that is not detachable from the description itself."[7] What does that mean? Among other things, it means that we cannot fully describe ourselves or our parishioners without reference to the stories that make up our histories. It means that we cannot capture the meaning of the doctrine of the atonement without reference to the story of the crucifixion and the resurrection. It means that Mrs. R's distress in her prayer life cannot be disconnected from her life story.

For the self-consciously religious person, the multitude of stories that make up one's narrative of self seek coherence in a set of sacred stories. For the Christian, these are the stories of scripture and of the church. Moral and religious growth, according to Hauerwas, "involves the constant conversation between our stories that allows us to live appropriate to the character of our existence."[8] The struggle to integrate stories has an honored literary history in the church. Witness the esteem in which the autobiographical writings of Augustine, John Bunyan, Jonathan Edwards, St. Teresa, and others are held. As pastors, we are helping parishioners shape their autobiographies.

In attending to the narratives of self that parishioners present to us, we listen with them for the themes of conflict and transcendence, tragedy and comedy. In presenting these ministry encounters for supervision, we gain the wisdom of supervisors and peers. One way to listen to crises in the context of life stories is as parable in conflict with myth.

Terrence Tilley writes about the difference between myth and parable. Myth, he says, is world-constructing.[9] We live in the world constructed by our myths. Parables upset the world of myth. By using the familiar, they challenge the ordinary with reversals of plot and meaning. Prodigals are welcomed, and good elder brothers are left outside pouting, challenging our notions of good. Life events also come along that challenge the particular myths by which we have constructed meaning. Gerald, age forty-three, has always worked hard. His addictive relationship to work coincided with the myth of achievement as the means to salvation. His heart attack became a parabolic event that challenged the myth by which he has lived. Events like this can become parables that are turning points for growth. The pastor can be the midwife of these events which result in continuing growth for a parishioner in crisis. With supportive and interpretive help, parishioners need not stubbornly defend myths that no longer lend coherence and meaning to their world or that do so only at the cost of self-destructive patterns. Thus it is that divorce, heart attack, or other crises can become parables that sharpen our vision of our selves and our world.

Gerald's heart attack occasioned a time of self-examination. He began to realize his driven and addictive relationship to his work and his neglect of self and others. He began to reorder priorities to include better diet, times for rest and renewal, and more attention to important personal relationships and spiritual values. He still struggles to keep those things in balance, but his heart attack did occasion reflection and change.

Donald Capps points out that autobiography (exploring life history) is not mere reminiscence. One of the major purposes of looking back is to perceive what was *not* perceived when an event first occurred. In looking back, we are not only recalling but reordering our perceptions about the past and its meaning for the present. "It is a restructuring of our perceptions of what we have been in order to gain a clearer picture of what we are becoming."[10]

Parabolic Events in Supervision

As the minister helps a parishioner to integrate parabolic events from his or her history, so supervision helps the minister discover those events in ministry which are parabolic for learning. The "critical incident report," in which the supervisee records a ministry encounter that was personally powerful, can help capture these parabolic events. Figure 6-1 is an outline that a minister in training might use to reflect with his or her supervisor on a pastoral encounter that had been significant for them.

Often the power of the critical incident roots in themes from one's history which await deeper examination and integration. I can recall several events from my own supervision that were parabolic for my own growth, learning, and ministry. The most powerful have been events in which I failed or perceived myself to have failed. When those were examined in supervision, I was able both to take responsibility where appropriate (against my history of taking too much responsibility) and to receive grace when I had clearly not earned it. Those parables upset the myth of self-sufficiency, of grace only as reward. Those conflicts are not neatly resolved. Nonetheless, those events help me to reflect on my history as well as on what I am becoming.

We see, then, that exploring life story in ministry is not simply a skill to be learned, although acquiring and honing skills are indispensable. In the acquiring and honing, the reflective minister will inevitably encounter ministry situations that are parabolic in his or her own life. They may occasion a re-perceiving of the minister's personal history. The life history involves several of the spheres in the supervisory field. If all that is examined

is the life history of the ministry student, then supervision has
become therapy and is unbalanced. If ministry encounters never
yield insights for the minister's own history, then learning has
become impersonal and lacks transformative power.

Setting: Where did the event occur? At whose initiative? What did you
notice about the setting that affected your preunderstanding of this encounter? What purpose and/or questions did you carry into this event?

Characters: Who was there, literally or symbolically? Who became central in this encounter? Who remained peripheral?

Plot: What happened? The traditional verbatim reporting can be placed
here. Supervisor and/or student may choose a narrative rather than
verbatim description, or a partially narrated description with key exchanges reported verbatim.

Themes: What recurring themes or symbols (named or not) appeared in
this encounter? What topics kept coming up or were consistently avoided
(by you or them)?

Tone: What were the feeling tones in this encounter (yours and theirs)?
Were the feelings congruent with the themes named above?

Further Reflections: What are the metaphors from the parishioners' life
story which characterize the way they experience and approach the
world? What images of ministry inform your understanding of the pastoral
relationship? What images from this pastoral encounter inform your images and understandings of ministry? What themes from your own life
story are evoked in and by this encounter? How do they affect your
understanding of this parishioner and the pastoral encounter? How does
the encounter affect your understanding of your own story? How do you
symbolize the presence and/or action of the Divine in reflection about
this encounter? How does your image of God inform your reflection upon
this ministry? How does your reflection upon this ministry inform your
images and concepts about God and the human situation?

Figure 6-1. Pastoral Encounter: An Outline for Reflection

Supervisors too come with unique personal histories. They
will be both blessed and limited by them. The responsible supervisor has awareness (always growing) of both those gifts and
those limits and seeks consultation regarding them. Supervision
is a personal event for supervisor as well as supervisee. Their
covenant is to continue to grow in skills of interpretation—
interpreting the "living human document." The primary and
consistent focus will be on the life stories of persons whom we

encounter in ministry. The horizons that bound that interpretive space include the sacred stories of the faith and the life stories of both supervisor and supervisee.

Appendix: Outline for Taking a Religious History

Several approaches to taking religious history have been named above. I am in debt to those authors for much of what follows. Readers are referred to the sources named above for more complete understandings of their approaches to life story and the assumptions that underlie them. The outline below is a brief one that can be administered in pastoral care settings. The thematic organization is identical to the one offered for reflection on the pastoral encounter (Figure 6-1).

Context, Setting

Where were you born, and who were the persons in your family of origin?

What were the religious and social class identifications of your family?

Have they changed?

What did your family teach you (in word and deed) about being religious?

How are you different from that?

Characters

Who are/were the persons who have been most influential in your religious development? How were they influential?

Who is your favorite saint or biblical character?

Have there been writers or figures in history that are important to your understanding of faith?

What is your favorite biblical or religious story?

What is your favorite hymn or religious song?

What is your favorite scripture or religious writing?

Plot

Have you had experiences that were turning points in your relationship to God? Describe them as best you can.

Describe the time in your life you felt closest to God.

Describe the time in your life you felt farthest from God.

Describe how you feel about God at this time in your life.

What religious practices are important to you? Why?

If you could change your past, how would you do it?

If you could change yourself now, how would you do it?
What does the future look like to you?

Themes

How would you describe sin(s)?
When you are most discouraged, what renews your hope?
Why do some people suffer more than others?
Do you think much about death? How do you feel about dying?
Is there a purpose or plan for human life? How do you understand that?
What things do you not understand about God or your faith?
What religious symbols are most important to you? Why?

Tone

How does God feel about you and why?
When you think about God, what do you feel?
What blessings were given to you by those who brought you up?
What curses were conferred upon you by those who brought you up?

NOTES

1. J. Hillman, "A Note on Story," *Parabola* 4:4 (1979).

2. W. E. Oates, *The Religious Care of the Psychiatric Patient* (Philadelphia: Westminster Press, 1978), pp. 108–109.

3. D. McKeever, "Personal Religious History as a Pastoral Tool," *Pastoral Psychology* 24:65–75 (1975).

4. J. W. Fowler, *Stages of Faith* (New York: Harper & Row, 1981).

5. S. Crites, "The Narrative Quality of Experience," *Journal of the American Academy of Religion* 39:291–311 (1971).

6. D. Capps, *Pastoral Care and Hermeneutics* (Philadelphia: Fortress Press, 1984); and C. V. Gerkin, *The Living Human Document: Re-visioning Pastoral Counseling in a Hermeneutical Mode* (Nashville: Abingdon Press, 1984).

7. S. Hauerwas, "Character, Narrative, and Growth in the Christian Life," in *Toward Moral and Religious Maturity,* ed. Christiane Brusselmans (Morristown, N.J.: Silver Burdett Co., 1980), p. 476 n. 13.

8. Ibid., p. 447.

9. T. Tilley, *Story Theology* (Wilmington, Del.: Michael Glazier, 1985), p. 39.

10. D. Capps, "Parabolic Events in Augustine's Autobiography," *Theology Today* 40:271 (1983).

7

Student Responses
to Clinical Pastoral Education

Alexa Smith

Thomas was nervous, "very nervous," on the first day. There were the gates and the wire. There was the mandatory paperwork required of all persons working for the Commonwealth of Kentucky, Department of Corrections. There was the guard, who demanded identification as Thomas made his first, very timid visit, to the women residents' living quarters. And there was what seemed like a blaring announcement over the prison public-address system: "Man on the floor. Please dress appropriately."

That was three weeks ago. Thomas laughs now when he tells the story about when he arrived "very unsure" of himself, wanting very specific directions about what to do during the day, wanting "somebody to check up on me, every item, like grading a paper."

Chaplaincy, he found, is not quite that way. Directions are not that specific. Emergencies arise. His days are as different as are the women encountered in each one.

"I'm a little bit more comfortable with what's going on," the three-week veteran chaplain now says with a smile, noting that he readily discusses situations and problems with his supervisor. But much of the time, his supervisor is not at the prison when Thomas is at work. Discussion is after the fact—in review, reflection, and evaluation. "And somebody to check up on me, every item. Well, I'm not sure I need that, but it is good to know it is there when I do need it," Thomas says.

Such discovery is the crux of what clinical pastoral education (CPE) means, according to students who have completed it. It means discovering one's pastoral self, one's strengths and gifts, one's conflicts and limitations. That occurs in two ways: through personal reflection and through clinical evaluation. Both influence a student's professional and personal growth. The two are inseparable.

This chapter reports a series of interviews conducted with students at the Louisville Presbyterian Theological Seminary who have completed one or more units of CPE. Participants were selected at random and reported a range of experiences, from very good to very difficult. The names of those interviewed, as well as identifying facts, have been changed at the discretion of this writer.

Professional self-understanding and personal self-understanding require reflecting on and evaluating both thoughts and actions. When the process works well, students say it opens up their lives. When it does not, it may be grueling. When it does work well, students say it requires certain disciplines, such as honest dialogue, personal vulnerability, responsible motives, authentic support, and a willingness both to hear and to give criticism. That requirement, they say, applies to both students and supervisors.

Such understanding, students say, is ongoing. It does not end when the unit does.

Such understanding, students say, is not acquired in isolation. It requires other people—supervisors, colleagues, clients, and not necessarily in that order of significance. Students say that genuine relationship is crucial, something the finest tools and techniques may hone but may not create. It is the essence of the experience—professional and personal, emotional and spiritual, theological and psychological. It is the catalyst for self-understanding.

Reflecting on Professional and Personal Growth

A lifetime of experience is what a person brings into ministry. And that is what the CPE student encounters—himself or herself and a lifetime of experience which informs the student's present.

Intense daily interaction with others—in prisons, hospitals, and mental health institutions—brings questions about that experience to the forefront: How does the student understand God to work in the world? What family traits, what old hurts, is a person bringing to his or her ministerial relationship? How is the student's past repeated in the present, with a new cast of characters? How easy is it to accept criticism? How does the student feel about being touched, hugged? How is the student threatened? On what issues is his or her mind closed? How realistic are the student's personal expectations?

Such interaction may generate new questions and reflections for the student. Common questions center around self-encounter, pastoral identity, personal limitations, and one's image of God. Professional self-understanding and personal self-understanding are interwoven, and such understanding is used to minister effectively to others.

Encountering One's Self

"There was a lot of emotion in it," says twenty-four-year-old Jeff, a second-year theological student. "I was feeling scared. It was difficult every day for me. I mean, seven months after my dad's death from cancer, here I was a chaplain on an oncology unit. It was something I wanted to do. I put a lot of thought into the decision to request that placement. And I needed to be there, working on issues of my dad's death as it relates to me, a professional, and how I effect ministry to others. And, a couple of times, I did meet Dad again. Seeing the wife, knowing that once this man dies, she's going to be alone. Well, I saw Mom in that."

Jeff was a chaplain. Daily he checked the patient census to find out who was scheduled for surgery and whose condition had changed from the day before. There were weekly meetings with nurses, with therapists, and with social workers—each soliciting the other's input for overall patient care. He preached twice that semester and attended peer group meetings and individual supervision sessions.

Daily he learned about his personal life and his professional role, how the two were enmeshed, the strengths, the weaknesses. A sensitivity to those dying of cancer—and to those watching the death—was one strength Jeff brought to the oncology unit. "I am sensitive to those with cancer," he admits. "And not just the statistics, the person right here, like my dad. Every story is different, yet it has a common theme and plot.

"There are sons and daughters who feel anger toward the dying patient, toward God, toward life, and they feel anger that they have anger, with people facing cancer, with themselves or the family." Jeff feels he knows what that is like, what it is like to be open to those feelings, the fears that prevent expressing those feelings.

"I dealt with patients in any kind of crisis, feelings about an upcoming surgery, what kinds of fears they had. I was there to share their feelings, any emotion they might need to express, if they were willing. Some were not willing, some couldn't," he says, adding that personal vulnerability is a struggle for him too. "I think I knew unconsciously that I would need to be fully in touch with my feelings working on that unit. And unconsciously, too, I knew I had built a wall around me because I've been hurt—and I was going to protect myself from any other hurt that might hit me. My supervisor helped me realize that.

"That's good and bad," Jeff says. "It's good to protect yourself, but the bad thing is that it prevents intimacy, risking. 'How am I going to feel if I know more about this person, if I like the person? Because the person may leave me, might die.' "

Jeff says he is more aware of the anger he felt throughout his father's death and he is more aware of the control he seeks in relationships, control over what is unexpected and hurtful. That fear of opening up, making himself vulnerable, was identified by both his supervisor and his chaplaincy peer group. Both needing and fearing closeness is a conflict still for Jeff, a conflict he is addressing. He adds, "I realize Dad is dead, realized that even at the beginning of the unit. But processing grief about that is ongoing with me. What I wanted to look at was how it affects my ministry; and it does significantly influence it."

Struggling with Pastoral Identity

Ministry is not Adam's first career. He came to seminary in his mid-thirties with a background in marketing. He came with lengthy experience in the job market and with what he considers to be a degree of self-awareness. What he was lacking was a sense of his pastoral self. Adam says, "In being a minister, what was my task? Doing my first services, taking the authority I need to take in worship. And that is still an issue for me personally." He smiles, slowly reflecting, "See, I thought pastoral care was being able to drum up the right scripture. I thought they would teach me the right things to say, to know how to respond to a cancer patient. Instead, I found my presence was the most important thing. Listening skills were very important, as well as some ability to get the patient to tell you what is really troubling."

That discovery happened for Adam during his first semester, which included a twenty-five-hour-a-week unit of CPE in a hospital. He says he chose it because chaplaincy was appealing and because he got paid for taking it. Then he says he heard the "horror stories of how people would try to tear me apart emotionally, that I'd have to watch people die and come home incapable of doing my studies, gruesome things. It was just not true.

It was interesting, delving into myself, finding out what makes me tick."

Much of that was done in patient care, Adam says. The emotion that was sometimes created was addressed with peers and with his supervisor. "Therapeutic issues did come up in that," Adam says, adding that his family's history of heart disease impacted him during work in the hospital's coronary care unit, generating anger, fear, and identification. Supervision, however, was not a time for therapy, he says; that time was spent clinically.

Now he says, "Working in an atmosphere like that seems to provoke emotional responses. It's an intense atmosphere. You're dealing with people in crisis. You see emotional reactions in them and also in you. But my supervisor allowed us to ask her for additional time if we needed it. For instance, I had a burn patient who had set herself on fire. It was the most horrible physical sight I had ever beheld. After I'd seen her, I needed to talk with someone and my supervisor was available."

Understanding the client and understanding a personal response to the client is not always accomplished in the clinical setting. It takes private time, too. That was true for Joan. "No one can tell you some of the understanding. You can't understand until you understand," says Joan with a smile. "And I'm not trying to be mystical." Joan worked twenty-five hours a week as a prison chaplain. She began the unit, she related, struggling with her pastoral identity, with her call, and struggling with what ministry itself meant. "Wearing a black robe and preaching on Sunday just didn't appeal to me. I was trying to understand my call, wondering if I even had a call. And I found that my identity as 'pastor' is no different than my identity as 'me.' It was no different, just more intentional," she says.

Joan was walking out of the prison gate at the end of a long day, wondering what she had accomplished talking with woman after woman about problem after problem. "I was thinking that the residents were talked to death all day by teachers, counselors, social workers, and caseworkers. And I was on that list too, another talker. Then it hit me that the chaplain is the only one of all those people addressing the women's relationships to God, that their guilt and anger, fear and pain, were spiritual and theological issues. I realized that I had a place and could maybe even do some good.

"I like people, talking with them, hearing their stories, looking for meaning in those stories. And for the first time, I felt I understood my call and my identity as a pastor—and it was just being me," she says.

Accepting Pastoral Limitations

Finding a pastoral identity is not, however, the culmination of the unit, according to Jane, a thirty-four-year-old, third-year seminary student. It includes working out that identity daily, both in a relationship to God and in conveying that relationship to others. Jane worked in a prison too. It was her second clinical placement. She says awareness of her pastoral identity was the easy part. The hard part was coming to terms with its limitations.

"Like, how to minister in this God-forsaken place. There were times when I really felt some people, after I'd heard their stories, were really God-forsaken. How in the world could I be God's agent to those people? Some of the issues I was confronted with in prison I'm not sure I've fully resolved," she says, speaking slowly and deliberately. "I'd be talking with people who were imprisoned on sex offenses. I'd read their files. I'd talk to them, and I could tell this is how they had been treated all their lives. And I certainly don't have a quick fix. They've been abused all their lives. They've been abusers. Then, the issue is, where does the responsibility lie?"

Jane says she knows that ultimate responsibility for decisions and actions lies with the individual, but she also says: "Some were so badly abused I don't think they really are capable of saying they won't be an abuser anymore. The pattern is so ingrained and I feel unhopeful for them. They're poor. They can't pay for decent help. The prison system is not going to provide it, at least not the kind I think they need. And I'd feel real sad."

Formulating a response to such stories was hard, Jane says. "You don't want to say, 'God loves you.' That is trite. Finding something meaningful to say was hard. The best thing I could do was to be there with that person who was sharing something painful with me." By "being there" she means listening and caring about what she heard, caring about who said it, communicating value and worth.

"Being there" for Jane also meant understanding her own anger at the stories told by the inmates—and it meant addressing her own anger with God that such situations exist, that such pain continues. "Take, for instance, the sexual abuse of children, of a small child, literally helpless—a child who will be haunted by these things for the rest of her life! That made me the angriest. How in God's name do people like this exist? I found myself really questioning God's interaction with humanity. God's role. God's power. The role of evil," she says.

Addressing One's Image of God

Marian is approaching mid-life. Early in their relationship, Marian's supervisor confronted her image of God. She says she was told her God did not serve her well, that she needed another, that she was terrified of her God; that her God was, in fact, a punishing father, a controlling male, a figure she could never please.

"Once you're told something like that," she says, "you just can't shove it aside. You have to figure out in your own mind why it's wrong or if it's true. And it made me angry that I had to deal with that, that I couldn't just leave it alone." She added that she had "no idea" how to replace her angry, punishing God with another kind of God.

Marian spent her semester examining her God image—and listening for the God images of others, her peers, her patients. She says she was careful to see if the image kept a person passive or powerless, if a person adopted a "This is God's will and I am helpless" position in life. Her own image of God expanded, she says. Her heavenly enthroned monarchial God became instead a personal source of power, present and available. Marian says she began thinking of God "as a verb."

"I began to see God giving me the strength to handle what is facing me and giving other persons the strength to handle what is facing them," she says, adding that God became "an extra source of power and strength," enabling people to transcend mortal inabilities and weaknesses.

She remembers sitting with a couple whose baby had died and how they struggled. She remembers sitting with a Vietnam veteran needing to vent memories—memories he had never before expressed—just before a risky surgery.

Marian says her changing God image altered her pastoral style, altered the way she responded to a hurting person's rationale, someone who said, "Well, this is God's will—I don't understand the reason." Instead, Marian says she saw God in a different place, that she was able to agree that terrible things happen, unwilling to agree that God is the cause. Her pastoral style expressed that, she says, placing "the power to cope squarely in the hands of God," acknowledging "God is there to help you get through this."

"We spent a good amount of time on our identities as ministers," Marian says of learning acquired during the unit. "I became aware of how my personal stuff affected how I interpreted what I heard during a pastoral visit, how I responded to a client I was willing to talk with."

She pauses. "There were times when I'd think, 'I'm totally inadequate. But I'm willing to do the only thing I know to do.' That was to be there, just listening and responding. And that's what they needed. Part of that is accepting the fact you've got limitations. Maybe it's not so much inadequacy. There are limits to what you can do. There are limits to what anybody can do."

Reflecting on Clinical Contacts

When students talk about clinical study, they talk about other people—their peers and their clients. They talk about relationships formed or those which did not develop. They talk about their own feelings and reactions. Students say evaluation and critique by supervisors and by peers are among the most crucial aspects of clinical work. They say it is a paradox, because it may be one of the hardest parts, too.

How clinical evaluation occurs varies from place to place, from supervisor to supervisor. There are, however, some standard approaches: verbatim writing, dual calling, interpersonal relations groups, role playing, clinical research, and preaching. Some are required to complete religious ideations, which are profiles of the stage of faith a client demonstrates. Others file short case histories, supplemented by readings of existing files. Pastoral assessments, utilized to identify issues related to the presenting problem (such as depression stemming from grief), are mandated for others.

Some of the reflection and evaluation occurs through peer group interaction. Some occurs one on one, student to supervisor.

Utilizing Verbatims and Dual Calling

Rachel and her supervisor often read verbatims out loud, back and forth, each assuming different roles. "When you read it out loud, you can see how it came across, not just the words, but the tone," says Rachel of her conversations with patients, reported line by line in the written verbatim. "Using that kind of feedback, you can become aware of other issues there, like why I stopped something, why I went in one direction in a conversation instead of another. Or, we'd evaluate if I missed something, something going on with the patient."

Jeff concurs. Verbatims were one way his intimacy issues surfaced. "My verbatims showed where I was lacking in intimacy, where I feared pushing patients with their emotions, where I avoided their feelings, where I wasn't completely in touch with mine. My supervisor would say, "What's going on? I see you as distant from this patient. What's going on there?" The supervisor noted that in the beginning of the unit Jeff often "came across as everything is okay," when in reality everything was not okay. Jeff found he offered reassurances rather than an intimate exchange. That was discerned in line-by-line analysis.

"I tend to rescue too quickly," Adam says, thinking back to verbatim sessions. "I'd just say, 'There, there now.' I think initially I was afraid I would not be comforting, sympathetic enough, but I found I was too much. My supervisor wanted me to be more confrontive." Adam also recalls learning how to pose open-ended questions, prompting conversation, instead of questions that could be answered with a "yes" or a "no."

Dual calling is another method of evaluation. Once, at Rachel's request, she was accompanied by her supervisor on a pastoral call. Rachel was a hospital chaplain. This was during a week when Rachel was unable to complete a verbatim for individual supervision. Though the supervisor's presence made both the chaplain and the patient nervous, according to Rachel, she says she found the feedback useful on how she related to the patient.

Another student who was accompanied by a supervisor on two visits, a unit requirement, is less positive about the experience, finding it inhibiting for both the patients and the student chaplain.

Processing Peer Group Interaction

Behaviors are also identified, observed, and experienced by peer group members. Common questions examine: Does a student communicate thoughts or feelings? What is not said? What makes it hard to be close? Is humor healthy or a defense mechanism?

Just how that is communicated to the individual varies from group to group, in a setting known as interpersonal relations group (IPR). Length and frequency of the sessions vary with the facility—some running weekly, others more often. Dynamics are passive and calm in some circles and confrontive in others, according to students. In some groups, self-defense is the posture. In others, an intimate unit evolves into a group that remains in touch even when CPE ends.

"It was good for me," says Gretchen of her group experience during a unit in which she focused on her own doubts of competency. "I got to the point where I could stand on my own two feet, where I could freely decide not to share and feel good about it and knowing that would not mean there was something wrong with me. But it's not an experience I would like to repeat. I went from very closed to guardedly open."

Conflict within the group is central to Gretchen's memory of it. Trust was an issue: generating questions about what to disclose and how much to disclose. "I felt I was expected to become intimate with people I would not choose to be intimate with. And it didn't keep separate my life at my placement from my life at the seminary. These were people I went to school with and had to live with. We'd share rides, go to IPR, meet each other naked in the shower. That's not the usual professional relationship," she says with a laugh.

Gretchen says that the time did teach her about self-assurance, about trusting her own opinions, her own feelings. It lessened, she says, how much control others may exert over her.

"There are a lot of horror stories about IPR," Rachel says with a smile. "Our group was pretty supportive. To be honest, I think we were scared, afraid if you got on someone's case they would get on your case. But some issues were worked out, some things between a peer and myself came to a head. If you went in with an issue, you could ask for feedback from the group. Had I not been so scared, I could have utilized the group more. There were questions I could have asked the group, but I didn't. I was afraid where it would go," she says now, adding that no time limits existed in her IPR for those who wanted feedback. The negative aspect of that is, Rachel says, that the "hot seat" position may last longer than the initiator intended. "Playing it safe is not drawing attention to yourself. You can get feedback, find out what the group has to say to you. Being scared is not taking that risk," Rachel says.

Jane's group met for ten weeks during a summer unit. The level of camaraderie she expected to develop in IPR never did. IPR included what she describes as "long periods of silence" and quite a bit of "intellectual" discussion. "I'm not sure how valuable I really found IPR to be," she says. "Also, I've been doing my own group therapy for one and a half years. I found I was working on issues in group and I felt no need to bring them to IPR, it would be just for show. Though I reacted to what others were saying and interacted with them," Jane explains, adding that she did not experience the IPR setting to be a therapeutic one.

"I guess it is really not designed for that. It's kind of a hybrid, focusing not so much on your personal identity as on your professional identity. Though what is done there could be applied to that—asking questions like, 'Who told you that? Where did you get that message?' What's the point in bringing all that out if you're not going to do anything with it?" she queries. "I don't know how to resolve that. CPE doesn't last long enough to really deal with anything. It might be really good to question yourself, 'What should IPR be? Who am I? How do I operate? What am I supposed to do with IPR?' I would tell someone considering CPE that IPR is their time. You choose what to do with it." She says that just as her group was forming some cohesion, the course ended.

Such close contact may bring about some painful interaction. That was true for Pamela, a recovering alcoholic, whose group included an adult child of an alcoholic. "My being alcoholic provoked feelings on her part," she says with a tired smile. "My credibility was not good with her, and our similar backgrounds provoked some interaction between us." The interaction, as Pamela recalls it, could be cutting, encompassing mistrust and accusations based on old memories of other people.

Pamela says that her learning for ministry is not to reveal her alcoholism, unless doing so would help another person, an Alcoholics Anonymous tenet. It was, she believes, appropriate in IPR. She says that in a parish setting she is capable of knowledgeably intervening with an alcoholic without revealing her past. She says she needs to be cautious not to overidentify with alcoholic persons she encounters in ministry, not to allow alcoholism to color relationships she may have with codependents angry with an alcoholic.

Adam found IPR "more dynamic" than any counseling situation he has encountered. "It challenged me. In therapy you can kind of sit on your thumbs. I think a lot of therapists feel their task is just to listen. Instead, IPR helps you search and be challenged."

While some groups reunite after the unit, including members from other schools, some find the aftermath distancing. One man says the people in his group "know so much about one another, we're threatened by one another."

Interacting In Role Plays, Research, and Worship

Group experiences, however, are not always at such an intense pitch. Interaction occurs daily among peers in working with clients. More structured forms of interaction occur through the use of such approaches as role plays, research presentations, and preaching reviews. During such structured time, relationships are built and support is exchanged.

"The first time we met, we gathered in a circle and pulled out roles written on paper from a paper bag," says Rachel of the initial role play experienced by her CPE group of five. "It was designed to sensitize students to the patients. What do people feel like there?" She says roles included a paralyzed person and someone confined to a wheelchair, while another was tied with restrainers and another sat on a bedpan. "And then we were asked, 'How uncomfortable is it?' If you've never been a patient, you don't know what that is like," she says. "And we each shared what we felt."

Research projects known as didactics require study of a topic and presentation to the group. Student presentations supplement staff and guest presentations. Discussion and questions follow the lectures.

"Most of the folks in my group chose topics in the areas they were working in, though they didn't have to do that," said Jim, speaking of his first unit of CPE which was spent working with psychiatric patients. "I enjoyed what I did, the religious backgrounds of psychiatric patients, and most were of pretty good quality, including bringing outside people in. You could examine a personal interest without having to focus on one's self."

In worship the focus is on God and on the community of faith. Preaching and leading worship are parts of the clinical experience as well. "For me, worship was where I really felt the support of the community, and sometimes even the presence of God," says Joan, who preached for the first time at the prison. "I never expected the response I received from the residents, from the other students, from my supervisor. I thought preaching was something I'd just have to do to complete the requirements. Instead, it was an opportunity to really touch people's lives and to enrich my own."

Students reported that sermon critiques operate in different ways. Some supervisors require a preliminary copy for review and revision prior to the service. Others elicit remarks from a peer group after the fact. Some record the worship on tape, and the entire group listens to the service days later.

Working Out the Supervisory Relationship

The supervisory relationship is a crucial one. It draws upon the entire CPE experience, reflecting on professional growth and personal growth and on how the two are entwined. Supervision is done on a one-to-one basis during a scheduled hour each week. Required materials guide the time, such as a verbatim or a sermon or a discussion focusing on the student's contracted goals for the unit.

It seems working together means establishing trust, resolving conflict, negotiating needs. When that alliance works at its best, there is partnership.

Developing a Sense of Partnership

Gretchen's trust of her supervisor is, in some ways, the core of her unit. The two had worked together briefly at the seminary. She requested a placement with him because she felt his care and his genuine participation in her learning. "He was willing to be vulnerable himself at times, and he allowed me to minister to him, not often, but on occasion. That made a big difference. And he was willing to admit he was wrong. That was a very good role model for me," she says, noting that her own feelings of incompetence and uncertainty could then be addressed more clearly. "I'm not sure I would have made it through CPE with someone other than him, someone who didn't really care. To play head games with me at a point when I was very vulnerable would be very destructive." She was able to trust his motives as "straight," even on occasions when the method did not seem clear to her, and that was foundational to her unit.

Gretchen says CPE made her aware of her own gifts for ministry and that denying her own competency was dishonest, a quality she cannot bear in others. She says laughingly, "Our supervisions varied. Lots of times I just came in feeling unreal, needing a lot of assurance that what I was doing was good. And he would throw back a question to make me be the one who said what I'd done was good, was okay. Sometimes he'd tell me a story, a parable, where I could easily identify with the main character, and I would find myself incorporating the same learning as that character. It was a powerful tool! Or, we would role-play a situation that happened.

"My theology, what I believed, was always a part of our talking. There were questions like: 'How is God present in ministry? Do you let God work through you? As a person, are you representing God? Where is God for your client? How is your client experiencing God? Do I experience God in the client? Does the client experience God in me?' " She smiles. "And I came to nothing final, but I came to a lot of good ideas I can continue to explore and test against new experiences."

Looking back, Gretchen says, "My main conflict in individual supervision was, at times, I wanted more therapy. I wished I could have had therapy instead of supervision. But there was a pretty good line drawn and I know it was necessary. The focus was how to function as a professional. We would identify issues coming up out of ministry, but not necessarily deal with them. We'd identify the issues operating and I would take them to therapy." The importance of Gretchen's feeling of partnership was reiterated again and again.

Acknowledging Each Supervisory Relationship as Unique

The supervisory relationship is person to person. That means each placement is particular to the persons involved: the student and the supervisor. Despite the fact that CPE experiences involve recurrent themes, such as pastoral identity or a God image, individual responses to those themes vary on the part of the student and sometimes on the part of the supervisor. Such individuality means that rumors of others' CPE experiences, others' opinions of supervisors, are not always reflective of what a particular individual may find, even in the exact same setting.

For instance, conflict may arise around the style of supervision within the working relationship. Keith sees a "big difference" in the styles of supervision in his two units of CPE, adding that he too changed somewhat in the year between units. He says, "My first supervisor was into the elements of tough love, being in touch with your angry side, which I think were her issues. But they ended up being mine and the others'. My second supervisor was always affirming within the same context. At the same time he was probing. I never felt cut open, exposed, and left on the floor to bleed. He was practical and pastoral in his care of me." Consequently, Keith says his "heaviest reflection" during the second unit occurred during individual supervision.

He cited the example of how inadequate he felt when he had to tell someone of a family member's death. He says his supervisor worked with him, offering both guidance and support. "I felt inadequate about that," Keith says of the task. "And fifty minutes of the supervision were spent on me, ten minutes on how he'd gone about this in the past. We'd talk about ways to do it, but he was really more present for my frustration."

Sid is the first to admit that his CPE experience was a painful one, one that is still confusing. He is still processing it and it is more than one year later. His main critique is that CPE is "so wrapped up in psychology. You have to believe in the process of psychology to the point that it becomes a god." And psychology was a field in which he had no background. He felt defenseless amidst the terminology, especially when it was applied to him. Terms like "owning" and "discount" and "denial" reinforced the psychological "mind-set" of CPE to Sid. He says he felt "psychoanalyzed. Every word I said, every thought I had, every thought that crossed my mind. Really looking back, I think you have to believe in the process for it to work," he says, adding that he knows others who have come through CPE feeling "renewed," even others in the same or a similar placement. He says he drew strength from his clients during the unit rather than from his supervisor or his peers. He did not feel supported, as though he was part of a joint ministry, the style of supervision familiar to him from the parish.

"Very direct" confrontation is part of Sid's memory. At the time, he says he felt "attacked" and "abused." He says, "Anytime I disagreed with him on any matter, I was automatically labeled a denial personality, which I denied. It was an endless loop." Sid says that confrontation did facilitate some growth. "It made me sit down and look at a mirror image of me. How does someone actually see me? It forced me to look at myself, my goals, my ministry, my life in general. Even though a lot of things he threw at me were not true, there were some things that were true. I had to say, 'Yes, this is a bad habit,' or 'I am passive-aggressive,'" he says.

Sid says he learned with his supervisor, although their relationship remained conflict ridden. For Sid, the conflict was never completely resolved, though he and his former supervisor intend to meet soon to achieve some resolution. Sid has since read some counseling texts, taken counseling classes, and begun personal counseling, and he feels more ease with psychological theory and terminology. Having a basic understanding of counseling techniques is a recommendation he would make to others considering a CPE unit.

In retrospect, Sid believes he and his supervisor each personified a personal issue for the other. He says his supervisor addressed that somewhat at the end of the unit. Sid says he learned he has difficulty with authority figures, especially those he perceives as "absolute" authorities. He learned that when he is confronted, he moves into denial and "shuts down." He learned that he is stubborn and strong-willed and that it is okay to be vulnerable sometimes. He learned about pastoral care, an area he previously emphasized less than preaching, evangelism, or Christian education. He says now he may even have matured. He says he is also learning about forgiveness and how to let go of his anger.

Learning to Negotiate Individual Needs

Jeff says that early direct dialogue eased him into rapport with his supervisor, adding that he had heard CPE stories of supervisors "taking you through the wringer." Jeff told his supervisor he would "shut down" if approached in that manner, that his defenses could not be taken away abruptly. He found his subsequent supervisory relationship to be "supportively confrontive," one that developed gradually as the relationship developed.

"For example, with a verbatim, she would say, 'I'm aware there is probably a lot of emotion in this section of the visit. What are you feeling?' If I tried to defend myself, she would say, 'Why do you feel you need to defend yourself right now?' She showed me it was okay to fear intimacy, to be scared, to be sensitive and hurt, to say, 'I'm sick of going onto the oncology unit. I'm hurt. I'm scared.' And she would say, 'It's not easy for you.' "

She did demand specificity from him. " 'What do you want from your supervision time? What do you want from me?' That was how it was," Jeff says. "We were very specific, and I felt that I got what I wanted, plus a lot more. She was a damn good supervisor, very insightful, aware of human behavior. And she participated in everything we did, such as a storytelling of our lives, the strengths and limits of our ministries. That was very important for me and for the whole group."

Jeff respects the model she set for ministry and felt it influenced his own sense of pastoral identity. "I felt she was empathetic with me, that she did care about me. But she was not overly concerned with my situation. She was concerned, but it was a relaxing concern. She had ease with her own role as a pastor. She didn't need to get tears out of me. She didn't need to help me, but she was hoping to, hoping I'd get what I needed. That showed me in giving pastoral care we need to be relaxed. That can be comforting to the person receiving care."

Rachel says she found pastoral care lacking in her initial relationship with her supervisor. "She was very task-oriented: 'What are some of the ways you may minister to these people?' Yet I did not feel ministered to," she says, adding that the matter was complicated for her by a fearful transference with her supervisor rooted in her childhood. When Rachel spoke with her supervisor about her fear, she was able to identify the transferential issues and to extend herself more to her clients: a parallel process. "When she understood me better, when she moved toward me pastorally, I was able to move pastorally toward others. It is important that a supervisor be pastoral to me. Not the 'Do as I say, not as I do' kind of thing," she says.

Rachel says that at the end of ten weeks, she saw herself differently and had shed some old images. She says she saw herself as a pastor, though she had never before been willing to hear she had something to contribute. Rachel thinks both she and her supervisor learned from the unit. Her supervisor, says Rachel, learned about patience and told her so. Rachel says when she felt that patience, she had more patience with herself. "There was grace for both of us," she says.

Gretchen maintains that her experience was a good one, one she still draws upon. She also maintains that it was sometimes very hard and that she sometimes felt like quitting. "But even doing it, I knew it was good for me," she says. "So I stuck with it and it probably changed my life. It occurred at the right time and in the right place."

8

The Self as Instrument

Darryl J. Tiller

The basic objectives of supervision in pastoral care are to form pastoral identity and to assist the growth of professional competence. The standards for clinical pastoral education call for the student "To become more aware of oneself as a minister and aware of the ways one's ministry affects persons. . . . To become aware of how one's attitudes, values and assumptions affect one's ministry."[1] To accomplish this, students are offered the clinical method of learning together with a variety of educational resources including parishioners, peers, supervisors, fellow professionals, and literature.

These goals were developed out of the educational tradition of John Dewey, who advocated experiential learning in the late nineteenth and early twentieth centuries.[2] Contemporary educators like Arthur Combs highlight the need to focus professional education in learning to use one's "self as instrument."[3] For Combs, the primary educational task is not to teach a body of information or to impart better techniques. The ever-present, critical tool or resource for the professional is one's *self*. So the focus of professional education should be in developing "creative, thinking human beings able to use themselves as refined and trustworthy instruments for dealing with complex problems."[4]

This notion of the "self as instrument" becomes a stackpole in supervision around which students may gather and integrate the various qualities of their characteristic styles of ministry. These qualities are gleaned from experiences in which they present themselves for supervision through a variety of methods. These may include reflection papers such as verbatim accounts of actual conversations with parishioners or clients, or theological reflection papers that deal with the function of our beliefs in pastoral care. Or students may submit tapes of actual pastoral conversations, group meetings, or sermons. More immediate media for reflection include the actual, here-and-now experiences of students in relationship with peers and supervisors. Interpersonal relations groups (IPR) and individual supervisory sessions are pregnant with educational potential for building one's sense of "self as instrument," one's pastoral identity and personal style.

The Event of Ministry

Ministry is an interpersonal event. It involves an exchange between at least two persons. This exchange may be a brief, one-time encounter, or it may occur with frequency over a longer period of time. The exchange may have purposes that are explicit, as in pastoral counseling that proceeds by contractual agreement to meet for one hour each week to enable a parishioner to work through depression; or the purpose may be less focused and unstructured, as in a hospital visit or a pastoral call in the home.

There are many other facets, actual or potential, that may make up any given event in ministry. At any rate, every process of pastoral care is an interpersonal event involving points of contact between persons. An interpersonal field is created which includes those portions of each individual self that is invested in the encounter, as presented in our model for supervision in chapter 3. That field is more complicated when we minister to couples or families. Couples are encountered in ministry both as individuals and as a relationship; families are encountered as a family system. In any case, the pastor, the parishioner(s), and the relationship comprise the three clinical poles by which we may understand any processes of ministry. Process theologians propose that God too is present within each "actual occasion" that transpires within this relationship. God is there as the "initial aim" (aim toward wholeness; best option in any concrete situation), Divine Eros (life-creating and -sustaining energy), and as Divine Logos (ordering principle).[5]

Harry Stack Sullivan's theory of "interpersonal psychiatry" provides a similar frame of reference.[6] Several of Sullivan's theorems can be applied to the event of ministry and serve to focus important educational issues in training pastors.

First, *the pastor is subjectively involved in the dynamics of any event of ministry.* The pastor is a "participant observer."[7] Second, in the process of using the "self as instrument," for the pastor, *what was originally interpersonal becomes intrapersonal, and what was intrapersonal becomes interpersonal.* [8]

This second theorem originates in a developmental theory of personality that can provide us with a rich educational focus in pastoral formation. For Sullivan, the personality develops in an interpersonal matrix. The growing infant is entirely dependent upon its others for meeting its basic needs. The importance of these significant others in this dependent context is that they shape the infant's self-concept through meeting or frustrating its needs. The infant either identifies with or fails to identify with the experienced aspects of the parenting personalities. Through what Sullivan called introjected personifications (subjectively created experiences of the other taken into oneself) of the mothering figure primarily, the infant develops his or her own self concept or intrapersonal self.[9] Much that determines our personality is developed by the age of six, if not before. It is not fixed in concrete. We indeed have choices and are subjectively involved in the creation of our personalities as we continue to grow across the years. It is upon these experiences of the possibility of change and growth that we engage in new learnings and educational ventures as part of our preparation for ministry.

As pastors, we bring our "selves" to the interpersonal events of ministry. According to the theorem, our current intrapersonal selves were developed in a uniquely interpersonal matrix and are foundational to our current interpersonal dynamics. By focusing on here and now relationships, we may derive a composite of our various strengths and weaknesses in *inter*personal ministry. This composite of characteristic interpersonal qualities provides all of us with a reliable grasp of ourselves and of our resources for ministry. Through exploration of our personal histories, we can access the skeleton of our underlying *intra*personal selves. This skeleton is created around various pivotal, relational themes (authority, peer relations, sexuality, etc.) and is fleshed out with our characteristic strengths and weaknesses. The educational focus moves back and forth from current interpersonal dynamics to personal history, and then back again to the here and now. For example, one of my here and now issues has been that of experiencing anxiety (of which I was not aware) in relation to my peers. I would express that anxiety in competing behaviors. I continued to do so even after I identified this dynamic. It was months later, when I probed further into my personal history, that I could learn to meet these needs in more constructive ways. As the eldest male in my family, I was expected to be a model and to some extent watch out for my younger brothers, as well as to respect and give way to my older sister. I gained some sense of blessing and of being special in this position of eldest male.

At the same time, as the middle child I experienced some deep pain from being squeezed out of parental nurture. That nurture went to "the babies" and to my sister, who held the special place of being the only daughter as well as the eldest child. With some measure of mixed blessing, I developed an identity around such themes as "being on the outside wanting in," a "caring for myself Lone Ranger style," and needing to compensate by "being special," always wanting to be loved. Becoming a minister and being competent were ways to regain this sense of being special and to carve out a niche for myself. Peers became, as siblings before them, persons with whom to compete for parental blessings and nurture. In recognizing these needs, taking responsibility for them, and finding other ways to get them met, I have experienced new freedom in relation to both peers and authority figures in my contemporary life. For example, I can participate with a group of peers in the writing of this book and laugh at myself in my fantasies of having written the best chapter, and can genuinely appreciate all other contributions (inferior as they are!), at rest in my own worth apart from any chapter I write. Making the educational connection between my contemporaries and my siblings in my competition for the favor of persons in authority provided me with the key awareness upon which I could build these resolutions.

The "self as instrument" stackpole, then, has two primary dimensions from which to build its gestalt: the here and now interpersonal dimension and the underlying intrapersonal dimension. The intrapersonal is accessed through an exploration of personal history, which, once clarified, provides a reliable reference point for understanding many interpersonal dynamics along parallel lines. Our relationship with our primary authority figures, our parents (or substitutes), sets in motion dynamics in our current relationships with persons in authority, such as supervisors, teachers, and bosses. Likewise, the dynamics that exist(ed) for us in relation to our siblings provide us with some good indicators of what to expect with our current set of peers. Our characteristic ways of relating to males and females are likewise dynamically related to our relationships with the male and female prototypes in our developmental lives.

As may now be obvious, pastors engaged in the interpersonal events of ministry are not purely objectively involved. Indeed, as Sullivan contends in his first theorem, we are subjectively involved (our needs, motives, attitudes, values, biases, goals—

our *selves*). Accordingly, Sullivan has called us "participant observers." Given this fact, we have an ethical responsibility to
know our *selves* and how we involve our *selves* in pastoral relationships. Only to the degree that we have come to know ourselves and how we characteristically involve ourselves in caring
relationships can we assume creative and constructive responsibility, so that our care is really pastoral. For example, in a correctional setting a student looked up an inmate who had slashed his
wrists and engaged the inmate in a rather forceful and critical
manner. The student was unaware that his involvement was
inappropriate. Through reflection in supervision upon his own
needs at the time, the student recognized that the inmate's behavior was threatening his sense of competence as the inmate's
counselor. In recognizing this and taking responsibility for his
own needs, the student was free to learn to use himself for the
benefit of the inmate, which is part of what it means to be
professional. Another example is that of a parishioner wanting
to talk about her approaching death, while the pastor avoids the
subject or seeks to reassure her without allowing the parishioner
to talk out her feelings. The pastor is unaware that she has not
worked through her own feelings about death for herself.

In building this kind of self-knowledge, we equip ourselves
with an awareness of our many resources as well as our limitations. We learn options for using ourselves to become more
effective in meeting the variety of needs that our parishioners
present to us. In this respect, supervision in the actual performance of ministry is an indispensable educational venture.

Cases: Bob and Mary

A look at this educational process in two students will illustrate what we have been talking about. Bob and Mary were two
students enrolled in their first unit of clinical pastoral education.
The context for this training was a medium-security, state-oper-
ated prison for the incarceration of adult male felons. Bob was
a forty-three-year-old, somewhat compulsive overachiever who
had completed two graduate degrees and embarked on his third,
this one in ministry. Bob's initial verbatim reports revealed an
interpersonal style that was quite anxious to solve other people's problems for them. Bob overcontrolled the conversation,
missed the parishioner's point by making his own assumptions
about what was meant, imposed his own value judgments, and
took over to offer advice about what the parishioner should do.
These were what we have called "learning problems" in chapter
2. Bob didn't like his counseling style and acknowledged it was

something that he wanted to change. His contract in supervision was "to learn ways to involve myself as pastor other than to control and offer advice."

Given Bob's overdirective counseling style, Carl Rogers' client-centered model was suggested to provide a corrective direction. Bob had already been introduced to the Rogerian approach and thought he knew how to implement it. It was suggested that he read Robert Carkhuff's *Helping and Human Relations*, [10] a work that further develops the client-centered approach. Over the following weeks, Bob made noticeable changes in his interpersonal style, although even as the unit ended he continued to work out learnings in this area. Below are two brief examples of Bob's conversational style, one from the first verbatim he submitted and one from the fifth week of his training.

Verbatim 1.

This was Bob's first conversation with inmate JE. Bob initiated the contact and carried the conversation through its getting-acquainted phase. (C=chaplain; I=inmate.) Bob asked about JE's family and learned that JE had a girlfriend and a daughter. About the daughter Bob asked:

C15: Does she come to visit also?

I15: Oh, yes, they both come together every time. My girlfriend wants to get married.

C16: *(I am silent.)*

I16: I don't want to. I talked to the chaplain and got all the information, but it's no marriage when you do it in the visitor's room.

C17: *(I am silent.)*

I17: Besides, it's not good to get married in prison. I know it can be done, but it ain't no good. Never know what may happen in two years.

C18: Well, what you and your girlfriend have going so far seems to work, doesn't it?

I18: Yes, it's working fine. We love each other and we're true to each other.

C19: You can't argue with success. Probably better to remain as you are. If you have been able to keep a good relationship with her without marrying, you at least know that works.

I19: Yeah. We love each other.

C20: Of course things may change in those two years. But at least it has worked up to now.

I20: Yeah.

C21:   The big thing is whether you are communicating. Have you told her why you don't want to be married?

I21:   Yes. I have told her that it's because it's no good, not that I don't love her or don't want to get married.

C22:   Of course, her feelings are important. In the next two years, it may be more important to her.

I22:   Yeah. That may change.

C23:   It's a real tough decision. You don't want to get married, she does. I don't know what to tell you. I guess the most important thing is to communicate and make sure you both know why each wants to do what you want to do.

I23:   Yeah.

C24:   Any chance you may be furloughed sometime and you could get married then?

I24:   Don't think so.

Bob's pastoral skills seem restricted to identifying the problem and rendering an answer to it. In cases where the problem is obscure, Bob creates one so as to exercise this singular approach to the difficulties of others. Supervision focused attention on alternative ways to listen, respond, and support another's efforts to resolve things personally.

Verbatim 5.

In this verbatim Bob did not take over the inmate's dilemma. The inmate, RB, contacted Bob earlier in the week to indicate he wanted to talk about some problems he was having with his daughter. Bob visited RB in his living unit.

C1:   You mentioned this week that you were having problems with your daughter. You want to tell me about your daughter?

I1:   I don't think anything can be done about it. I've just about given up.

C2:   I hear despair in what you say.

I2:   I'm just about at the end of my rope. My daughter sent back my most recent letter "return to sender." I've apparently lost contact with her.

C3:   Tell me more.

I3:   Well, my daughter is about twenty-one and she has a little girl (my granddaughter), and she has been writing me real regular for a year. About two weeks ago I received a letter from her and in the letter she said that she couldn't write me anymore. My ex-wife had found out she was writing me and told her she would have to choose between me and her. I just don't understand. She's twenty-one and has a kid and my wife is telling her not to write me. She's the last contact I have with my family.

C4: I hear a sense of loss in your voice, and a puzzled feeling as to why this is happening.

I4: Yeah. *(Opens up further.)*

In this fifth-week verbatim, Bob demonstrated that he was learning to leave the problem with the parishioner rather than to take over and offer advice. He was learning to facilitate the parishioner's grasp of his own problem by reflecting how the parishioner may be feeling. As is evident, even these skills need sharpening, but Bob was learning a new way.

The above examples are focused primarily on learning at the level of skill development in current *inter*personal dynamics. A deeper level of learning with more extensive consequences occurs when students explore their *intra*personal dynamics out of which the interpersonal ones arise. For Bob, this occurred as we focused attention on the roots of his anxiety to "get something going" and "to do something" about his parishioner's problem, which, by the way, is a common anxiety among students beginning ministry.

Resistance to such attention to ourselves is always a part of supervision. To own our experiences of anxiety in ministerial duties is threatening to everyone. In chapter 2 we have discussed the shape these resistances can take as "problems about learning." For Bob, these were expressed as he alternately owned that he was controlling in his conversations with his parishioners and then wanted to define sharply the meaning of "control" and "intellectualize" about the problem rather than change. As safety and trust were built into the supervisory relationship, Bob was able to identify the negative meanings of control for him which made it difficult to acknowledge controlling behaviors in himself. Through owning this quality and encountering external acceptance by the supervisor for who he was, including his control, Bob was able to achieve more openness to the fact that he was, indeed, controlling at times.

Bob's self-understanding of this tendency and his gradual acceptance of its reality was also facilitated when he made connections between these current behaviors and his personal history. One way Bob would move in and take over was with incessant questioning. This found its roots in Bob's identification with his grandfather, who functioned parentally with him throughout childhood. In Bob's own words, his grandfather had a pair of pliers and a screwdriver in my hands by the time I was old enough to hold them. Some of my earliest memories are of me and Grandfather under the car taking things apart and figuring out how to put things back together. This is where I get my "efficiency expert" characteristic.

Later on, Bob worked professionally in computer analysis and had many stories, both funny and regretful, in his use of his "efficiency" behavior.

Understanding that it was through his relationship to his grandfather that he learned some of these behaviors helped Bob grow to appreciate himself more. He had warm memories of his grandfather, and there were positive reasons why he adopted this "efficiency expert" characteristic, even though he now viewed it as somewhat less than helpful. This new appreciation of his unique personal history, bolstered by an expressed and experienced theology of love for himself, helped Bob not to be so at odds with himself and consequently so resistant to owning the controlling parts of his personality. Within this context of love, he could start making the changes he wanted to make. Those changes, as exhibited through comparing verbatims 1 and 5, were in evidence in all of Bob's relationships as he learned to experiment with alternatives to his old pattern of managing anxiety through overcontrol.

Mary was a twenty-four-year-old married student who was overweight and often looked scared. Her verbatims revealed her "learning problems" as avoiding her parishioner's feelings, failing to pick up on them, especially when these feelings were expressed strongly. An example follows in a verbatim that Mary presented from her second weekly counseling session with RG:

I1:   I just came from talking with one of the officers in the school *(showing anger toward the guard)*.
C1:   What was that all about?
I2:   I was just showing another inmate where the school was so that he could sign up to get his GED [General Equivalency Diploma]—he is new here. This officer told me I was in an unauthorized area and that I better get out. So I moved, and he was following me all over and really on my case. He said that next time he'd write me up. I told him to do what he had to but I wasn't going to do anything wrong so he didn't have to follow me around. And he said he was going to write me up for bad-mouthing him. I wasn't doing anything wrong, so I got out of there. When I went back he said if he found me there again without a reason he'd write me up.

C2: Sounds like you've had a rough day.

I3: Yeah, I did.

C3: I wonder if complaining about it helps.

I4: Yeah, it helps, 'cause I don't pay any attention to things the first time; then for the second time I answer back. 'Cause I figure that if I don't, it will just keep happening over and over.

C4: *(Silent. There is a pause for a few seconds. Then RG asked me how my weekend was.)* It was okay. Pretty hot. *(I mentioned that I found a place to live.)* So how was your weekend?

I5: Same as always, I guess.

In supervision Mary identified feeling anger in C4 and acknowledged she was bogged down, not knowing what to do with her feelings. She could readily recognize these *inter*personal difficulties. She went on to declare she was not so much uncomfortable with her parishioner's expression of feeling as she was afraid of her own response to it. Mary seemed to have particular difficulty with her own anger and hurt feelings. Just knowing this was not sufficient to help her change as she desired, so as to be more available to her parishioners at the emotional level. Indeed, with all her regular counselees, Mary reported that her sessions seemed to be going nowhere, each counselee tending to repeat the same issues and concerns from week to week. Something more needed to happen to effect a breakthrough in her work.

A number of instruments are utilized in concert with one another in standard CPE programs. In addition to verbatims and other reflection papers, students have an opportunity to learn from events that occur in their relationships to supervisors and peers that involve immediate encounters in the here and now. Interpersonal relations groups (IPR) and individual supervisory sessions are two such media for learning. Together these instruments proved beneficial for Mary in helping her effect a breakthrough in this learning issue of avoiding feelings.

Mary clearly owned the difficulty managing her feelings. She had trouble determining what she was feeling, distinguishing one feeling from another, let alone giving expression to those feelings or using them to enhance and facilitate her pastoral work.

Anger was the emotion with which Mary had the most difficulty. We soon identified her need to please people in authority as a central "problem about learning in her supervision." She had experienced some anger toward me in our initial screening interview but did not mention it. Before our first supervisory session she decided she was going to tell me about it. The fact that she did without getting rejected, Mary later described as a major turning point for her. The same thing happened in her IPR group when she confronted one of her peers with anger she felt toward him early in the unit. The whole experience of taking these risks was frightening to Mary but also powerfully liberating, presenting her with other new learnings.

As Mary affirmed herself by expressing anger, she found she still felt and behaved as an excluded person, withdrawing to the periphery of her IPR group. Another feeling surfaced. Now Mary was scared. What do you say after you say, "I'm angry"? At this deeper, *intra*personal level of self-encounter, Mary realized she both wanted to be "in" as a group member and resisted it in fear. She lived with a number of internal discounts of her worth which she began to let the group know about, bit by bit, over the next several weeks. She felt she did not have the right to be a part of the group, that her wants, needs, and interests were unimportant, that somehow she was not "good enough." Mary expressed feelings of fear and embarrassment as we encouraged her participation in the group. Connections with her personal history made clear sense of her current interpersonal difficulties. As the eldest child, Mary was given to assume primary responsibility for the care of her two younger brothers. She was forced to give up going to private school during later childhood in order that her mother and, later, her father could go back to school. These are examples of how Mary learned to suppress what she wanted in order to ensure that the needs of others were met. Knowing this and connecting it to her current interpersonal difficulties (such as reducing RG's expressed concerns to mere "complaining") bolstered Mary's resources for affecting her desired change.

An example of Mary's growth came in the eighth week of the IPR sessions when she was experiencing painful feelings and, in her characteristic style, withheld them. With invitation, Mary moved beyond her issue of "Is it all right to feel anger?" to encounter her hurt and her notion "To hurt is weak." As we waited, Mary allowed herself to cry with us and to be comforted. In so doing, she moved beyond the binding grasp of her *intra*personal self to embrace and be embraced by others. It was in the context of these IPR sessions, bolstered by individual supervision, that Mary made progress on her learning contract. In that contract, Mary stated that she wanted to be herself, "not edit in order to please," not squelch her emotions, and "thereby bring more resources" to her ministry. Subsequently, these changes began to show in her pastoral care. She encouraged more expression of feelings from parishioners, and shared more of her own feelings, confronting several inmates who talked abusively to her, and asserting herself with her counselees to assist them in focusing their own work and stop avoiding things.

Both Bob and Mary made significant strides in their growth toward professional competence. In large part, this involved addressing their subjective involvement in specific events of ministry. They did this by using the clinical method to reflect upon the dynamics between their parishioners and themselves, but this led to concerted reflection upon the second clinical pole in our supervisory model, of using "themselves as instruments" as pastors, coming to understand some of the roots in their interpersonal styles. This process enabled them to learn to use themselves in ways that were more helpful to their parishioners and more congruent with the best of their theological intentions.

Parallel Images of Faith

The theological parallel to this clinical focus is not always so obvious. While we grow in the use of our "self as instrument" in ministry, we are also growing simultaneously at the level of our personal spiritual edification, along with our parishioners. In the biblical account of creation, the term "image" is used rather than "self" or "intrapersonal self." We are created "in the image of God." But we have experienced "the fall" and our image is marred and our relationship with God is broken.

One consequence of this broken relationship with God is that now our image of God is marred by our own marred image of ourselves. Projections from our brokenness distort our image of God. Differentiating between aspects of our own self-image, our projected image of God, and the actual image of God becomes an important task of discernment in preparing ourselves for responsibility before one another and before God. The clinical study of our involvement with others mirrors our own image in our image of God, and vice versa, presenting in depth a perspective for the "testing of spirits" to see if they are actually of God. Edgar Draper, M.D., and a group of psychiatrists demonstrated in their study that accurate diagnoses could be made of psychiatric patients by interviewing those patients as to their religious faith perspectives alone.[11] And Wayne Oates writes, "The Bible is a mirror into which one projects one's own concept of oneself, and which in turn reflects it back with accuracy."[12]

Perhaps one of the clearest clinical studies of how we create God in our own image is that done by Ana-Maria Rizzuto, M.D. From psychoanalytic tradition, Rizzuto begins her study with

Freud and moves to object-relations theory to provide her perspective on this matter. She shows how each person creates a God representation alongside the intrapsychic representations of self and objects they develop. This God representation is especially, though not exclusively, created out of the dynamic relationship with one's parents. Our God image is changed, shaped, and reshaped through the years along with the evolving and changing self.[13] Events and processes of change that penetrate the intrapersonal level open up possibilities of change in one's representation too. Psychotherapy, and to some degree clinical supervision, are two such experiences in which change is likely to occur.

Some of the parallels between our image of ourselves and our image of God are evident, for example, by taking a glimpse at the religion of inmates in prison. There are parallels between a characteristic criminal personality and typical inmate images of God. In brief, the criminal personality is characterized by impulsivity, excitement seeking, power thrusting, irresponsibility, fleeting commitments, using others as objects, and so forth. Correspondingly, the criminal's god is often a god of magic and power, a god of early parole and dropped charges. Inmates typically prefer emotion-filled worship services with heavy-metal music and preaching to satisfy their thirst for excitement. A characteristic of the criminal personality is to want to be number one or not at all. In chapel, inmates compete, sometimes viciously, for leadership and create factions within the chapel body. In typical, compartmentalized life-styles inmates can "praise God" at 10 A.M. worship and take their neighbor's last pack of cigarettes at 3 P.M. before gathering again for the evening worship.

On the basis of creating God in our own image, Jim Jones can persuade a cult of followers seeking to be faithful to "God" to create a Jonestown. Or positively, Martin Luther can find liberation for himself in coming to a corrective understanding of God. Through hearing a message of grace and being changed by it, he can lead a movement of challenge to the image of God as represented by the church of his time, bringing liberation to the Protestant people of Europe. And in the process the image of God is liberated too. Among children, God is imaged after their image as intimate and egocentric, through their global, concrete, magical, and omnipotent thinking.[14] Adolescents, while pursuing independence, power, and responsibility, may lose faith as they no longer accept the image of God of their childhood and have not yet done the work of adulthood to create a new image based on interdependence.

One of the liberating effects of Mary's educational experience resulted from addressing her expectations of what she "should be as a minister—or even as a Christian." Mary would feel embarrassed when her parishioners would "talk religion" to her. She would respond by either withdrawing or defending herself, hearing expressions of faith by inmates that were different from hers as a challenge or a put-down to her own faith. In writing a reflection paper about these expectations, Mary discovered that many of her "shoulds" stemmed from her childhood learnings. She began to identify the sources of their authority among her internal voices, experiencing the freedom to separate and differentiate those authorities from herself and to choose on her own authority what was informed by a larger world of knowledge and experience than that of her childhood. Mary had been disowning many of her own perceptions in faith and values. Now she was free to claim and create her own personal faith perspective. As Mary learned to differentiate *her* faith perspectives from those of others, she had less need to defend herself or withdraw when others wanted to "talk religion." In fact, she began initiating "religious talk" with newfound freedom and excitement and chose to do a special research project in the field of religious experience.

As our self-image is marred, our image of God is marred. Salvation involves restoration of both images. In Jesus Christ we have our self-image restored. Jesus reveals the image of God. By grace through faith in him we are restored. The Christian life becomes a dynamic process of growing toward the Christ image. Our image is not the image of Christ; but we are called

> to grow up in every way unto Christ . . . to a mature person, to the measure of the stature which belongs to the fulness of Christ . . . to lay aside the old self . . . and be renewed in the spirit of your mind, and put on the new self. (Paraphrased from Eph. 4:13–14; see also 2 Peter 1:3–8 and 1 Tim. 1:1–3)

NOTES

1. ACPE, *Standards* (Atlanta: Association for Clinical Pastoral Education, 1985), pp. 8–9.

2. T. D. Burridge, *What Happened in Education: An Introduction to Western Educational History* (Boston: Allyn & Bacon, 1970), pp. 106–110.

3. A. W. Combs, *The Professional Education of Teachers: A Perceptual View of Teacher Preparation* (Boston: Allyn & Bacon, 1965), pp. 8–9.

4. Ibid., p. 7.

5. J. Cobb, *Process Theology* (Philadelphia: Westminster Press, 1976), pp. 26, 43–48, 71–75, 99.

6. H. S. Sullivan, *The Interpersonal Theory of Psychiatry* (New York: W. W. Norton & Co., 1953), pp. xi–xii, 13–20.

7. H. S. Sullivan, *The Psychiatric Interview* (New York: W. W. Norton & Co., 1954), pp. 3, 19–25, 103–104.

8. Sullivan, *The Psychiatric Interview*, pp. 49–158.

9. Ibid., pp. 118–122, 161–168, 174–175.

10. R. R. Carkhuff, *Helping and Human Relations* (New York: Holt, Rinehart & Winston, 1969).

11. E. Draper and others, "On the Diagnostic Value of Ideation," *Archives of General Psychiatry* 13:202–207 (1965).

12. W. E. Oates, *The Religious Care of the Psychiatric Patient* (Philadelphia: Westminster Press, 1978), p. 96.

13. A. M. Rizzuto, *The Birth of the Living God* (Chicago: University of Chicago Press, 1979), pp. 6–8, 41–53, 177–201, 196.

14. D. Heller, "The Children's God," *Psychology Today*, Dec. 1985, pp. 22–27.

9

Supervising
the Counseling Relationship

John D. Lentz

Two people went fishing. Each had three poles. One became
frustrated and caught nothing. The other person had fun and
caught more than usual. The difference between the two was a
perceptual one. The first person tried to fish three poles. The
second person fished, using three poles.

This chapter is about fishing with three poles in supervision.
This concept was set forth theoretically in dimensions of supervisory reflection discussed in chapter 3: the dimension of *administrative oversight,* the *therapeutic* dimension, and the dimension of
the *working alliance* of supervision itself. Here we will address its
practical application in these three dimensions of supervision in
the teaching of pastoral counseling. Clinical theory and practice
can best be understood when combined. In our basic course
introducing students to counseling with individuals, the students are required to utilize theory in the actual practice of
counseling with inmates at the women's prison in Kentucky.
Each student is assigned two residents who have requested
counseling and can benefit from it in an individual setting.

Administrative Contracts

The first step in going fishing with someone is to agree on
when, where, and how you are going. The clinical contract for
training contains these arrangements. It is structured to help
students and their supervisors work together for optimal learning, while at the same time providing maximum assistance to the
client. By the course structure, each student will: (1) Be respon-

sible for counseling two persons and meet with each of them once a week. (2) Meet each week with two peers and the supervisor for one and a half hours of supervision. (3) Make an individual contract for change that will enhance professional practice. (4) Prepare a written presentation each week according to the guidelines for presentations. (See "Appendix: A Guide to Preparing Tapes for Supervision," at the end of this chapter.)

This agreement encourages students to share responsibility for their learning. Each week they decide what they will present and what they want to learn from it. This reduces the over/ under nature of the supervisory relationship, structuring it in the direction of mutual responsibility. It also seems to cut down the number of picky criticisms that students make while their peers are presenting. Perhaps this is because asking for assistance in a particular area discourages general and unsolicited comments about other areas.

These administrative contracts contain an implied message to anxious students. The students can choose what will be discussed, and they do not need to fear that private matters will be revealed. Their own preparatory analysis of each tape of their counseling to be presented ensures that some initiative is already taken toward being vulnerable. Committing our own thoughts about our work to writing beforehand means placing before peers our self-reflection as well as our work itself. The usual response to this vulnerability is acceptance and appreciation.

Other administrative agreements are entered into with the institutions where our students work. At the women's prison, for example, each student agrees not to bring in or take out anything and to respect the confidentiality of the prisoner/client. Continuity for the client is provided when the semester is completed by permitting the prisoner to continue counseling with the supervisor who, the client is aware, has been following the case.

Professional Contracts

The professional contract that each supervisee makes is for specific growth in professional skills as counselors. While any change that is made bears on one's personal life, that is not the focus of attention.[1] Ordinarily the supervisee will be making this contract before the first client is seen. The manner in which this contract is worked out will influence the way a supervisee makes contracts with clients.[2] What the supervisor models in this process is important. This is based on the premise undergirding the parallel process in supervision discussed in chapters 2 and 3. Briefly, the notion of parallel process reflects the fact that supervisees frequently change their behavior as a result of having contact with both the client and the supervisor. Thus supervisees are likely to do in supervision what clients did with them. Or, supervisees are likely to "go and do likewise" with their clients, doing what they have experienced being done with them by their supervisor.[3]

Supervisory contracts need to be established in terms of concrete goals that are attainable. Contracts that include words like "better," "more," or "less" cannot be defined so that everyone in the room knows how much. For instance, a contract to listen better is so vague no one can know for certain when the goal has been reached. However, a contract to recognize and respond to at least two messages that are "spoken between the lines" is specific and can be measured for completion. Vague goals set by a self-critical person will be only partially recognized, no matter how much is accomplished. The self-critical person seldom believes he or she has done enough. Abstract goals tend to become like mirages, unattainable in their vagueness, or are used to show completion, when there is none.

While we are establishing the administrative and professional contracts, the relationships with supervisor and peers are being subtly negotiated. It is a time when everyone sizes everyone else up.

The three dimensions of supervisory reflection spoken of earlier are *administrative oversight,* the *therapeutic dimension,* and the *working alliance.* Fishing with three poles, a supervisor often addresses all three areas within a particular issue. We cannot reel in three lines at the same time. Yet sometimes by addressing one, all three are worked with in varying degrees. Human communication is very complex and seldom conveys only one message at a given time.[4] The following verbatim account illustrates this complexity as well as some methods for dealing with it.

Administrative Oversight

The supervisor is alone in the meeting room and waiting for the next three students to arrive for the first meeting. All names are fictitious. This verbatim contains Joe's major problem about learning.

The door bursts open, with Joe leading his two female peers through the door. His tone of voice is loud and he doesn't seem to be speaking to anyone in particular, although his two peers and the supervisor are within hearing distance.

Joe 1:   I have never been angrier in all my life. I have been humili-
           ated, criticized, and put down. Every time I ask a question,
           I'm put down. If this is what they call supervision. It cer-
           tainly isn't teaching. I think it's sadistic, that is what I think
           it is. I think Karen is just—*(Joe was intentionally interrupted
           because he was talking about someone not in the room.)*

Sup 1:   What is going on? Would someone care to fill me in on
           what is happening?

Peer 1:   Joe is angry about the first supervisory session that he had
           with Karen. He—

Joe 2:   *(Interrupting.)* You're darn right I'm angry. I don't want to
           be treated—I don't have to be treated that way.

Sup 2:   Have you told Karen *(other supervisor; Joe was taking two
           courses simultaneously)* that you are angry?

Joe 3:   Not yet. But I will . . . tomorrow. I just want to know if you
           intend to treat us like that . . . like she did. Teaching is
           giving answers. I know, I taught for several years. *(A three-
           or four-minute angry explanation of what teaching is followed, how
           he wasn't going to learn through being criticized or humiliated. At
           times he could hold some eye contact, and at others he wouldn't look
           at anyone. He made references to the philosophy of teaching.)*

Sup 3:   You do seem to be very angry. I—

Joe 4:   I want to know if I ask questions will I get answers or what?

Sup 4:   I'm not sure, but I *am* sure I know what *not* to do now.
           (Backs away, holding arms up; general laughter by all of us.) Two
           things. Whatever is going on between you and Karen will
           have to stay there, short of encouraging you to work it out
           between yourselves. Look, I'm innocent in this. How come
           I'm getting all this anger? Second, I'm not sure if I will give
           you the answers. You're a teacher; you know that some-
           times you teach by helping the student to find the answer.

Joe 5:   Well, Karen just won't tell me. No help, just criticism. *(He
           sees my raised hand, indicating stop.)*

Sup 5:   That is between you two. You can drop the other course,
           talk to her, or learn from the experience; it is up to you.
           The way I work is to strive toward your reaching your
           learning goals, so that you become as successful as you can
           be. I like to think of myself as a coach, or teacher like
           Socrates. *(We continue to talk more specifically about him and
           negotiate the changes that he wants to make. He has become notice-
           ably more calm and capable of talking in a rational manner.)*

Joe contracted to ask for what he wanted directly, to stop
discounting himself and others, and to find ways of protecting
himself from what he considered critical authority persons. All

three changes came directly out of what he presented above.

Although the previous conversation is unique, it is also representative of the way people negotiate their learning contracts by revealing what they need. Frequently, supervisees who are on the verge of making a personal change will give immediate clues about what they need to accomplish in order to become better counselors. Folks that are not ready to make such changes are usually more guarded and don't reveal as dramatically what they need to do for professional growth. Sharper and less wounded supervisees usually sense what they need and make contracts in a very straightforward manner.

Joe invited one supervisor to side with him against another supervisor. This is clearly an issue in the dimension of administrative oversight. To take either side administratively would create a problem. Siding with Joe undermines the authority of a colleague, which ultimately alienates Joe by simply becoming another supervisor whom he can't trust. Remaining neutral is the only way to build a relationship with as much integrity as possible, allowing as little discussion of persons not present as possible. This protects the working relationships necessary to deliver pastoral services throughout the system.

There is also a therapeutic dimension to the same process. As indicated, one of Joe's major problems receiving help is covering fear with anger. Since the supervisor with whom he was angry is female, he may also have a problem of perceiving female authorities as critical. With the level of anger he expressed toward this supervisor, one could guess another major personal impasse was going to be with denial. Where a high level of blame is present covering up feelings of inadequacy, so also is denial.

Finally, issues are present that are shaping the dimension of the working alliance in supervision itself. Joe is asking whether he will be hurt or humiliated. Can he be vulnerable in this setting? Will he be treated gently and with respect? The reassurance he was given in Sup 4 begins to establish such a climate. Being respectful of Joe's indirect manner of asking for it is in part recognizing that all of us do the same thing at times.

Attention was focused primarily on the administrative dimension because that area presented the most immediate need. Were it not handled effectively, the learning contract might be missed. Moreover, if trustworthiness in administrative relationships were not established, the supervisory relationship itself would be affected by a low trust level that would inhibit work at each step.

Of major concern is choosing which dimension to address at a given time—the administrative, the therapeutic, or the working alliance. While starting with the administrative one is probably a good rule of thumb, the issue most needing attention will surface by the unspoken messages given while talking about the client or devising strategy for working with the client. Thus the therapeutic aspects of supervision will intrude upon any discussion of the client, or some implied message will be present in how we discuss the client. A common way to know that the supervisory relationship needs attention is through the client's relationship with the supervisee. If, for example, the client is angry with the supervisee, it is a fair assumption that there is some anger in the supervisory relationship itself. When we are being supervised, we usually bring into the supervisory hour the same issues that are bothering us personally. Good supervision frequently becomes a matter of choosing what will and what will not be examined by listening to the unspoken messages that emerge and handling them effectively.

Often when supervisor and supervisee get stuck, switching to a different dimension is all that is necessary to find a solution. The following verbatim was chosen because it illustrates both intentionally choosing one fishing pole first and then switching to another.

The Therapeutic Dimension

Sherry is a married female student completing her second year. Her learning problem was with intimacy. She had a great deal of difficulty deepening or sustaining relationships at the level of self-disclosure. When this would show up, she would go from one extreme to another, sharing everything and then withdrawing, and then denying any problem whatsoever. She would become teary and keep others away from any threatening aspect of her work by displaying pain. Her problem about learning was expressed by her avoidance of any imperfections. She frequently distracted the group from proceeding to topics that she feared would be threatening, if examined.

In the following exchanges, the primary focus is on the therapeutic dimension of supervision. However, the way of getting to it is through administrative oversight of the counseling relationship. As supervision began, Sherry's voice indicated strong emotion that was unrelated to what was being said. The supervisor became suspicious that she might be about to sabotage her personal goal unconsciously. The dialogue began after the four of us read her prepared material and were ready to hear her tape.

Sherry 1: I would like you to listen to the responses that I make and then . . . I'm aware that as I listened to the tape at one point I was responding one way, but I must have been giving another message at the same time. *(There is a great deal of quivering in her voice.)*

Sup 1: *(Ignoring the emotion by not addressing except by voice tone, which was nurturing in response to her display of hurt)* You want us to figure out how the critical messages came across even though you didn't mean for them to be communicated.

Sherry 2: *(Tears are falling down her face, and her voice is filled with emotion.)* I felt that it wasn't going well . . . but that it wasn't going right.

Sup 2: You want to know how to reach her? *(The only acknowledgment of her emotion is by facial expression and tone of voice. No verbal acknowledgment is made, since she has not spoken directly about her feelings.)*

Sherry 3: Yeah! *(With emotion that says that is it)*

Sup 3: I notice you obviously have a lot of emotion caught up with this issue.

Sherry 4: *(Openly crying)* As I was listening to this tape this afternoon—um, I was getting messages that I had spoken and yet with so much confusion.

Sup 4: So you are feeling jumbled up, confused, and wondering if you have done a good job. Feeling stuck.

Sherry 5: I have no clues about what next to do.

Sup 5: *(Enthusiastically)* You couldn't have brought in a better tape than this one. Excellent. Let's listen to the tape.

The supervisor has guessed that Sherry was afraid she was going to be criticized. His response implies that she has done an excellent job, although it is ambiguous for which job she is being praised. No irony or dishonesty is intended; the compliment is meant. Her tentativeness matches that of her client, who was feeling stuck in her own life.[5] By acknowledging that she is stuck, Sherry is already doing something different herself. For the first time Sherry has tentatively acknowledged that she was having difficulty. She is admitting that she isn't perfect.

In the past, Sherry had used emotional displays to divert supervision from addressing anything related to her lack of perfection. Circumventing her emotional display to stick to issues surrounding the administration of treatment helped her move through this impasse. She seemed determined to begin facing her imperfections no matter what. As can be expected, at about the same time that Sherry moved beyond her personal impasse so did her client.

The Working Alliance

The maintenance of the relationships between peers and between each supervisee and the supervisor is of course an ongoing and continuous task. Any difficulties that ensue bear addressing at the first appropriate moment. The following is an instance of a student raising an issue in relationship to his peers.

Twelve weeks into the semester, Bill had just completed his presentation. All three students in the group were very bright and had been doing excellent work.

Bill 1:   *(Talking to the three of us)* I appreciate your help. I feel much more confident.

Jerry 1:   *(Jumping in)* I have a difficult time believing your lack of confidence. *(Turns to me.)* Do you mind if we handle this now?

Sup 1:   Now is a perfect time. *(This has not been prearranged.)*

Jerry 2:   We come in each week with both of you making perfect presentations and then talking as though you feel very little confidence.

Sup 2:   This might be easier to understand if you address a specific issue, time, and place with each person, rather than trying to take on both of them at the same time. *(Mild laughter)*

Jerry 3:   Okay, Bill, what I need to know from you is if your feelings of inadequacy are real. You come in here, and everything you do seems too perfect. For instance, tonight.

Bill 3:   *(Grinning)* Of course they are real.

Jerry 4:   Whenever you present material, before the end of the time you think of the answer you're seeking.

Bill 4:   *(Laughing)* That's because he *(gesturing toward me)* won't let me ask, or you all give me answers until I have thought the answers out myself.

Jerry 5:   *(Stern and serious)* Are you laughing at me?

Bill 5:   No! I'm laughing out of relief, and that I'm being complimented about what I feel the most inadequate about. Each week I think you and your client deal with such deep issues, and yet you think I have been doing so well. It's ironic, because I have been thinking the same thing about you. Yet I haven't had the courage to bring it up.

Sue 6:   Each week I come in here, and I feel dumb. I have been

	thinking you two were always so-o-o sharp that I have felt inadequate. *(She gave a specific example.)*
Sup 6:	All three of you are at least half right. *(Pause)* Your peers are very competent, and they bring in excellent tapes, with analysis that is insightful. Jerry, I'm impressed that you brought this up. That took courage and a willingness to be genuinely vulnerable.
Bill 6:	Jerry, this is just another time you have spoken when I wish I had brought up, or said, what you did.
Jerry 6:	I'm sorry. I just needed to check that out.
Sup 7:	*(Mockingly)* "Aw, gee, shucks, it weren't nothing." *(Serious tone of voice)* I'm not willing for you either to apologize or to be so humble about having done what is appropriate.
Jerry 7:	Oh. Okay! *(Laughing)* I'm ready to present now.
Sup 8:	Again? *(Laughter)*

What isn't obvious is the parallel process occurring with both Jerry and his client. Jerry believed both he and his client needed to confront their parents. His presentation included a segment of tape that contained evidence to support his belief.

Again, while this segment of supervision deals primarily with the dimension of maintaining peer relationships, it contains elements that are therapeutic. One problem that Jerry had about receiving help was to assume the worst about how others felt toward him and then withdraw rather than check out his assumptions. To have initiated this request for clarification was an act of personal change on his part. When the parallel process between client and therapist is examined, it would follow logically that Jerry's client would be making changes at a similar level. Whenever the supervisee gets beyond his or her personal impasse, the client usually does so as well.

I have intended to show that whatever dimension we choose for supervisory reflection, the others are also involved. Getting stuck in one dimension may simply mean it is time to check another pole because the fish are biting on that one. These clinical examples were chosen to illustrate that whatever pole we pick, to ignore the others in any case would have reduced the "catch of the day."

Termination

During the last few weeks of supervision we confront termination, in one fashion or another. The clients will be indicating their awareness that time is growing short, covertly, if not overtly. It is usually helpful in supervision to model for the supervisee effective ways of terminating with clients. Such effective ways of ending supervision are valuable experiences for supervisees before termination with their clients. These supervisory sessions should be undertaken in time for the supervisees then to "go and do likewise."

As part of this termination process, it is important for supervisees to recognize what they have accomplished. The more they grasp their achievements, the more likely their clients are to recognize theirs. Ideally, everyone has something to celebrate at this point. If the goals were concrete, then supervisees, peers, and clients all are aware of the changes they have made.

The emotional side of termination likewise is best modeled with the students. One way of doing this is to take time for each person to state what he or she has learned and how each will remember the others in the group. This is an effective way of saying good-bye, because it is specific. Compliments that are specific are more meaningful. At the same time, to do this exercise each person must acknowledge what he or she has learned from the others in the group. This can be easily undertaken in conjunction with deciding on grades.

In summary, through examining any of the three dimensions of supervision, the other two are often dealt with at the same time. Even when a fish is biting on one pole, good fishing dictates that the others are watched for activity. Through careful fishing of all three poles in supervision, clients and supervisees are best attended.

APPENDIX:
A GUIDE TO PREPARING TAPES FOR SUPERVISION

This procedure can be followed whether you are studying your work in group or individual treatment. It can be employed by a cotherapist in training with a therapist in a group they lead conjointly.

Review the Tape

Listen for a segment of five to ten minutes in length that is especially productive or especially troublesome. Make your selection on the basis of what you want to learn from your work. You may wish to demonstrate an effective series of interventions you have made to strengthen your theory and practice. You may wish to explore some place where your work has broken down or you did not have the resources to deal with what happened. We learn equally well from our mistakes.

1. Play your selected tape segment several times, making notes about what you hear.
2. Settle on a way of doing your own analysis of this segment, concentrating on a structural analysis of your client's ego states; or a transactional analysis of what happened; or the analysis of a game, if that has developed; or the recording of information about the script; or any other appropriate conceptual tool.
3. Prepare a one-page summary of your work for presentation in accord with the outline below.

Outline for Presentation

This material will be one page, with sufficient copies so that each person present can have one. It is presented in abbreviated form at the start of the session in five minutes or less, allowing for succinct answers to questions your supervisor or others present may have. The outline includes:

1. A brief description of your client and a summary of salient facts, such as age, contract, and significant events in treatment data. If you are presenting a group, include the seating diagram as described by Eric Berne in his book *Principles of Group Treatment,* pp. 139–142.
2. A one-sentence statement of what you want to learn in presenting this material.
3. Two or three sentences placing the particular segment you are playing in context of what has transpired earlier in the session.
4. Your own analysis of what happened during this segment. Give your conclusions from the conceptual tools you have employed, including structural diagrams, transactional diagrams, tools for game analysis, the script matrix, or any other theoretical apparatus you use in analyzing the treatment process.

NOTES

1. See chapter 3.
2. M. J. G. Doehrman, "Parallel Processes in Supervision and Psychotherapy," *Bulletin of the Menninger Clinic* 40 (1):71–72 (1976).
3. Ibid., p. 71.
4. P. Walzlawick and others, *Pragmatics of Human Communication: A Study of Interactional Patterns, Pathologies, and Paradoxes* (New York: W. W. Norton & Co., 1976), pp. 43–47.
5. Doehrman, "Parallel Processes in Supervision and Psychotherapy," pp. 71–72.

10

Group Supervision
Bruce Skaggs

The clinical pastoral trainee often questions the value of and need for group supervision. The previously mentioned therapeutic dimension of supervision speaks to the need for exploring the personal self in order to increase effectiveness.

Additionally, pastors frequently find themselves involved in various group situations. These run the gamut from the family that is seeking counseling for personal or spiritual problems to the building fund committee, and to the Sunday school where personality conflicts are causing undercurrents of dissension among the staff and affecting attendance and curriculum. An understanding of these potential group dynamics will enhance the pastor's effectiveness in all group situations.

Finally, group supervision enhances the exploration of parallel process where problems with fears and anxieties are projected onto others, making the pastor ineffective in situations that "strike a familiar chord."

Relevance

The successful pastor has learned to understand group dynamics, interact meaningfully within whatever group situation is present, and have an adequate self-awareness so as to relate to all members of these groups in order to get maximum performance from them. An understanding of group dynamics needs to extend into all aspects of the pastor's life. This goes from the basic family unit to the entire social network.

A group of twelve counselors was assembled at a conference in order to brainstorm new ways to upgrade a teaching program at a local college. Since all of the counselors were of approximate skill, the only obvious difference was that two of the participants were women. The morning session was spent with a highly competitive group expressing many thoughts resulting in some very good concepts being brought forth. After the lunch break, only eight counselors returned, all men. The remainder of the day was spent with each member bragging about his accomplishments and no productive ideas emerged.

What happened? The answer lies in the psyche of the remaining members who unconsciously assumed that the two males and two females left together, thus giving all the remaining males a sense of being one-upped by their colleagues. Thus, the remainder of the day was spent trying to reassure themselves of their virility. Ridiculous, you say, but no work was accomplished once an unresolved sexual element was introduced into the group.

How many times a similar situation occurs, no one can say. Since a great number of the dynamics affecting group behavior happen at the unconscious level, we are no doubt often involved with phenomena like this, totally outside our awareness. A similar result of low productivity occurred in the supervision of three trainees in counseling.

Three trainees were assigned to a supervisor for the purpose of group supervision of work they were doing with their individual clients. From the beginning there were multiple scheduling problems, with the trainees making several appointments for supervision and then changing them because of their own schedule conflicts. Finally a mutual time was established with the supervisor, only to have none of the trainees show up. After more delays, the first meeting was held, at which the supervisory contract was made and the trainees were oriented to the expectations of their assignments. The next week they again did not show up for supervision.

At this point the supervisor was frustrated and angry and made the assumption that he was dealing with a severe resistance problem. Contact was finally reestablished with the designated spokesman for the trainees, and in the ensuing meeting the supervisor confronted the trainees on the assumed resistance to supervision.

In this session the following facts emerged: Trainee A, a woman, had been reluctant to sign up for the class because she disliked personal disclosure and knew that this class would deal with the trainee's own personality issues. This was also complicated by the fact that her usual behavior when around men was to yield to their wishes even if their wishes went against her own thoughts.

Trainee B, a man, was extremely passive and assumed a posture of "following the crowd." His personality characteristics led him never to take any leadership roles.

Trainee C, a man, was given the spokesman role by default. Trainee C was a person who always over-scheduled himself, had poor self-discipline, and seldom completed projects. However, he was the most aggressive of the three and also made many convincing points when discussing anything related to school. He had over-scheduled himself with classes and outside work and had put the supervision class at a very low priority.

This analysis of the group dynamics led the supervisor to conclude that the individual personalities of the three trainees created the nonproductive group atmosphere rather than individual resistance, as had been originally assumed. In this situation the leadership of the small group had been assumed by an unlikely leader and the personality of the group had taken on a negative direction.

The complications that the group situation created did impede the early supervision of the trainees' work, but the scenario opened up an area of supervision for the three trainees that was of far greater value to their overall learning process.

Through this experience, they were able to integrate how their own personal dynamics blocked their learning. They could see how they carried this configuration into every aspect of their own life from their respective families to the various committees on which they served. This provides group supervision with a dimension not available in a one-on-one supervision model. Through this parallel process, far greater learning can take place, which gives the trainee a sense of what experiences are like in the "real world" of our social systems.

The example above demonstrates a two-dimensional communication system: Supervisor $\rightleftarrows$ Trainee/Therapist. The breakdown between trainees and supervisor occurred in the trainee subsystem, but there is potential for a breakdown in either direction.

Types of Group Supervision

Group supervision constitutes the bringing together of two or more trainees in a peer atmosphere where the goal is a specific educational/interpersonal experience. Often a spokesperson will be appointed, initially, in order to get the participants together. However, these individuals do not constitute a group in the strictest sense until they have met as a group and the dynamics of a group have begun to take shape.

Group supervision can be conducted in two specific ways. The first, which may be called the Super Group (often referred to in CPE experience as the IPR group), is designed to bring a number of trainees together in order to experience the group process. Here the group is established around the guidelines of a typical therapy group. The trainees are expected to learn through the group experience, with the emphasis being on what events develop within the group.

The second approach to group supervision assembles a number of trainees who present clinical material in a group learning experience. In this type of group the agenda is structured around assignments to the trainees, who are responsible for presenting material from their work with patients or clients in a clinical seminar or a case study group. This is an ideal group to study the parallel process of learning, and here we can add a third dimension to the two-dimensional communication system shown above. This third dimension is that of the client/patient. Thus we expand the Supervisor $\rightleftharpoons$ Trainee/Therapist to Supervisor $\rightleftharpoons$ Trainee/Therapist $\rightleftharpoons$ Client/Patient. Once the third dimension is added, the additional possibilities for communication breakdown increase proportionally, once again pointing out the need for increased self-awareness at all levels.

The key to the success of both groups is the sharing of experiences. This free expression must take place in order to maximize learning. Several things must be present for this to happen. First, trainees must feel safe to express their feelings openly. Therefore the supervisor must provide a structure for the group that assures an atmosphere of acceptance and the knowledge that feelings and emotions will be protected. Once this protection has been established, the supervisor must give the trainees permission to express themselves freely. This permission must come genuinely from the supervisor at both the conscious and the unconscious level, and the supervisor can undermine the whole experience if there is not a real commitment to making the group work.

The participating trainees in the group must take the group experience seriously if the process is to be effective. They must be motivated and willing to take risks. It is essential that they be willing to verbalize their feelings energetically. Passivity and a "wait and see" attitude on the part of the trainees will result in a less than ideal learning experience. Ultimately, the responsibility of the success or failure of the group process rests on the shoulders of the trainees, who must be willing to demand the best possible learning experience.

Once the administrative contracts are established and the trainees feel safe and know that confidentiality will be maintained, then the scene is set for further group dynamics to unfold.

Leadership

Although in any supervision group there is always a designated instructor, there will also be an internal leader. Awareness of this is important, since how the group will function, or whether it will function at all, will be dependent on who the leader is and what his or her attitude is about the Super Group. How and why a particular individual will emerge as the leader is dependent on many factors, a few of which are (1) leadership qualities of the individual, (2) alliances that take place among group members, (3) knowledge of the subject matter, and (4) assertiveness.

It is a fact that no real work will occur until the internal leadership issue has been settled. An order of dominance will be established within the group. It may be overtly obvious or it could be obscure, depending on the personal makeup of the various members of the group.

The most common situation is for a single person to emerge as the leader, with other members falling in line according to how assertive or passive their personalities are. The "leadership development phase" is extremely important, since it is here that the positive or negative attitude of the group will begin to develop. *It is absolutely necessary that a positive attitude be established for the overall success of the group.* If a negative attitude develops at this early stage, it will have a lasting effect and may stifle the group throughout its existence. Whoever emerges as the group leader will have a major influence on the group, and the attitude of the group will be a melding of the attitudes of all the group members.

Group Culture

This group attitude is often referred to as the "group culture." Every group has its own unique culture, and no two group cultures are alike. The specific culture of a group influences the behavior of the individuals in the group. Since cultural changes come slowly, the behavior of the group as a whole, as well as the individuals in the group, will tend to remain the same for extended periods of time. This is unlike group leadership which can change as the membership changes.

This cultural effect can carry a person's performance in group to exceed his or her own personal capabilities, but it can also have the opposite effect. A negative group culture can render an enthusiastic group member apathetic after only a few group sessions. Obviously, then, it is vital that a positive group culture be established.

> Six randomly selected trainees were assigned to a supervisor for the expressed purpose of learning about group dynamics as part of the group course in pastoral education. From the beginning, the supervisor was positive, nurturing, demonstrating strong leadership through the task of showing group members what was expected of them. Support and caring were stressed, with open communication and a high degree of confidentiality established.
>
> Within three weeks after the group had formed, members were supportive and confrontive of each other, and there was a high level of interaction among the trainees. The supervisor slowly withdrew from directing the interaction as the trainees took a more active, positive, and supportive role with a great deal of self-disclosure and a very positive growth and learning experience.

As stated previously, a negative group culture, once established, is very difficult to change. Uncertainty, anxiety, underlying anger, or frustration are all emotions that the trainees may experience. These emotions may result in an unconscious desire for them to move the group culture in a negative direction.

If the apprehensive trainees can engage the unwitting supervisor into supporting this negative group culture, this will in turn keep the interactive process at a "safe" level.

Apprehensions may also extend to the supervisor. It is essential that he or she be open and straightforward as the group process develops. Failure to do this can produce the results seen in the following example:

> A supervisor of extensive experience with individual trainees, but with no group supervision, was asked to "fill in" when an overabundance of trainees signed up for the group course. Based on the supervisor's desire to help, he did not express to the department head his reluctance and anxiety over the task he was asked to do. The peer pressure from his colleagues also added to his insecurity over doing the job "right." As a result, the supervisor reverted to his usual behavior when threatened (parallel process) and became

passive. This passivity and the unconscious anxiety were picked up by the trainees, who also experienced anxiety, since the protective atmosphere was absent. The result at the behavioral level was overt competition among the trainees. Often one person would "get put on the hot seat" and the entire group would nitpick at that person. This in turn led to tardiness and a high degree of absenteeism. The result was to reinforce the supervisor's feelings of inadequacy as a group leader and to reinforce the suspicions and fears of the various trainees.

Forming a Positive Group Culture

Since the attitude of the instructor is vital, if he or she doesn't want to supervise this group of trainees, or doesn't believe in group supervision, a negative attitude will be communicated and a negative group culture will develop, inadvertently, reaffirming what the supervisor believed. Assuming that the supervisor is positive and wants a positive experience for the trainees, the supervisor will be positive and upbeat. This is achieved through positive reinforcement of behavior leading to the positive group culture and lack of reinforcement to behavior of a negative nature. It is also important that the supervisor give more information and structure early so the trainees will know what is expected of them and lower their anxiety. Contrary to the beliefs of many "old school" group leaders, it is not true that anxiety is conducive to positive group learning and a positive culture, since effective learning will not take place if a person feels threatened and needs to provide emotional protection for himself or herself. Here again, the achievement of a protective and safe atmosphere within the group contributes to the learning potential.

Tandem Group Learning

Given the opportunity, each trainee will tend to identify with at least one other person in the group. This pairing or "tandem" connection will often free trainees from defensiveness that limits learning:

A group of students in a Super Group had been involved with one member's struggle with authority. This had originated when the trainee got angry with the supervisor. The trainee's inability to make a connection between his anger toward the supervisor and his inability to please his demanding and rejecting father was finally resolved when another trainee began to discover his own problems with authority. The first trainee just could not see any connection, because at that point he felt "on the hot seat" and his desire to "see" the problem was clouded by his greater need at the unconscious level to defend himself. Only when the other trainee began to talk about his experiences did the first trainee feel permission psychologically to switch from a defensive protection of himself to a learning stance.

This transition was made possible by the tandem effect within the group process. The tandem concept revolved around the realization that group members will tend to protect themselves when on the spot and insights are hard to come by, since the participants' natural protection systems will protect them from over-disclosure. However, when like personalities are in the same group, those participants who are not "on the hot seat" are able to discover insights about themselves, since they have no need to have their defenses up.

Therefore it is wise, whenever possible, to have two or three persons with similar issues and/or personality traits together in a group so their insights may be shared. Once an observing member (one not "on the hot seat") discovers the insights, he or she can often communicate these insights more effectively to the defensive member than the supervisor or other members.

Supervisory Contracts

Since the early developmental phase of any training group is very tentative, strict adherence to meeting times and days, as well as assigned projects such as reports, case studies, and demonstrations, must be maintained. Here again, the supervisor can sabotage the success by failing to adhere to the administrative contracts with the trainees.

Group supervision seems better suited in the closed-ended group, a group with a definite starting and ending date and a group whose participants are held constant. This type of group is similar in nature to the committee or project group commonly found in churches and social agencies.

The open-ended group, which lends itself more readily to the therapy group, has no ending date, and members are replaced with new members as people terminate their group experience. This type of group is more prevalent in social situations and is the most significant type we encounter. There are many similarities between this type of group and our most familiar group, the basic family unit.

Types of Groups

Groups may be typed according to the style of leadership that is adopted by the supervisor for the purpose of supervision. The types of groups are laissez-faire, autocratic, and democratic.[1]

The type of group should be determined by the supervisor, depending on that supervisor's own personality, since each group will mirror many characteristics of the supervisor. Awareness on the part of the supervisor of the types of groups and how one's personality fits the various types will enhance the group's success.

The first type, laissez-faire, is least effective in terms of productivity, since it has a passive, nondirective approach. Here the supervisor gives little direction and "lets the group go." This passive leadership behavior may be indicative of fear. The all too common example of this is the parishioner who is "talked into" taking the Sunday school superintendent's job and fails miserably. His or her lack of assertiveness and unwillingness to deal with the various personalities of the Sunday school teachers lead to a slow erosion of the entire Sunday school.

The second type of group, the autocratic, is highly productive. Here the group's functioning relies on the drive and leadership of the supervisor. In an educational setting, much more material is covered and each member is more individually stimulated. However, since the energy for the group comes from the leader, if something happens to that leader, the group will become nonproductive. The personality of the supervisor of the autocratic group is one of aggressiveness and drive. He or she is usually strongly goal-oriented and may be rigid and sensitive to criticism, and the success or the failure of the group will probably be taken very personally.

An example of an autocratic group is the board of directors of a company headed by the owner of the company. He leads the meetings and directs the operation. He dictates when he wants feedback from his board, and they will be only partially candid with him. If the president is not at the meeting, the meeting may not be held, or if it is, no work will be done, since everything needs the approval of the president.

The third type of group is the democratic. In the democratic group, each member has the opportunity to express his or her opinion. Especially in the early stages, very little work is accomplished, because the order of dominance from within the group must be established with its emerging leadership. Since the supervisor only gives guidance and creates a proper atmosphere, the initial meetings are relatively nonproductive in terms of overall accomplishment. This type of group is usually creative, and many ideas can flow from it. However, without the authority of the supervisor, the group may go slowly—which especially in the beginning is a disadvantage.

The advantage of the democratic group is in its internal strength. Since its power comes from its individual members rather than the leader, the group will function just as effectively if the leader is absent. The democratic group also has the distinct advantage of not being as influenced by the biases of the supervisor.

The personality of the supervisor who encourages this type of group is one of certainty. A person who is not in a hurry, does not have anything to prove, and can take pressure and criticism without being defensive is a supervisor who probably has matured from the autocratic school.

Administrative Needs in Group Supervision

The physical and administrative setting will influence the effectiveness of group supervision and therefore needs to be addressed. Assuming that communication among the group members and the supervisor is desired, the following will be helpful:

1. Chairs should be placed in a circle to enhance communication.
2. Couches and overstuffed chairs with arms should be avoided, because they block and prevent communication.
3. Large conference tables should be avoided, because they block movement and give group members a natural barrier.
4. Brightly lighted rooms should be avoided, because group members feel too exposed.
5. Large rooms make group members feel conspicious and therefore inhibited. If a large room must be used, select a corner and arrange the chairs in a circle in that corner.

Administratively, it is important that the sessions start and end on time. Otherwise, the group members will straggle in, impeding effectiveness. If the group is frequently allowed to run late, members will put off working until toward the end, thus promoting longer and longer sessions. The supervisor should realize that the structure enhances the group process and be very strict about providing a good, safe, and constant setting.

In summary, group supervision often is the supervision of

choice. It can and often does provide a learning experience far in excess of the supervision provided one on one. However, there are limitations to group supervision, and the prospective supervisor must be desirous of a successful group experience for his or her trainees and be willing to make that commitment.

NOTES

1. K. Lewis, R. Lippitt, and R. White, "Patterns of Aggressive Behavior in Experimentally Created 'Social Climates,' " *Journal of Social Psychology* 10:271–299 (1939).

11

Some Aspects
of Live Supervision

Carolyn Lindsey

Live supervision is, as the term suggests, literally supervising the student's work simultaneously as the therapeutic process is occurring.[1] It cannot take the place of other forms of supervision that oversee a trainee's entire educational and clinical program. However, it does constitute one important way to improve the student's techniques in therapy while the helping process is going on. Live supervision imparts direct understanding of how to perform therapy. It can provide a vital link in one's overall training. The task of this chapter is to give an overview of the process of live supervision, particularly in marital and family therapy. It would be helpful when reading it to imagine yourself standing in a room with mirrors on the walls, floor, and ceiling. Each time there is movement in this room, it is reflected in all directions, reverberating up and down as well as off the walls. The same thing happens throughout the system of *live* supervision each time there is movement, emotional or physical.

Live supervision can be conducted in a number of settings: a training center in a university, a counseling agency, a teaching facility, a two-room office with a one-way mirror, or a single room in which the supervisor is actually present. There are many different ways of doing it. Detailed descriptions of these methods and a history of their development can be found in *Family Therapy Supervision* by Rosemary Whiffen and John Byng-Hall.[2] This book contains a readable summary of differing theoretical stances and teaching methods among notable family therapists from several different countries, orientations, and teaching centers.

Why Live Supervision?

In marriage and family therapy, the three major means of addressing clinical data are audiotaping, videotaping, and live supervision. Audiotaping a therapy session is one step above a verbal "self-report" by the student of what happened in a session. Only what was spoken is recorded for reflection. No nonverbal or visual communication is available for observation. Videotaping adds the visual component to the clinical materials that allows supervision to assess a variety of subtle and nonverbal processes, both constructive and resistant.[3] As with audiotaping, however, supervisory reflection is delayed for hours or days. Valuable information may be given to the supervisee and effective interventions supported. But the opportunity to implement them is lost and may never occur again.

Live supervision evolved to close the gap between clinical work and reflection, moving supervision even closer to the helping process it seeks to effect. Live supervision is "where the action is." Its model of immediate supervisory intervention is extremely powerful and can be accomplished through the earphone, the one-way mirror, the telephone call technique, or the presence of the supervisor in the same room with the family and the trainee.[4]

It is important that clients and families be prepared for live supervision. They need to know they are coming for a consultation and their therapist is gaining additional training. With such understandings, it will not be awkward for the therapist to leave the room, interrupt the session to discuss a situation, or ask the family to view the tape of their own work. The family is aware from the beginning of what the procedure will be. Often clients meet the consultant/supervisor ahead of time and are prepared for these procedures which can eliminate surprises, elicit cooperation, and reduce resistance.

Working with live material is rewarding, because it is the most immediate and useful way into a family system. Supervisor and student no longer work retrospectively. Supervisors can instruct students to try something new or different, with the opportunity to apply the idea immediately. In addition to immediate feedback, overall guidance of the ongoing process between therapist and family becomes possible.[5]

Live supervision protects a client from the incompetence of a beginner by shaping the trainee's skills quickly in directions of proven effectiveness. It avoids having the trainee get distracted by personal impasses, or what we have termed "learning problems" in chapter 3. By enabling immediate issues to be addressed in the performance of therapy, many believe live supervision enables the trainees to learn techniques of therapy more rapidly and economically. At any rate, live supervision is one key tool for training the student in (1) perception—how to perceive as a therapist; (2) cognition—how to think as a therapist; and (3) behavior/action—how to act as a therapist.

The supervisor can make immediate rather than delayed responses to students in each of these three areas. Students are freed from the inaccuracies of self-reporting and the anxieties of efforts to perform tasks beyond their capacity. The supervisor must accurately perceive what is going on in a therapy session in order to give it effective direction and recognize the student's progress.

The chief rationale for live supervision lies in its opportunity to intervene directly within the ongoing therapeutic process, thereby limiting ineffectual responses by the trainee and curtailing continuing irrelevant interactions with clients. The major task of the intervening supervisor is to suggest strategies that may assist the students in facilitating change or to offer feedback that will motivate the students to search for other strategies on their own.

Supervision in the live setting can prove more effective than other models in producing confident and competent student therapists, because intervention can occur as students are formalizing their own methods of therapy. The performance of a task and the student's understanding of the intervention need to occur simultaneously. This model demands a level of commitment on the part of everyone involved. Clients as well as students feel a sense of security in the knowledge that they are being attended to and cared for. The emotional intensity is often high for all involved, heightening the pressure on the supervisor, student, and clients alike. Students trained under pressure are better prepared to handle crisis situations in their future professional career when the assurance of authority is absent. When the students know that their supervisors are putting their knowledge on the line, they are more likely to take risks and be less rigid in their own work. This is assuming the students have worked through their own transferential and authority issues in previous supervision.

Phases of Live Supervision

There are at least three different stages through which students move in live supervision. As in Erik Erikson's theory of developmental stages, if the supervisee skips one stage or proceeds into the next stage without completing the first, the process will stop until some remapping is done. Erikson has termed this developmental process the epigenetic principle: "Somewhat generalized, this principle states that anything that grows has a ground plan, and that out of this ground plan the parts arise, each part having its time of special ascendancy, until all the parts have arisen to form a functioning whole."[6]

Erikson advances eight stages of individual development describing what happens when the tasks of one stage are not completed. Each stage "exists in some form before its decisive and critical time normally arrives and remains systematically related to all others, so that the whole ensemble depends on the proper development in the proper sequence."[7]

As students move through the stages of supervision, each stage must be completed before they can move on to the next one. We must constantly draw on previous stages, for those stages do not appear in mere succession, once completed never again to surface. The process is not just a linear pathway but also a dynamic one. As each stage is completed, that stage will resurface and continue to develop further as each successive stage is approached.[8] The same thing is true, as you can see, among the three stages of live supervision and their principal tasks.

1. Beginning

Gathering of supervisee's history of therapy and supervision experience

Establishing supervisee's goals

Helping the supervisee to become aware of his or her internal processes

Focusing the expectations

2. Middle

Outlining of each supervisory session

Reconnecting with the supervisee to access his or her awareness of the process

Checking with supervisee to see if he or she has any leftover business from the previous session

Identifying the supervisee's agenda for the session

Planning for the next session (supervisory or therapy)

Keeping in check the supervisee's interpersonal emotions toward client(s) and supervisor

Tracing the parallel process

Diagnosing symptoms of client(s)

Teaching the use of the *DSM—III—R (Diagnostic and Statistical Manual of Mental Disorders)*[9]

Observing the client's process leading to the student's presuppositions to be verified with the client in the next session

Gathering feedback and input of supervisor

Deciding on options, alternatives, and choices for the therapist's interventions

Reviewing evaluation of parallel process of supervision—past, present, and future

3. End

Terminating of the supervisory and therapeutic process in the closing segment of the task at hand

Attending to all unfinished business

Clarifying of student's understanding of anything that still needs attention

Imparting to student a summary of his or her performance

Surfacing with the supervisee any unfinished tasks to be concluded with the client

Listening to the student's evaluation of the supervisor's work

Parallel Process

The live supervision model provides the supervisor with a more controllable environment in which to monitor the way the therapist maintains the treatment process. In order for live supervision to be successful, both supervisor and student need to be aware of the phenomenon known as parallel process. Margery Doehrman contends that the effectiveness of supervision depends on insight into the interplay of forces in the parallel processes of therapy and supervision.[10] As nearly as we can gather, some form of parallel process can be found in every patient-therapist-supervisor relationship.[11] What is happening between the client and the student therapist may also be reflected in the relationship between the student and the supervisor and vice versa. As Doehrman puts it, "The very problems experienced in the one relationship affect and are reflected in the other relationship so that a two-way process exists . . . in which the therapist's problems in supervision are related to the patient problems in psychotherapy and vice versa."[12]

As students confront the chaos a client sometimes feels, the students must deal with the chaos in their own personal professional lives. As they confront their supervisor, students not only struggle to develop their skills but also to deal with their own issues with authority figures from the past. If the supervisor is also being observed for purposes of further training, the parallel process will be present in this relationship. Whatever problems develop permeate all levels of the supervisory system. Below is the hierarchy of levels that can be found in live supervision:

CONSULTANT TO SUPERVISOR

SUPERVISOR

STUDENT SUPERVISEE

CLIENT

(family, couple, or individual)

PROCESS WITHIN CLIENT'S FAMILY

While viewing this, one can also keep in mind the beginning, middle, and end stages of therapy. This permits us to remain alert to the presence of parallel process throughout each stage of supervision as well as each level of the system. There is a mirroring or reflecting effect of the transactions at each level. For example, what clients describe about their personal situation may be acted out in the therapy session toward the supervisee and again repeated between the supervisee and the supervisor. Whatever the issue, it permeates the entire system of live supervision in parallel process at all levels simultaneously. The deeper we probe into this parallel process, the greater our awareness and learning.

The Beginning Stage

During the beginning stage, the supervisee's issues with inadequacy will be exhibited in an exaggerated way. Authority issues, along with feelings of inferiority, vulnerability, and personal awareness, are often present in opposition to interpersonal issues of competition, limitation, and uniqueness. There are optimal points to enhance change within a dysfunctional system of supervised treatment which are heightened by the presence of a live supervisor. The supervisor can alert students to be aware of their nonverbal behavior, recognized or unrecognized. Without the frame of reference provided by our concepts of parallel process and stages in supervision, both supervisor and student will be at a disadvantage when reflecting upon their work. Breakdowns can result in both the therapy process and the working alliance of supervision.

The following clinical example from my own supervision illustrates how in parallel process one specific issue can permeate all levels in the system. The supervisee was a twenty-five-year-old woman who had been in the practice of marriage and family therapy for two years. There was less differentiation than usual between the supervisee and myself. I identified closely with her in our personal similarities, since she too was a young wife, a new mother, and a struggling, insecure psychotherapist. The exhaustion she felt from balancing three careers was all too familiar to me.

My supervisee would often come to sessions so overwhelmed that I had great difficulty not mothering her. Both of us shared a struggle with feelings of isolation, being the only two female colleagues in a male-dominated work world. On one occasion, when our supervisory session was to be done live at our center's monthly staff conference, my supervisee came in discussing how intimidated she felt by her male clients. The session was being viewed by myself and a staff of six colleagues, all male, who were literally lined up behind a one-way mirror. One of our center's recent staff development projects called for each of us to explore the system of our own family of origin. As my supervisee continued to struggle with her male client, it became clear how difficult it was for her to confront him, to challenge him to change, to question his perceptions, or to disagree with his opinion. I was immediately reminded of my own parallel struggles, coming from a male-dominated family and being isolated in my professional training as the lone woman.

I called my supervisee out of the therapy session into the room with the all-male viewing panel. Both of us shared some feelings about that. Attempting to keep the countertransference at a minimum, I asked my supervisee what some of her expectations of males were and how her disappointments with them were connected to her feelings of intimidation. She quickly realized she was waiting for her male client to take charge. I asked her what he was paying for and she laughed and reentered the therapy room ready to shift gears and to do her job.

The Middle Stage

During the middle phase, the potency of live supervision is established only when there is an awareness of parallel process and how it can repeat itself on several levels, both past and present. The issue of waiting for males to take charge expressed itself for my supervisee both up and down the hierarchy of live supervision and across time at this stage of her training. Whatever is learned around this issue can be joined with theoretical ideas in ways that formulate the student's pastoral or therapeutic identity. Reflection upon the therapeutic dimension of their own psychodynamics helps students to meet clients more humanly and effectively. Skills are acquired through recognizing the realities of transference and countertransference.

Live supervision demands a level of vulnerability for both supervisor and supervisee alike. One of the best measurements of progress in the supervisee's efforts to deal with transference toward the supervisor can be determined by the depths of intrapsychic material elicited from the client. If a supervisee exceeds limits of the presented problem, works too hard, lowers self-expectations, or explores unpresented material with the presence of intense feelings, it is likely some personal problem from the past is appearing. Because of the tendency for these problems to play themselves out in the working alliance of supervision, differentiation is essential to keep the parallel process in balance and at the lowest point of enmeshment. *When a supervisor is as vulnerable as the student, the supervisory process will work.* This demands some self-supervision (of one's own style) on the part of every supervisor in order to be effective.

A major goal in live supervision is to help student therapists maintain control of the treatment session, while exposing them to as many stimulating experiences with clients as possible. The integration of helping theory and clinical practice is a second major goal during this middle phase. These two goals are more easily achieved with the use of live supervision. When these goals are not achieved simultaneously, students tend to become frustrated during the delay of unstructured interaction with clients while waiting for supervisory direction.

Broadening the student's horizon is the task at hand. The supervisor does not address the reason for the student's behavior at this juncture. Instead, the supervisor's attention turns to (1) being as objective as possible, (2) remembering that transference is naturally high, and (3) remembering that advice, interruptions, criticism, or implications will only hinder the supervisory process.

After the clients have left, supervisors and students debrief usually during an individual supervision session. This is the time for students to share what was going on inside them while doing the therapy process as they implemented supervisory directions. Mutual learning can occur when the supervisors are honest in owning their own responsibility and intent while intervening in the process. Often it will be helpful for the supervisor to share first to ease the tension for the student. Raising the student's awareness is best accomplished by patience and modeling.

The complexity of performing therapy challenges a student to learn to operate at several levels simultaneously. A student must diagnose individually and systemically, assess historical information and interpersonal dynamics, and also interpret the developmental stage of the family system together with its repetitive patterns. Supervision is invaluable in assisting the student to track all of these dynamics at once. The momentum of connecting interpersonally with the supervisor will stimulate the student to go on to the next phase of supervision.

The End Stage

Although evaluation is an important part of each stage, the stage of termination requires particular attention to this element. A careful review of the supervisee's goals and expectations in the supervisory contract is made to see whether any issues failed to surface along the way. This phase of the learning process lasts several weeks in order to enable review and discussion and thus assure thoroughness. Closure is extremely important. Taking time to share with the supervisee insights and learnings the supervisor may have had earlier will lead to new understandings of the parallel process that now may be appropriately incorporated into the supervisee's schema of learning.

As a student enters the termination phase of supervision, sharing serves a dual purpose. It is a time for the supervisor to be sure the supervisee understands systemic concepts. In order for students to achieve this, they must switch from their cognitive thinking to use their imagination, their creativity, and their musing.

As in other stages, parallel process prevails here as well. The more thorough and complete the closure the supervisor and the student put upon their working alliance, the more successful the supervisee becomes in the termination process with clients.

NOTES

1. An excellent definition of live supervision is provided by S. F. Loewenstein, P. Reder, and A. Clark, "The Consumer's Response: Trainees' Discussion of the Experience of Live Supervision," in *Family Therapy Supervision: Recent Developments in Practice,* ed. R. Whiffen and J. Byng-Hall (London: Grune & Stratton 1982), p. 124.

2. Ibid.

3. See C. A. Everett, "The Use of Videotape in Supervision," in *Psychotherapy Supervision: Theory, Research and Practice,* ed. A. K. Hess (New York: John Wiley & Sons, 1980), p. 373.

4. A discussion of the positive and negative aspects of each of these methods can be found in Whiffen and Byng-Hall, *Family Therapy Supervision,* pp. 17–79.

5. See B. W. Cade and P. M. Seligman, "Teaching a Strategic Approach," in Whiffen and Byng-Hall, *Family Therapy Supervision,* p. 174.

6. E. H. Erikson, *Identity and the Life Cycle* (New York: W. W. Norton & Co., 1980), p. 53.

7. Ibid., p. 29.

8. Ibid., p. 39.

9. *DSM—III—R,* 3rd rev. ed. (Washington: American Psychiatric Association, 1987).

10. M. J. G. Doehrman, "Parallel Processes in Supervision and Psychotherapy, *Bulletin of the Menninger Clinic* 40 (1):17 (1976).

11. Ibid., p. 4.

12. Ibid., p. 16.

12

Transference and Countertransference in Supervision

Clarence Barton and Amanda W. Ragland

Seldom is the process of supervision so clear-cut that it is black or white; instead, it is infused with "the wonderful world of color." One rich source of this color is to be found in the supervisee's inner world of feelings.

One supervisor recognized the learning potential for the student when the following experience occurred.

While making rounds in the hospital, the supervising chaplain was cryptically asked by a nurse, "Aren't chaplains supposed to minister to people who are dying?" The supervisor acknowledged as how that did seem like a reasonable expectation, then asked the nurse what led to her question. She replied, "I have asked our unit chaplain to visit Miss Smith three times now and he has yet to go into her room." Shaking her head, she concluded, "It just doesn't make sense. The woman has cancer and is slowly dying; she wants to see a chaplain!" The supervisor assured the nurse that a chaplain would see the patient; he then made an appointment with his supervisee, the chaplain assigned to that unit.

In the supervisory session, the student confirmed what the nurse reported; he had been repeatedly asked to visit the dying patient and had not yet done so, concluding, "I cannot bring myself to go into the patient's room." As he reflected on what his behavior might mean, he said, "I'm doing something else that is crazy. For the past few weeks, every time I come to the hospital I have to bring this corncob pipe in my pocket. I bought it for Mr. Jones, an elderly patient that I have spent a lot of time with; the day I came to the hospital to give it to him, he had been transferred to the infirmary with pneumonia. He didn't improve; every time I visited him I brought the pipe, but did not want to give it to him while he was so sick. He died before I could give it to him. Ever since, I have had to bring the pipe with me to the hospital." The student appeared tense and sad as he reported this experience.

The supervisor explored with this student his experience with death and grief. Although the student was in his mid-twenties, he had not lost a significant person. The death of the elderly man, his patient, was the first significant encounter with grief this student remembered. His failure to work through his grief and his emotional denial of the patient's death was communicated by his repeated bringing of the pipe. Until he was able to do his own grief work he was unable to enter into another pastoral relationship with a dying patient; therefore he avoided visiting the female cancer patient.

The supervisor accepted the student's need to do his own grief work and accepted himself the responsibility for acting on the referral from the nurse. He explored with the student the cancer patient's need for ministry and offered to provide for her care. The supervisor then asked the student whether he wished to accompany him to visit the cancer patient. The student thought about the offer and accepted it. After the visit, the student voluntarily told the supervisor that he felt confident in providing ministry to the cancer patient, which he continued to do until the woman died some weeks later.

This young man had a *colorful* and highly relevant learning experience when his feelings of grief over the old man's death were still present as he moved into other relationships. His own grief played a significant role in his interactions with the female cancer patient. What he experienced is countertransference.

Given our tendency to collect impressions, or *colors,* from past relationships and experiences, it is not surprising that transference and countertransference show up as topics for discussion in the supervisory relationship. We always carry our colors with us. The fact that we can transfer our impressions to other people, or can instantaneously place a face from the past on a person in the present, predisposes us to transference and countertransference issues in the training of helping professionals.

Development of the Concepts

The concept of transference has its origin in the work of Freud. Freud coined the term when he discovered that his patients tended to transfer their childhood feelings for their parents to him during the course of analysis.[1] The feelings these patients had for Freud consisted of libido (love and sensual attraction) and aggression (hostility and primitive rage) which they had originally experienced toward their parents in infancy.

Freud's use of the term "transference" was limited to the infantile feelings that a patient transferred to the analyst within the context of psychoanalysis. This first definition of transference has evolved, through the years, to a much broader concept. In the 1940s, Wilhelm Reich believed that the transfer of whole sets of ideas and attitudes was part of the human personality, so that transference was not limited just to the psychoanalytic setting.[2]

Harry Stack Sullivan's development of the concept of parataxic distortions in the early 1950s also influenced the concept of transference. Parataxic distortions occur when the present reality of an interpersonal relationship is ignored in some way because of the transferring of feelings and behavior from past relationships to the current situation.[3] A person overlooks the actual personality of the other person and relates to the other as if he or she were another person encountered in the past.[4] During the interpersonal transaction, the participants can place on each other several different faces arising from past experiences.

These ideas that Sullivan originated are typical of the broader definition of transference used today. In the broader definition, transference refers to any distortion of a current relationship through acting out any aspect of a past relationship.

Like transference, the concept of countertransference also has its roots in the work of Freud. Freud saw countertransference as the unconscious reactions of the analyst toward the patient. These reactions were seen as stemming from the patient's transference toward the analyst rather than from the analyst's own motivations. Countertransference was considered a threat to the analytic neutrality that was necessary for the success of analysis.[5]

The concept of countertransference has also changed through the years. Robert Tyson claims that there have been three basic changes. First, the definition of countertransference has expanded beyond the inclusion of the helper's unconscious reactions to encompass also the helper's conscious reactions toward the patient. Second, the source of countertransference has shifted away from the helper's response to the helpee's transference to include the helper's own unresolved personal difficulties. Third, the concept of countertransference has changed from being seen as a total hindrance to being seen, if managed and used properly, as a useful tool in the therapeutic process.[6] As early as 1949 and 1950, people like Winnicott and Heiman were beginning to see that dealing with issues of the helper's countertransference could unearth understanding about the counselee's own psychic process which could actually enhance therapeutic progress.[7] Webster's dictionary simply states that countertransference is the complex of feelings that therapists have toward their patients.[8]

Both the concept of transference and of countertransference have expanded beyond their first use in the original Freudian sense. Broader definitions will be used in the remaining portion of this chapter. Since countertransference is one form of the larger phenomenon of transference itself, we will refer to both under the overarching concept of transference unless a precise distinction is required.

Recognizing Transference

Questions arise when we begin to consider transference. How do its elements come into play in the supervisory process? How can we establish awareness of this phenomenon?

In the supervisory relationship, your transference toward your supervisor may be operative even before the relationship begins. You may hear stories about your supervisor that shape your impressions before the two of you meet. By the time of the initial interview, you may have inaccurate expectations of your supervisor which may be considered transference. Your unresolved issues with authority figures work their way into the supervisory relationship and can become topics for discussion. For example, students who were taught by previous authority figures to seek their advice may approach supervision expecting the supervisor to think for them.

Transference may be operative in the supervisory relationship any time you display behavior that is extreme or out of the ordinary, whether this is an overly emotional response, an unusual lack of thinking or problem-solving ability, or a behavior that is seductive. Transference can take as many different forms as there are supervisees, all with their own unique unresolved issues. Whenever the supervisee operates with inaccurate assumptions about the supervisor based on past impressions, or colorings, transference occurs.

There are similar clues that indicate that countertransference toward your parishioners or clients may be operative. One is that you simply must be the one to provide care for this person as though what you have to offer is unique in all the world. Another clue is your reluctance to discuss a particular parishioner, patient, or client. A helping relationship in which the helper is overinvolved gets intense, and reference to it may be avoided in the ordinary exchange of information.

Sometimes gifts—even something so small as sharing coffee, going on a walk, or giving handmade things—from either you or your parishioner can indicate transference. Frances Brown gives an excellent example of a female therapist working with a male patient.[9] The male was sexually attracted to the therapist. He made a sketch as a Christmas gift. He had the fantasy that she would hang it in her bedroom and her husband would ask her about the picture. After the man shared his fantasy with the therapist, she responded that she did not have a husband. That was what the man wanted to know all along. The female therapist had let the conversation depart from the here and now therapeutic relationship and end in her bedroom. This is a countertransference issue which may need to be addressed in supervision. If this kind of thing happened repeatedly, this might be an issue that the therapist would need to address in her own therapy.

Countertransference may be present when the boundaries of the relationship move beyond a specific type of caregiving or outside the bounds of the contractual relationship. For example, the chaplain and the patient might lean toward romantic involvement. Clinical supervision is governed by clear contracts. The supervisor's countertransference might be operative if the relationship is allowed to turn into a friendship and serious reflection stops. This type of shift might also indicate transference on behalf of the student. E. Mansell Pattison lists several indications of countertransference that we have not mentioned: being careless in keeping appointments, having repeated erotic or hostile feelings, experiencing boredom during counseling sessions, permitting or even encouraging misbehavior, trying to impress the person you are helping, giving premature reassurance, dreaming about the person you are helping, making unusual appointments, or behaving in a manner unusual for you.[10] There are many indications that transference and countertransference are operative; we have considered only a few.

Once we are aware that transference is present, we have to decide what to do about it. The supervisory model detailed in chapter 3 provides a framework in which to deal effectively with these ideas. We turn our attention now to exactly how that can work.

Using the Supervisory Model

Each of the dimensions of reflection of the supervisory model is significant in dealing with issues of transference and countertransference: (1) the therapeutic dimension, which focuses on whatever insight, behavioral change, or other personal conditions need to be met by the supervisee in order to increase personal effectiveness; (2) the dimension of administrative oversight, which is concerned that the clients, patients, or parishioners receive proper and effective treatment or care; and (3) the dimension of the working alliance, which concentrates on the supervisory relationships themselves between supervisee, peers, and supervisor.

The Therapeutic Dimension

In the therapeutic dimension, the question often becomes how much of an issue is suitable for supervision and how much would best be resolved by the student in a psychotherapeutic or counseling environment. Although it is recognized that transference and countertransference occur in a variety of settings, they are often neglected as a potential learning experience for the supervisees. Marcia Goin and Frank Kline's study of twenty-four supervisors of second-year psychiatric residents found that twelve of them made no comments on countertransference issues. Eight dealt with the subject directly, and four dealt with it indirectly.[11] In this research, one of the main reasons the supervisor neglected these issues was a desire to avoid confusing supervision with therapy. In such neglect, the educational needs of the student suffer.

It is consistent with effective supervision to provide support, to relieve anxiety appropriately, and to establish a positive working relationship with the supervisee. Even though these goals are synonymous with those of therapy, they cannot be avoided in supervision. At times, issues involving transference provide excellent opportunities for learning that have the potential to enhance the supervisee's professional functioning. There do need to be, however, some checks or boundaries governing how far we go in dealing with the underlying personal issues surrounding them.

One such check is to determine whether the transference reveals issues that fit with the learning goals articulated by the supervisee. Supervision is a structured relationship based on a contractual agreement between the supervisor and the supervisee. In clinical supervision, the conversation takes shape around each student's own needs for personal development and growth. These contracts determine the specific types of learning that are being sought in the professional relationships at hand. Any personal growth issue that arises through reflecting upon these changes is suitable to be addressed in supervision.

Another check is to determine whether dealing with the issues that arise from transference is becoming the primary focus of the supervisory process. When such discussions are permitted to dominate the relationship, learning in other areas of our model is inhibited or subverted. Within the therapeutic dimension of supervision, anything that fosters the student's own personal growth in the professional role is a good use of time and energy, but this has to be kept in balance with the other two dimensions, those concerning the working alliance of supervision and the administrative oversight of pastoral care.

There are issues that become apparent in dealing with transference that are resolvable within supervision. There are also those which are not. The issues that are not are more deeply ingrained in the student's personality and require the more specialized environment of psychotherapy. Whenever the supervisory conversation is repeatedly pulled back to the same personal problem, we have a good indication that the student is dealing with an issue that really needs to be worked out in counseling where one can explore early decisions and feelings or examine the origin of the issue in ways that go beyond the focus of supervision upon one's contemporary involvement in professional relationships. Two examples might be helpful here.

A male chaplain at a medium-security woman's prison on several occasions brought verbatims into supervision in which he discounted the inmate's responsibility. In one particular case, the chaplain had talked with a woman who had been locked up and denied usual privileges as a disciplinary measure. The prisoner had started a fight with another inmate, even being verbally abusive to a guard in the whole process. The woman knew the consequences for her actions, but she did them anyway. The chaplain visited her while she was still locked up. He was very touched by the way she had been terribly mistreated in the whole situation and how no one gave her a chance to explain her side of the matter. When the chaplain presented the verbatim of the conversation in supervision, he asked the supervisor whether the guards were usually so tough.

The supervisor had noticed a similar pattern in the chaplain's interactions with other inmates and raised this tendency to overlook the inmate's responsibility as a countertransference issue. At first, the chaplain did not understand what the supervisor was talking about, but after some careful explanation, the chaplain did see that he was treating the inmates in some ways like children. In supervision, the two explored the roots of this behavior. The chaplain realized that he treated the inmates the way he treated his little sister when they were younger, because it had been his responsibility to look after her. He also realized that he did not need to look after his sister or the inmates anymore.

This was a priceless learning experience for the chaplain. After this, he was able to function more effectively in his pastoral role by viewing the inmates as responsible for their own actions. This is an example of an issue that surfaced in considering countertransference that was fruitful for the supervisee's education and could be resolved within the supervisory relationship.

Another chaplain, this time a woman, was visiting an older male patient in the hospital. This patient had just had one of his legs removed from the knee down. When the chaplain visited him, the patient, who was angry about his loss, spoke sharply to her and criticized the hospital administration. The chaplain felt like a child and was at a loss as to the best way to respond. She fumbled for some polite words and left the room in a daze. She brought up the experience in supervision and explored the countertransference involved. The chaplain explained that she felt like a child in the room who had not done the right thing. She heard the patient's criticism of the hospital administration as a personal assault.

The supervisor and the chaplain had previously discussed how she at times placed her father's face on the supervisor. Together they discovered that the chaplain was placing her father's face on the older male patient as well. Her father had been overpowering and critical of her in ways that still diminished her overall sense of self-worth. The chaplain had been realizing for some time that her father treated her poorly. She reported a few early memories and scenes that were quite painful. She had never really confronted her father for his behavior. The supervisor, a seasoned professional, realized that sorting through these experiences was necessary but beyond the scope of supervision and suggested she might want to explore some of these issues in her own counseling, which she did.

This experience needed to be discussed in supervision, but the extent and depth of the issue did not allow it to be fully explored or resolved within the supervisory relationship. In this case, the repetitive nature of the chaplain's transference to the supervisor had become a theme in their working alliance. This built a backdrop against which to explore the countertransference to the patient and also served as a clue to the extent of the chaplain's personal issue. Although addressing this issue was in line with the student's learning contract to gain self-confidence in her pastoral activities, both she and the supervisor recognized the need to explore it in her own counseling, lest the supervisory process be continually drawn into the therapeutic realm, neglecting its other aspects. In a situation like this, the supervisor may choose to concentrate on the here and now effect of the countertransference rather than the origins of the issue. This helps to maintain the delicate balance between the three reflective areas and forms a good complement to personal therapy.

It is normally very helpful for students receiving supervision to be concurrently involved in personal psychotherapy. These students usually know very quickly the distinction between a therapy issue and a supervisory issue. Those students who are not in psychotherapy may need to be encouraged to seek counseling, particularly if experiences like the last example begin to occur and the quality of the supervisory process is diminished.

A student's transference to the supervisor and countertransference to parishioners and peers are significant issues for the therapeutic dimension of reflection. When these issues involve the learning goals determined by the contractual agreement, they need to be handled in such a manner that they do not become the sole focus of supervision. Otherwise, inadequate attention is paid to administrative oversight and the working alliance.

Administrative Oversight

In the experience of the chaplain who carried the pipe and hesitated to get involved with the woman dying of cancer, the supervisor appreciated the supervisee's need to experience his own grief but did not lose sight of this woman's need to see a chaplain. Good supervision will keep an eye out for the patient as well as the supervisee.

Relationships in which the student experiences countertransference with a patient or client can become very intense. In a clinical setting, it might be appropriate to suggest that students take someone along the next time they visit these patients, since this can serve to decompress the relationship. The person could be a peer or the supervisor. The supervisor and the student together may need to give some attention to structuring the student's relationship with the patient. Setting limits on the amount of time the student spends with a particular person is one way this structuring may occur.

When countertransference comes into play, it is important that we sort out what the supervisee can and cannot be to the person. A clinical example best illustrates this concept.

One of the authors recalls visiting a patient who had just been admitted to the hospital. The patient was an elderly woman who had two grown sons. She was a grande dame kind of person. After talking with this woman for a brief time, the chaplain realized that he wanted to kill her. She was a lovely, well-groomed, gray-haired woman. He was anxiously puzzled over why he would have such intense feelings toward her. He ended the visit feeling vaguely scared. Upon reflection, he discovered that this elderly patient reminded him of his grandmother who was a grande dame, a United Daughters of the Confederacy member for twenty years. She was a strong woman, the kind of woman that he as a teenager found invincible. His grandmother would not let him grow up. His rage toward the patient in the hospital was the same that he felt for his grandmother.

Later, the chaplain decided that by acknowledging his feelings to his peers, he could still probably function in a formal pastoral role with this patient. He could probably do her funeral if that was needed! He also was aware that he would not be able to be a pastoral counselor to this patient unless he received counseling himself and was willing to invest the energy to resolve his own issues.

When countertransference is a significant issue in pastoral care, such structuring and limiting of the relationship are appropriate. In pastoral counseling, should such a significant countertransference issue emerge, the student and the supervisor may consider the option of referring the client to another counselor, especially when it cannot be appropriately managed in the supervisory process or the student is unwilling to invest the personal energy that its resolution would require. Often the supervisory process can offset the potentially harmful effects of a helper's countertransference for a helpee. If this countertransference issue is deeply ingrained, the helper may need to seek psychotherapy in addition to supervision.

There needs to be an exploration on the part of the supervisor and the supervisee regarding the amount of energy that will need to be invested in order to provide adequate care. There also needs to be some agreement about whether the amount of energy that needs to be invested is worth it. If it is not, other options need to be explored to ensure that the helpee receives quality care. If careful and deliberate attention is not given to structuring the relationship and sorting out the extent of the helper's involvement, the care provided to the helpee can suffer.

The Working Alliance

Transference issues also manifest themselves in the working alliance of supervision. This is true specifically in the supervisee's transference to the supervisor and countertransference to peers. Supervisees involved in a peer group may develop feelings of competition, jealousy, superiority or inferiority, and so forth. Here countertransference may reflect sibling rivalry or other unresolved issues stemming from the supervisee's family of origin. All these kinds of experiences are grist for the mill of supervisory reflection. There is really nothing that happens within the context of one's professional relationships which cannot be effectively addressed in supervision.

When a supervisee experiences transference toward the supervisor, efforts to resolve it spill over into the therapeutic dimension of supervision. But it may be necessary also to nurture the working alliance by making agreements about ways to sustain effective supervision. For example, one supervisee experienced the supervisor as critical and sly because of a transference issue. Once this issue had been acknowledged, the supervisor and the supervisee came to an agreement that they would stop periodically to give voice to their current thoughts and feelings toward each other. They also reached an understanding that the supervisee check with the supervisor when she was feeling criticized or wondered whether the supervisor was being sly. In this way, the two maintained their working alliance until the transference issue could be brought to resolution.

Countertransference and transference can also become evident in the parallel process described in earlier chapters. When supervisees interact with their supervisors in the same way that their patients or clients interact with them, or in a similar way, they may be attempting, at an unconscious level, to resolve their own countertransference issues. Examining the parallel process can quickly reveal the places where the supervisee is stuck in the caregiving relationship. This happened in the following example:

Two students in a pastoral counseling program were working as cotherapists and providing marital therapy for a couple. The couple had established a pattern of arguing by blaming each other. When the blaming began, it would usually escalate and become destructive to the relationship. In working out the details for supervision and discussing the continued care of the couple, the cotherapists ended up having a similar blaming argument. They carried this argument over into supervision in a way that paralleled the arguments of their couple. They discovered alternative patterns of communication and were able to pass these new discoveries on to the couple receiving marital therapy.

This parallel process moves in both directions. Supervisees can return to treat their patients or clients in the manner in which their supervisors treat them in supervision. When this happens, it is often the result of the supervisee's unresolved issues, but it can also reveal the supervisor's countertransference. In one hospital setting, when the patient of one psychiatrist repeatedly set the psychiatrist's wastebasket on fire, the nurses got upset with the psychiatrist, knowing that the fires were actually a reflection of the *psychiatrist's* anger. The adage from therapeutic circles that a therapist cannot accompany a client beyond where the therapist has gone also applies to the supervisory relationship. Countertransference among supervisors may become evident if they find themselves discouraging supervisees' personal growth in areas they have not experienced.

Regardless of where the countertransference originates, exploring it throughout the various dimensions of the parallel process can move the whole learning process forward. Reflecting on the working alliance in supervision, like reflecting on its therapeutic dimension and its administrative oversight, has a profound influence on the management of countertransference and transference issues as they manifest themselves throughout the supervisory process.

Conclusion

It is not possible for us to have conscious awareness of all that motivates us at any given time; we are far too complex for that. Not only is total self-awareness impossible, it is unnecessary in order to have significant, meaningful, and helpful interactions with others. Sometimes it is even more helpful not to be so self-aware. One psychiatric resident was called to the hospital because a patient was out on the window ledge threatening to jump. As the resident approached the hospital he asked himself in desperation, "What am I going to do? What can I say?" When he arrived, he decided to climb out onto the window ledge with the patient. He did so and spontaneously asked, "Are you feeling a little jumpy today?" They both laughed, thereby establishing an immediate rapport that proved to be useful.

While we cannot expect to be totally self-aware, we can develop an educated intuition through the process of supervision.

With this educated intuition, we become more aware of when transference issues are present in the learning process. Seasoned clinicians recognize the value of these experiences for personal growth in any professional role and even look for these issues to take into supervision. They know, through dealing with these commodities, that they ensure the fullest possible dimensions of professional development.

Each of us bears an accumulation of impressions, or colors, from past relationships. This is not something to be avoided; it just is. It is part and parcel of the very beauty in the complexity of our being. As we interact with other people, our colors become our starting point with them. Considering transference in clinical supervision is not only beneficial, it is the place where we can use all our creativity to transform these colors into a chosen work of art.

NOTES

1. B. Apfelbaum, *Dimensions of Transference in Psychotherapy* (Berkeley: University of California Press, 1958), p. 1.

2. Ibid., p. 2.

3. E. M. Pattison, "Transference and Countertransference in Pastoral Care," *Journal of Pastoral Care* 19(4):195 (1965).

4. Ibid.

5. R. L. Tyson, "Countertransference Evolution in Theory and Practice," *Journal of the American Psychoanalytic Association* 34(2):252 (1986).

6. Ibid., pp. 254–255.

7. H. P. Blum, "Countertransference and the Theory of Technique: Discussion," *Journal of the American Psychoanalytic Association* 34(2):317 (1986).

8. *Webster's Third New International Dictionary of the English Language, Unabridged,* s.v. "countertransference."

9. F. Brown, "Erotic and Pseudo-Erotic Elements in the Treatment of Male Patients by Female Therapists," *Clinical Social Work Journal* 12(3):254 (1984).

10. Pattison, "Transference and Countertransference in Pastoral Care," p. 199.

11. M. K. Goin and F. Kline, "Countertransference: A Neglected Subject in Clinical Supervision," *American Journal of Psychiatry* 133(1):41–43 (1976).

13

Passivity in Supervision
Nancy Fontenot

My call has developed along two pathways, one in management and one in clinical work. The management path was in the area of social services programming, then staff development. The clinical path was in the practice of psychotherapy, in groups, with individuals, couples, and families; then, the supervision of psychotherapy. It was in my clinical work that I first came upon the theory of passivity described by Jacqui Schiff and her staff in their book *Cathexis Reader*. [1] In my application of their theory with nonpsychotic clients, I discovered how useful the concept could be. I began to apply it to my management experience as well and discovered that passive behaviors could be seen at all levels, organizational and personal. Eventually I applied the theory to my experiences in supervision, and that is the focus of this chapter.

Non-Problem Solving

The supervisory model presented in this book is primarily a process. The supervisor and the supervisee are equally involved. Both bring to supervision questions about how to effectively help an individual or a group of persons. What specifically can we do to offer them pastoral care? The supervisee seeks to answer those questions in relation to clients, patients, or parishioners. The supervisor seeks to answer those questions in relation to the supervisee as well as the supervisee's clients, patients, or parishioners. Thus supervision becomes a problem-solving process through which we seek to answer those questions. When it is successful, both the supervisor and the supervisee achieve some resolution to these problems rather than avoiding them. Behaviors that are non-problem solving prevent personal growth in the pastoral role. This phenomenon of non-problem-solving forms the basis for the theory of passivity developed by Jacqui Schiff.[2]

Robert was a D.Min. student who came to supervision with much experience in pastoral care and supervision. For several weeks he presented the new supervisor with volumes of repetitious and unsolicited materials on his clients. Finally the supervisor asked Robert why he was generating these particular materials. He told the supervisor that this style of presentation had been required by his last CPE supervisor and he assumed this style was what the current supervisor wanted. Robert was overadapting to his guess of what the new supervisor wanted. This is one form of passivity.

Passivity prevents people from functioning in autonomous, healthy, and appropriate ways. Robert was expending much energy that was not directed toward problem solving. In chapter 2, resistance to change in supervision was discussed around the concepts of *learning problems* and *problems about learning.* In this supervisory session, Robert's *learning problem*—the recurring characteristic, automatic, and inappropriate pattern in relationships that an individual brings to supervision—involved his need to please authority figures. The supervisor's confrontation of Robert's overadaptation brought this learning problem to the fore so that he could begin to deal with it. The *problem about learning*—that is, particular defenses against supervision—that Robert demonstrated was a form of submission, in which he was adopting a former supervisor's method without determining its appropriateness in the current situation. The supervisor's confrontation also brought this problem about learning to attention so that Robert could focus on change in this area as well.

Passivity is a non-problem-solving process that may be found in thinking, feeling, or behavior. It results from unresolved dependency and constitutes an attempt to re-create or to maintain a dependent/symbiotic relationship with another person. In a symbiotic relationship two persons behave as though between them they form one complete person, each being unable to act as a whole person without the psychological or real presence of the other person.[3] There is a normal dependency in the relationship between the primary parent and an infant. The aim of this relationship is the eventual autonomy of the developing young person. The child's needs are met without the parents' discounting their own. However, when normal dependency issues remain unresolved between parent and child, the growing person seeks to resolve them through re-creating dependent relationships later in life. By paying attention to supervisees' attempts to create dependent relationships in their practice of pastoral care and in supervisory relationships, the supervisor can confront this process and assist the supervisee to move to autonomy.

The three dimensions of supervision described in chapter 3 are those of administrative oversight, which involves maintaining the welfare or treatment of clients together with the institutional structure that supports the service; the therapeutic dimension, which encompasses the personal growth of the supervisee in the pastoral role; and the dimension of the working alliance in supervision, which focuses on problems emerging in the supervisory relationship itself. Passivity or non-problem solving may occur in any of these three dimensions; however, the primary focus of this chapter will be on the therapeutic dimension of personal growth. Because supervision always takes place within a larger system (e.g., church, agency, hospital, school), administrative relationships are present that permit the passivity of any member in any of the relevant systems to have an impact on the supervisory process. Passive behaviors of the client are often brought to supervision through parallel process in the form of the same passive behavior in the trainee. Trainees also use passive behaviors learned in their families with their peers (who represent siblings) in supervision, and the supervisory process helps bring the learning problems represented in such behaviors to the surface to be worked through and resolved. Working with passive behaviors as they occur furthers the therapeutic dimension of supervision, with appropriate referral for psychotherapy when reappearance of the learning problem continues. Through such referral the supervisor then returns the primary focus of supervision to the helping process itself.

The Structure of Supervision

The supervision described throughout this chapter is primarily in conjunction with clinical coursework at Louisville Presbyterian Theological Seminary. The coursework includes individual, group, family, and marital therapy courses at the Master of Divinity (M.Div.) level and advanced counseling/psychotherapy coursework at the Doctor of Ministry (D.Min.) level. Most students attend supervision once a week for one hour if supervised individually or for one and a half hours when supervised in a small group (three trainees). Counseling sessions are recorded on audio or video tape, and trainees select a particular section of the session (usually 5 to 8 minutes) to present for supervision. Trainees negotiate a supervisory contract early in their work, indicating what they want to change about themselves in order to become more effective as counselor/therapists. Each trainee prepares a supervisory question or questions for each session. The question or questions focus on an issue that furthers the trainee's personal development as a pastoral counselor.

Depending upon the course focus, the trainee's clinical experience will be in individual or group or marital or family therapy, and the tapes for supervision will match the course and clinical foci. Some trainees in the introductory course in individual counseling receive clinical experience in a round-robin triad: trainee A counsels trainee B, trainee B counsels trainee C, and trainee C counsels trainee A. All three prepare tapes and supervisory questions and attend the same weekly supervisory session. This method of training for individual counseling has been exceptionally effective. Not only do the trainees reap the benefits of small-group supervision, learning from the experiences of each other and learning to supervise each other, but they also have the experience of having their client attend supervision, and the trainee-clients give helpful feedback on effective and ineffective interventions.

Apprenticeship in group coleadership or assistant leadership with the supervisor is especially effective training for D.Min. and other advanced students. There are many benefits to apprenticeship, including immediate observation and, when appropriate, immediate feedback on the trainee's work, modeling effective psychotherapeutic techniques by the supervisor, the opportunity to work with "experienced" clients, and a fresh approach for the clients, to name a few.

When trainees travel some distance for coursework and supervision, as is often the case for D.Min. students, face-to-face supervision is built around times the students are in town, generally two hours a week two times a month. In between sessions the trainees may send tapes with written descriptions of the supervisory questions. The supervisor listens to or views the tape selections and prepares a response. This response may be a supervisory tape to be returned to the trainee, a written response, or a verbal response discussed in a long-distance telephone conversation or discussed in person in extra time on trips to Louisville. If the supervisor travels to the trainee's location, the sessions are held there as well. Since trainees learn so much from each other, we prefer to supervise D.Min. students in pairs or small groups. Clinical examples used throughout this chapter have been disguised to protect the guilty as well as the innocent.

Discounting

Passivity is preserved through a process of discounting. When a person believes or acts as though some aspect of self, others, or the reality is less significant or more significant than it is, the person is discounting. The discount may involve ignoring or distorting some aspect of our own internal experience, or it may be of our external experience. We may discount the other person's internal or external experience. We may redefine, minimize, or exaggerate some particular aspect of our experience, so that the distortion then becomes inconsistent with reality. A person uses discounting to establish or maintain a dependent/symbiotic relationship. Any of us may discount in three areas: stimuli, problems, or options. One may discount the existence, the significance, the change possibilities, or one's own abilities to change in any of the three areas.[4] Each person who discounts surrenders autonomy or refuses to recognize the autonomy of another.

Discounts are found between individuals, family members, and members of an organization. Some forms of discounting are ignoring, overexplaining, underexplaining, teasing remarks and gestures, put-downs, and facetiously saying the opposite of what is meant. When grownups discount children, they invite some form of personal pathology. The degree of discount helps determine the severity of the pathology. Between grownups, discounts contribute to unhappy relationships. Because the focus of this chapter is on non-problem-solving behavior, we will consider discounting in the area of problems.

The four levels of discounting in problems are (1) discounting the existence of a problem, (2) discounting the significance of a problem, (3) discounting the possibilities for change in the problem, and (4) discounting the capacity of someone (self or other) to solve the problem.

Each level may be illustrated in a family setting:

1. Mother is watching her soap operas on television. Little Johnny is riding his bicycle beside the open window. Johnny falls from his bicycle and cuts his knee. As Johnny screams and cries for his mother, she doesn't hear him, being engrossed in the program. She discounts the existence of the problem.

2. Same scene. This time mother hears Johnny's screams and cries but continues to watch the program, thinking the problem is not big enough to warrant her attention. She discounts the significance of the problem.

3. Same scene. Mother hears the screams and cries, goes to the door and sees that Johnny is hurt, but returns to the televi-

sion believing there's nothing anyone can do now, since he's already fallen off the bicycle. She discounts the solvability of the problem.

4. Same scene. Mother runs out to Johnny upon hearing his screams and cries, then dissolves into tears and apologizes to Johnny that she's such a terrible mother, since she let him get hurt. She acts helpless when she sees his cut knee and thinks there's nothing she can do to help the situation. She discounts her ability to solve the problem.

In supervision, similar discounting can occur at each level. Trainees may discount themselves by putting down their own ideas, feelings, or contributions. Trainees may discount previous experiences and knowledge which they bring to supervision. The trainee may also discount the supervisor's ability to recognize the trainee's existing knowledge and skills and to work with the trainee to build on those existing qualities. The supervisor may discount what the trainee brings or does not bring to the supervisory experience and may then overexplain or underexplain.

1. In supervision the existence of a problem is discounted when the trainee ignores a problem in the work with the client, in the supervisory session, or with the supervisor. If the supervisor accepts the trainee's discount of the problem, then the supervisor is discounting the existence of the problem as well.

Ed and Suzanne brought to supervision a tape of an adolescent group they were leading in a middle school. The adolescents were all referred to the group because of drug-related problems. In the tape they presented, one youth named Mike talked in the background while the others discussed family situations. Mike kept repeating, "Mike is crazy. Mike is crazy." Until supervision, Suzanne and Ed did not hear Mike's comments. The supervisor asked what was happening on the tape and brought to their attention their discount of the existence of a problem with Mike in the group.

2. The trainee or the supervisor may recognize that a problem exists but minimize or misinterpret its importance or its relevance. Either may see the problem as too large or too small to handle. The trainee may have noticed the client's inappropriate behavior but was so intent on clarifying issues raised in the previous supervisory session that the trainee missed confronting the current behavior.

The next week in Suzanne's adolescent group, she determined to talk with Mike about his disruptive behavior. Mike was absent from school that day, so Suzanne talked with the total group about disruptive behavior and did not deal with Craig, who remained silent and withdrawn during the entire session.

Suzanne later learned that Craig had been arrested the previous weekend. She learned that fact only after the school officials had notified her that Craig had been suspended from school and withdrawn from the group.

3. The trainee may see the problem as unusual or extraordinary and believe that no solution exists. One student announced to the supervisor that no one could handle all the work that the professor had assigned, that the expectations for this counseling course were unrealistic, and that the work simply couldn't be done.

Solvent fume abuse was the particular drug problem of Ed and Suzanne's group members. When the supervisor asked Ed what he was doing to confront or deal with the issues of this problem in group, Ed gave the supervisor an elaborate explanation of the hopelessness of adolescents who sniff paint.

4. The fourth level of discounting is of one's own capacity to solve a problem. It may also involve a discount of some other person's ability to solve the problem or to react differently. Trainees believe there is a solution, but they are too slow or personally inadequate to handle the task. They confess to the supervisor that the client or the task should be assigned to someone else, since they cannot get anything to work because of some tragic flaw that makes them inadequate or since someone else can do what they can't. The supervisor may decide to reassign a client or a task for similar reasons, in that way discounting the trainee's ability to solve the problem.

Ed and Suzanne began the counseling group late in the spring. There were only twelve weeks left in the school year when the group held its first session. When positive results of the sessions were minimal, Suzanne told the supervisor that more advanced students should have been assigned to the group, discounting her own abilities to have an impact on the group members.

Passive Behaviors

There are four styles of passive behaviors that an individual may use to re-create a dependent/symbiotic relationship. None of the four involves thinking through a problem to solution while taking into account all the elements of the individual's personality. The four are:

1. Doing nothing. The teacher gives the student an assignment, and the student does not turn in the completed work.

2. Overadaptation. Same assignment; the student guesses what the teacher wants from talking to students who knew the teacher in the past and completes work different from the assignment.
3. Agitation. Given the assignment, the student complains to friends, others in class, other faculty members, to anyone who will listen about the assignment.
4. Incapacitation or violence. The student withdraws from friends, sits in the library staring at books related to the assignment, but rather than doing any work, becomes dysfunctional. Or the student goes home and explodes, tearing up class materials, the dorm room, anything close enough to destroy.

These passive behaviors comprise the internal as well as the external actions people employ to avoid making an autonomous response to stimuli, problems, or options. Their aim is to retreat and meet their needs within an unhealthy, dependent relationship. The use of any one of these passive behaviors constitutes an attempt to establish a symbiosis, and any response to them beyond confrontation is necessarily symbiotic. In confrontation, the aim is to react to the behavior so that the individual responds actively. Active behavior involves thinking, feeling, and behaving autonomously. Without discounting, the individual establishes separate goals, figures out how to reach the goals, thinks about what he or she is doing, and does it.[5]

Doing Nothing

Doing nothing means that the individual does not respond to stimuli, to problems, or to options. Instead of using energy to take action that solves a problem, the individual uses psychic energy to inhibit responses and thinking. While doing nothing, people are usually aware of being uncomfortable. However, they do little thinking about what is happening or what they could do to solve the problem. People do nothing in organizations such as churches or agencies by such behaviors as denying that something significant is happening, isolating themselves and withdrawing from conflict, feeling or thinking something and not expressing it, ignoring issues, getting confused, or not attending meetings important to or for them.

Examples of ways that trainees do nothing include not "making it" to counseling sessions or to supervisory sessions; having difficulty coordinating the supervisory group so that members of the group miss supervisory sessions or the entire group misses a number of sessions; hearing the client say something significant in the counseling session (e.g., she has been thinking that things are so messed up that she thinks life just isn't worth living anymore) and making no intervention; ignoring issues the client is bringing or changing the subject in counseling sessions; and similarly ignoring issues in supervision.

Supervisors may also become involved in doing nothing if they are aware that the trainee is having problems, involved in unhealthy or unhelpful relationships with clients and/or with the supervisor, and the supervisor makes no intervention with the trainee. Thinking through the trainee's learning needs and choosing to allow the trainee to make mistakes in order to learn from them is not passive behavior. It is the nonthinking and non-problem-solving stance that would qualify as passive behavior.

Andrew was a practicing minister in a local parish. He considered returning to seminary for a D.Min. There were several seminaries within commuting distance from which to choose. He talked with the faculty member responsible for admission to the D.Min. program in one of the seminaries; he also talked with the faculty member responsible for the D.Min. specialty in counseling at that seminary. Because of his reservations about his capability to perform adequately in the counseling specialty, he attended a counseling class at the seminary, receiving supervision on clinical work as part of the class requirement. In supervision he discussed his interest in the D.Min. program. Six months later, he still had not applied for admission to the program. He talked again with the appropriate faculty members. He continued to express interest in the program. Two years later, he had not yet submitted his application.

Overadaptation

In overadaptation we use energy to "psyche out" what others want of us and adapt to that fantasy. We do not identify our own goals but are anxious to please the persons whom we have designated as parent figures. We perceive that those parent figures are more important than we are, and it is our responsibility to guess what they need and want and produce it. Because they are so obliging, overadapted people often get a lot of reinforcement from others. When given a great deal of information about their abilities, their capacities, their situation, and the consequences of their behavior, overadapted persons have difficulty continuing to discount. So this style of behavior is the most amenable to change. One method of confronting overadaptation is to present these individuals with unreasonable or even ridiculous expectations which invite them to have to decide for themselves what is appropriate and what is not. The anger that usually results from having to deal with such expectations and to think for oneself leads to a breakdown in the symbiosis.

Overadaptations in families and other organizations include being "good," being quiet, giving in to what others want, listening attentively to parental figures, volunteering to take on additional tasks and committee work, meeting quotas whether they make sense or not, looking Christian, and cooperating with others especially when it is more appropriate to disagree.

Robert, who overproduced in accordance with his previous supervisor's expectations, illustrates overadaptation. Another form of overadaptation is demonstrated by the trainee who takes techniques or options discussed in one supervisory session relevant to the previous client and uses them in a literal manner with the next client whether or not they are appropriate. Still another version is observed with the trainee who uses on the client a new counseling technique just learned in a class or a professional seminar, again without relevance to the client's situation. The supervisor who accepts this passive behavior without confronting it is either doing nothing or overadapting to a supervisory system of passivity.

It is important to note the difference between passive overadaptation and the conscious, nonpassive behavior in constructive adaptation. Adaptation involves thinking through the problem or situation and deciding to comply because it makes sense to do so.

John was an experienced minister returning to seminary for an advanced degree, the D.Min. with a specialization in counseling. A requirement of this degree is to receive weekly supervision on the student's leadership of a counseling group. John's group was one he began with local parishioners who were interested in a counseling experience. John initially brought selections of tape from the group counseling sessions with specific supervisory questions concerning the practical application of theory and techniques and possible solutions for problem areas encountered in the group sessions. He appeared to participate actively in the supervisory discussion and to work out the solutions and techniques he would apply. He returned to his counseling group and experimented with the techniques and solutions. It soon became apparent that John was applying techniques from one week's supervision inappropriately to the next week's group; his methods were always one week old. He also told his group about the wonderful supervisor he had and gave the supervisor the credit for these "wonderful" interventions.

When the pattern was clearly established, the supervisor confronted John's overadaptation by telling him the story of Epaminondas:

> On daily visits to his auntie, Epaminondas' auntie gave him presents to take home. Once he carried a piece of cake so tightly that it became crumbs. His mother told him to carry cake by wrapping it in leaves, putting it in his hat, and wearing the hat home. His auntie next gave him butter which he wrapped in leaves, put in his hat and wore home. Of course, it melted. So his mother told him to carry butter by wrapping it in leaves, taking it to the brook, and cooling it awhile in water. His auntie's next gift was a puppy dog which he wrapped in leaves and tried to cool in the brook, almost drowning it. His mother told him to carry a puppy dog by tying a string around its neck, placing the puppy on the ground, and walking it home. Auntie's next gift was a loaf of bread which Epaminondas walked home on a string. The final instruction his mother gave him was to be careful how he stepped on some pies cooling on the doorstep—and he was.[6]

The confrontation triggered a decision by John to make his own choices about what would be the basis of his work with specific clients, where they were and what they were saying in the session. He also decided to use supervision for learning rather than for pleasing the supervisor.

Agitation

In agitation the individual uses energy in purposeless, non-goal-oriented activities such as pacing, pencil tapping or chewing, hair twirling, smoking, nail biting, gum chewing, eating, drinking, stuttering, or repetitive thinking. The activities are not directed toward the situation and do not address solving the problem. They are being used to work up energy while the individual is experiencing a threat to symbiosis and is "trying" to "do something" effective. Often the person experiences an internal discomfort that some report as a tingling sensation, described as "electric" or "crawly." Others experience agitation behaviorally only. In those instances the purpose of the agitated behavior is to deny the feelings the individual is having and to shift the discomfort to someone else.

Mild and even moderate agitation can be stopped by helping people become aware of the behavior and allowing them to decide whether they want to continue with it. Helping the person to identify the underlying issue that the behavior represents also has positive results. Identifying the problem to be solved and alternative solutions also stops the agitation. More severe agitation may need a calm instruction from another person to stop. A severely agitated person is experiencing a threat to an important symbiotic relationship, one that the person may be unwilling or unprepared to abandon. Therefore confrontation without support for the severely agitated person's neediness may result in an escalation to violence.

In groups and organizations such as families and churches, agitation may be seen in such behavior as getting busy with trivial activities, convening extra meetings, generating extra paperwork, intellectualizing, lying, reorganizing, taking work home, carrying papers or books or other business back and forth, overeating, collecting data, telephoning, and other behaviors such as gossiping about family or office, a.k.a. the "grapevine." When agitated behavior is present in an organization—for example, when people are *doing* something but without clear purpose or goal—it is helpful again to define the problem and look toward realistic solutions. It is often true that agitation in groups is not recognized as a passive behavior, again because "at least they are *doing* something." Helping the group to stop the process of spinning and to focus on their goal, either defining it or redirecting activity toward achieving it, leads to active rather than passive behavior.

Some of the agitated behaviors found in organizations become evident in the supervisory process. Trainees may attempt to manage the discomfort they experience by shifting the responsibility for it to the supervisor or to their peers. Trainees' discomfort may come from challenges to their frame of reference, expectations that they are to change, and unresolved dependency issues. Agitated behaviors may function to shift the discomfort to others who are in the supervisory process. Supervisors who are uncomfortable with their position of authority or with any aspect of supervision may also utilize agitation to manage their discomfort.

Hyperactivity and busyness may be the form of agitation chosen. Producing or requiring long reports and extra paperwork would demonstrate agitation along with excessive verbiage in written or oral presentations. Spending excessive time discussing cases and problems with supervisors and with peers may be another form of agitation, especially when the discussions are circular and repetitive and do not lead to any change in behavior. The response of being bored (low-level anger) from a supervisor or a peer may be an indication that the trainee's uncomfortable feelings of anger have been successfully transferred to the other person. Blaming the system, the process, the supervisor, or another individual for the trainee's difficulties is another indication of agitation rather than problem solving. Helping trainees to identify what problems they are not solving or utilizing other confrontations indicated above reduces the agitation.

Alex is in the D.Min. program in counseling. He travels from another city for client sessions, supervision, and classwork. His wife is a helping professional who is competitive with him and increasingly resentful of the time he is taking in the program. Alex called one week to cancel supervision; the next week he indicated that his reason for canceling involved a conflict with his wife over the program. His clients were provided through a local residential treatment program. A few supervisory sessions later, he came to supervision without a tape presentation; another conflict with his wife was preventing his weekly visit to his clients. The supervisor chose to confront Alex's use of family problems as agitation. This agitation was interfering with his counseling and supervisory experiences. The supervisor referred Alex to a pastoral counselor in his city for therapy. The focus of supervision returned to his own growth as a pastoral counselor.

Incapacitation or Violence

Beginning from the lowest level of passive behavior, doing nothing, to the highest level, incapacitation or violence, there is an increasing demand upon the environment to intervene. Both incapacitation and violence as passive behaviors involve an adamant refusal to think and solve problems, placing an immediate demand upon the environment to take over responsibility. Both discharge energy built up through maintaining passivity. Incapacitation involves an implosion of energy; violence an explosion. The person is experiencing underlying terror, and these behaviors are last-ditch efforts to get protection from fantasized catastrophies by forcing symbiosis from someone in the environment (police, hospitals, prisons). Examples of incapacitation include fainting, getting sick, migraine headaches, bleeding ulcers, and catatonia. Violence includes going crazy, attacking people or property, self-mutilation or harm, homicide and suicide. During episodes of discharging energy using these passive behaviors, the individual does no thinking and accepts no responsibility for the behavior.

In organizations and families, violence is found in physical and emotional abuse, attacks on an individual's professional reputation, forced resignations and retirements or firings, walking out on another person or a group, any type of harassment on the job, or destroying a person or property. Because of the power the supervisor has in the supervisory process, including accreditation processes that affect the trainee's professional career, it is important that the supervisor use that power with grace and responsibility, taking care to be pastoral, not destructive.

In the case of violence, intervention requires containing the escalation until the energy is discharged. After the energy has run its course, the individual needs to be expected to take responsibility for the inappropriate behavior and its consequences. Incapacitation is an overadapted form of violence. After the escalation, there is usually an unwillingness to think about it and to take responsibility for it. The most effective confrontations include withdrawal of support and refusal to take care of people when they incapacitate. This undercuts the symbiotic payoff and supports the individual's taking responsibility for the behavior.[7]

Sam was a second-year seminary student who came directly from college into seminary. His behavior provides an example of passive incapacitation. He was single and came from a family with several generations of ministers on both sides of the family. He was not sure of his vocational call, having attended seminary because it was assumed by the family that as firstborn son he would carry on the tradition and become a minister. He was more and more conflicted about his career. After one unit of clinical pastoral education and a pastoral care prerequisite course, Sam registered for a course in group counseling. He began to cut classes, staying more and more in his room. Attending group counseling supervision was the only activity he pursued with regularity. With care and concern his fellow students in the supervisory group confronted his near-incapacitation. With their support and encouragement he made the decision to withdraw from seminary until he decided what vocation he wanted to pursue. He also entered therapy for help with unresolved family issues.

Sometimes escalations at this level cannot be contained. Sandy was a seminary graduate who began coleading a group with the supervisor while taking a group counseling course. She continued coleadership for additional training following the end of the course and graduation. The contract for coleadership and supervision was clearly outlined between Sandy and the supervisor. When Sandy did not carry through her agreements in the contract, the supervisor confronted her. Sandy spent several supervisory sessions in various forms of agitation, blaming the supervisor for problems in one session, using indirect methods of communication with the supervisor (leaving notes, phone messages) when communication had been direct previously, and complaining about the supervisor to friends in and out of seminary. When the supervisor confronted the agitation as a passive behavior, without warning Sandy announced to the counseling group that she was quitting coleadership and walked out, violating termination agreements with both the group and the supervisor.

Confronting Passivity

Supervisors and supervisees alike have the option to confront or ignore the passivity when they observe it. Confrontation provides both the opportunity to work through the passivity and to reestablish the problem-solving process of supervision. The working alliance of supervision turns upon what success we have in doing so.

There is a hierarchy in the levels of passive behavior, with increasing demand upon the environment to take charge. Two theories exist concerning confrontation. The original theory developed by Jacqui Schiff indicated that when agitation is present, the individual must be returned to overadaptation in order to confront the passivity.[8] It was her theory that confrontation takes place through taking the individual back down the levels of passivity, that violence or incapacitation can be prevented by recognizing agitation as a warning and demanding that the individual overadapt to a strong parental command to stop the agitating behavior. A more recent theory is that passive behaviors may be successfully confronted at each stage.

Effective confrontation entails bringing the passive behavior into awareness and inviting individuals to act with autonomy, accepting responsibility for their own involvement while refusing to accept responsibility for anyone else's. Confrontation may involve education as some people have had no models for problem solving in their history and possess few problem-solving skills. Teaching those people basic steps in problem identification, discovering options, and problem solving will be of great help to them. The individual who confronts and teaches will take care in the teaching not to get "hooked" into doing for the learners what they can do for themselves and thereby stroking the old pattern in a new way. Discounting the existence of dependent/symbiotic relationships and invitations to join them need to be identified and challenged as well.

Throughout this chapter, I have used the concept of confrontation in supervision, especially the confrontation of passivity.

By this I do not mean criticism or even confronting with a critical style. What I mean is the use of any technique at the supervisor's disposal to bring into the trainee's awareness the dynamics taking place in the counseling session, in the supervisory session, or in supervisory and peer relationships. There are many styles through which supervisors may engage in confrontation, such as thoughtful, caring, critical, judgmental. Judgmental confrontations are the least effective, because they invite trainees to respond in adaptive ways. The styles that most invite thinking, problem solving, and autonomy on the part of the trainee will be the most effective, whether they make use of direct questions or observations, metaphor and storytelling, leading questions, or other specific techniques.

The antithesis to passivity is autonomy, that is, taking responsibility for one's own behaviors, thoughts, feelings, and perceptions. Autonomous individuals differentiate between themselves and their acts; they solve problems; they are aware of a choice of options, and they exercise those options; and they directly and effectively express feelings, needs, and wants as these occur. Since autonomy is built upon successfully solving problems oneself, supervision is an ideal arena in which to help supervisees become autonomous.

NOTES

1. J. L. Schiff and others, *Cathexis Reader: Transactional Analysis Treatment of Psychosis* (New York: Harper & Row, 1975), pp. 5–22.

2. J. L. Schiff and A. W. Schiff, "Passivity," *Transactional Analysis Journal* 1(1):71 (1971).

3. S. Woolams and M. Brown, *Transactional Analysis: A Modern and Comprehensive Text of TA Theory and Practice* (Dexter, Mich.: Huran Valley Institute, 1978), pp. 107–108.

4. Schiff, *Cathexis Reader*, p. 16. Also see Woolams and Brown, *Transactional Analysis*, p. 114.

5. Schiff, *Cathexis Reader*, p. 10.

6. S. C. Bryant, *Epaminondas and His Auntie* (New York: Houghton Mifflin Co., 1938); and E. Merriam, *That Noodlehead Epaminondas* (New York: Scholastic Book Services, 1968).

7. Schiff, *Cathexis Reader*, pp. 13–14.

8. Ibid., pp. 12–13.

14

Gender Issues in Supervision

Barbara A. Sheehan

"God created them male and female. In God's image were they created—male and female" (Gen. 1:27, paraphrased). "Are you the opposite sex or am I the opposite sex?" the young girl asks the young boy in a commercial advertisement.

Yes, God created us male and female. Yes, males and females are opposite sexes. Biologically there are distinct differences between males and females. Developmentally there are distinct differences as well. Culturally the sexes have been influenced by stereotyped identities in terms of what is masculine and what is feminine. These cultural definitions can limit our personal discovery of being created in God's image and the discovery of the fullness of one another. Too often, men and women learn to view themselves in relation to others of the same and opposite sex in ways that are incomplete, missing the uniqueness of the total person as male or as female.

Gender and Ministry

Some of our learning about who we are as female or male blocks effective ministry. Our biased learning inhibits our growth in self-awareness and self-understanding. This gets translated into ministerial and collegial relationships that fail to make effective use of our total selves. Awareness of our gender identity (how we identify ourselves as male or female in relationships) is an essential element in supervision. Both the supervisor and the supervisee impose their stereotyped images upon the process of giving and receiving help, contributing to what was discussed in chapter 2 as "learning problems" and "problems about learning." To allow the issues of gender identity to go unattended gives sway to hiddenness and restriction of one's full self. Being closed to gender uniqueness in ourselves and in the opposite sex, we ultimately close off the uniqueness of the women and men with whom we minister. The other person becomes a "thing" rather than a particular human being with unique ways of relating to self and others. Although we may be able to relate personally to other people's feelings of fear or loneliness or sadness, we may be out of touch with their experience in the light of their identity as woman or man.

Whenever we lack awareness or acceptance of who we have become as a man or a woman, that element of pastoral care known as transparency or openness is blocked. The underlying issue may be fear of one's masculinity or femininity, born out of negative messages we received as we grew up or out of a confusion between our own experience and the world's definition of how we ought to be. This fear, when confronted, takes the "pastoral space" in one's inner self that could be available for healing another's life. The result is an unnatural guardedness or restraint in the ministerial relationship. The same pattern of withholding or fear will manifest itself in peer or supervisory relationships.

To remain unaware of our uniqueness together with the uniqueness of each member of the opposite sex can foster unhealthy and conflictual relationships between persons of both the same and the opposite sex. A man can expect a woman to respond in certain male-oriented fashions. For example, he may not understand her desire to discuss feelings, if he usually tends to ignore them. A woman can unconsciously expect a man to receive care the way she may wish to be cared for. Models for ministry and pastoral interventions may be formulated by unconscious attitudes and expectations rather than by clearly conceptualized and conscious choices.

There are accompanying dangers that "mixed messages" between men and women may interfere with pastoral care. A male minister may give unconscious signals to a female parishioner that her sexuality is bad or seductive when in fact she is responding in ways of relating foreign to a man. A female minister may signal a man that his competitive behavior is not acceptable to her because she is unaware of her own struggle to be a woman in a man's world.

We will examine four cases that illustrate the issues of gender identity and sexuality as they affect the ministerial relationship. These introduce the discussion of some theoretical material on the subject, followed by some implications for ministry and some practical exercises for self-awareness and growth.

Cases

K was a thirty-four-year-old male intern. While a seminary student, he had full responsibilities for a congregation on the weekends. He and his wife were expecting their first child. After a three-hour workshop on the issue of "Ministry and Sexuality," K expressed his anger, frustration, and sense of having wasted a half day at the workshop. He found the workshop "useless and archaic." "I thought you were going to help us minister with homosexuals and those who talk about masturbation! I know who I am as a male and how I use that in ministry. We've had all that stuff." I asked K to say more about the use of himself as male minister. Silence prevailed. Then I asked, "What is it that you like about yourself as male?" He thought and responded, "My warmth." I affirmed his answer, then asked what other identification he had as a male. "I don't like any of those characteristics; I don't want them," he responded.

K had a firm dislike of what he had learned were "male" characteristics within himself. He found it repulsive to consider himself as a person who was aggressive and competitive. These things he did not want to be. The male he learned about was to be kept out of him. This left him not knowing who he was as a male or how his masculinity could inform his ministry. The result for K was a consistent emotional distancing in ministerial, peer, and supervisory relationships.

L was a thirty-six-year-old woman minister who became attracted to one of her patients. She spent a great deal of energy trying to repress her sexual feelings, because "I can't feel this way." L also spent a lot of energy avoiding the fact that the patient experienced her as emotionally and sexually appealing. L's energies were being withheld from the ministerial relationship because of her lack of sexual integration and her need to hide a basic part of herself. Her sidestepping the real intrapersonal issue was evident in her verbatim, however. L reported feeling angry about what she conceived as the patient making up stories. The patient often initiated a new, yet not significant topic as L began termination of her visit. L responded by staying longer with the patient. She used indirect language and withheld her normal empathic approach. She felt a strong need to be in control, although pastoral control had not surfaced as an issue prior to this relationship. As L unmasked the reality of her feelings and dealt with her uncomfortableness she became a more free and effective minister with the patient. She was able to be more direct and empathic. Her skill at terminating the pastoral visit was also enhanced.

T, a male, made a presurgical visit to a woman who was to have a hysterectomy. He inquired about her fears of surgery and her support system, but he never asked what this surgery might mean for her in terms of her feelings about herself or her relationship with her husband. T was uncomfortable with any discussion of sexual identity or sexual relationships, both of which proved to be key issues for this patient. Like L, T had unresolved issues about his own sexuality that inhibited his ability to talk candidly about such matters. Unresolved issues relating to sexuality prevented both L and T from offering a more effective pastoral intervention in meeting the needs of their patients.

S, a female, seemed to relate more intimately as a pastor to men than to women. She also had more men as social acquaintances. Through processing this in supervision, she discovered that she thought men were both more accepting of her and better able to minister. She drew her pastoral identity from men rather than from women, whom she did not think could function in positions of authority or leadership. She actually feared being a minister, yet felt called to do so. S's growth in pastoral identity was directly related to her work on her attitudes about women ministers and her identity as a woman. She had to address a conflict between her attitude about her gender capabilities and her own role as a minister. Only then could she stop compensating by overidentifying with and seeking to find herself in males.

These cases illustrate how issues of gender and sexuality present themselves in supervision. They represent problems we encounter in being fully present and using ourselves fully in ministry. They also express how gender perceptions and a lack of psychosexual integration impose themselves within pastoral relationships.

Developmental Theories

Michael Cavanaugh emphasizes the critical importance of psychosexual development in human growth. He maintains that a healthy psychosexual development includes four dimensions: cognitive, emotional, social, and moral. The cognitive dimension is that of *perceiving* positively both one's body—gender and growth-producing sexual behavior—and those of others. The emotional dimension is *feeling* comfortable and confident with both one's body and sexuality and those of others. The social dimension is that aspect of one's development which involves *relating* to the opposite and the same sex in unselfconscious and potentially mutually fulfilling ways. The moral dimension as discussed by Cavanaugh is that of *valuing* the behaviors necessary for continuing sexual growth.[1]

These dimensions of psychosexual development affect the relational life of the minister, making them a needed aspect of supervisory reflection. The minister's perceptions, feelings, manner of relating, and values regarding gender and sexuality impinge upon effective care as much as anxieties about death and dying. These aspects of gender identity and sexuality are essential elements of a pastoral assessment in which we as pastors explore who we are in relation to the other. They are equally necessary in our efforts to develop more holistic pastoral functioning.

Our culture and history have led us to some stereotypical identities as male and female. Our history makers have been family, society, and church. They have taught that certain behaviors, feelings, and responses are to be relegated to males, others to females. Even though Jungian psychology has helped illumine our understanding of the anima and animus in each person, many adults today (ministers not excluded) seek to identify themselves and those both of the same and the opposite sex with earlier learned stereotypes. In this acceptance one may stifle both awareness and growth. As ministers, we may tend to relate out of set perceptions and/or uncomfortable feelings. Mutuality in ministry is inhibited and the freedom for appropriate intimacy lost.

Our understanding of the cognitive dimension of psychosexual development has been influenced by psychological and moral theory. Erik Erikson theorized that a person matures from childhood through successive struggles with the issues of trust versus mistrust, autonomy versus shame and doubt, initiative versus guilt, industry versus inferiority, and so forth.[2] The goal of maturity is individuation and separation. Lawrence Kohlberg held that moral development moves from ego-centered decisions based on individual need, through compliance with conventions of society, to a principled understanding of what is right based on a logic of equality and reciprocity. Decision making in a mature adult is founded on rights and rules.[3]

Carol Gilligan's research with women, however, demonstrates that these theories of maturation based on male subjects are not generally applicable to a woman's growth.[4] A young girl perceives herself in relationship to another. From her mother she perceives her femaleness as not separate from but connected to others. The young girl experiences her femininity from her mother, who is the one in relationship. The young boy learns early in life from his mother to be separate; he is not like her. Although society is changing with more men being single parents, these differences in self-identity are prevalent among most men and women.

Gilligan points out that a woman ordinarily judges herself on her care and concern for others rather than on independent assertion and action. An adult woman seeks her identity in her relatedness to others; an adult man often finds satisfaction in his independent strength.

Most persons in ministry today have been influenced (both consciously and unconsciously) by what is now recognized as the masculine development toward individuation, separation, and independence. Our whole society seems to be striving for this. The maturing female minister may find herself struggling to fit into the masculine mode of learned identity; the maturing male may find his desire for relationship to be countercultural. Most of us have grown up with one model of development—primarily the masculine.

Search for Identity

The search for our true identities tends to develop in our relationships through a process that moves from belonging, to control, to affection. In this process, two or more persons go through stages of deciding who belongs, then who is in charge, finally arriving at a point of affection in which those involved experience a sense of self-lovableness that is transparent and growing. Major stumbling blocks may be confronted along the way as a consequence of the different relationship priorities of females and males. A female minister seeks relationship. She may enter it seeking affection as a first step. Because of this, she may experience rejection from a male parishioner whose identity is more cautious. The problem is not that this man doesn't want a relationship with her. He is cautious because he perceives himself as needing to be in control of the relationship. He feels she is coming on "too strong." Conversely, the male minister may be perceived by a female parishioner as too distant because the female is looking for a relationship by which she evaluates the caregiver's response.

Male Movement to Self-Identity

The emotional and social dimensions of a person's psychosexual development have their beginnings just as early in life as our cognitive development. Evelyn and James Whitehead in *Seasons of Strength* describe how the adolescent comes to a sense of identity through a process of distancing, of setting oneself apart from those "not male" or "not female."[5] Young women are perceived by the young man as "not me." Early in the process the focus seems to be on sex; women are viewed as sexually "other" and felt to be dangerous because of the male's feelings that are aroused. Fear often results from these feelings. It is a fear of losing his own identity as male. This same fear is evident in the female, although not as strongly. The young woman places far less emphasis on the "not female" and more emphasis on the social function of her identity. As Gilligan's research demonstrates, her emphasis is on connectedness rather than separation.

The adolescent male's early dating relationships help him to view women as individuals as diverse as he has found males to be. Through this discovery, the male identity loses its need for distancing and comes to embrace the uniqueness of other males and females. His fear of the "not me" diminishes as he matures in self-awareness both among the males and among the females in his experiences.

Gender issues in the area of feeling comfortable, confident, and competent with one's own body and those of the same and opposite sex often arise because of the unresolved fear experienced at about age fifteen. The fear of "not me" in dating is seen as a not very "manly" emotion. This fear if not addressed is carried into adulthood. It becomes associated with the feelings in the male that are aroused by his experience of a woman. She is felt to be the seducer and must be avoided. The man learns to suppress his feelings in order to protect his masculine identity from this seducer. A wall gets built between the male and all women whom he identifies as the fear object, whereas in reality the fear object is his own feelings. As he continues to fear his own feelings, he becomes less open and less confident in speaking about sexuality, whether his own or someone else's. Sexual feelings and sexuality become barriers to relating on a healthy level.

This fear will impact pastoral relationships, causing the male minister to remain at a distance or to speak superficially about sexual issues with a parishioner. Student T in the earlier example was fearful of discussing his patient's sexual concern relating to her surgery because of his uncertainty about "what will she think?" His avoidance was also related to his fear of any woman as a sexual entity. The topic of most concern to the patient presented a fear for student T, precluding needed pastoral care.

While distancing and fear of one's feelings are more prominent in males, the issue of social change is more predominant in females. Social identity calls women to make a personal transformation that embodies breaking away from conventional self-concepts and movement toward integrating their personal experience and their culture.

Female Movement to Self-Identity

Initially, a woman may perceive herself in congruence with cultural definitions of who she is and her experience. For example, culturally, women have been viewed as the hidden force behind the man. A woman's purpose is to make a man successful and to keep the house. She is dependent on the direction, wisdom, and guidance of a male. To learn from another woman may be difficult, if not foreign.

Early in life many women accept these societal definitions of who they are. Being relationally oriented, they hold themselves accountable to what their culture defines as female and often feel guilty for falling short of this definition or for failing the male. But as the female matures, she begins to experience her difference from these societal definitions. She starts to question the way her culture and her church have defined her. She develops new criteria for interpreting and evaluating herself. She moves into what the Whiteheads define as dichotomous thinking, or thinking in terms of opposites: good-bad, friend-enemy, female-male.[6] This movement alerts her to oppression, and she begins to experience herself as suspicious of males as well as of the institutions that constrained her. She may become angry at the culture that "lied" to her and "trapped" her in a false identity.

Through confronting both her appropriate anger and her experience of herself, the woman continues to mature by incorporating her anger into a larger sense of the self. Instead of perceiving all men, or all of society, or the entire church as against them or as the opposites who thwarted them, women begin to integrate their experience by naming and celebrating men and institutions who have given them life. They realize that good and bad, friend and enemy, do not neatly separate women and men. Good and bad, friend and enemy, are found among all persons, even women.

Male-Female Relationships

A common dynamic is found in the conflict between a woman whose thinking is dichotomous and a man who is angry because the woman colleague is angry and blaming. Effective dialogue leading to an awareness of one's own inner dynamics becomes necessary in order to understand and accept one another. Is ministry with a male patient, a congregant, or a client informed by an unconscious suspicion or a struggle to break out of cultural definitions? As a woman, is there an effort to change the male or resist giving openly of the intimate self out of a fear of being trapped once again? As a male or a female, how have cultural definitions been normative to personal identity for self and for others?

Related to developmental maturity is the reality that culturally the male has been the one to make a decision to start a relationship. The young man or adult male asks the woman for a date; the woman is dependent on the man to do so. Both the authority and the responsibility rest with him. Therefore, both men and women may find it difficult to relate to a woman in authority. Some share the opinion that women may not accept their authority because of a fear of success. More recently it is recognized that the woman may shun authority more out of the perceived fear of the consequences of performing an action that is inconsistent with her gender. Not only can this affect women's roles of leadership in the local congregations. This "authority issue" is present throughout pastoral relationships, determining what is appropriate confrontation and how one uses one's self in ministry; how one is passive, assertive, or aggressive. Gender issues surrounding the exercise of authority may also find repeated expression in male-to-male relationships as well. Men have learned competitiveness rather than mutuality. As the initiators of dating relationships, men have come to identify the woman as the one to pursue in a relationship. So it becomes more difficult for men to befriend one another and to form intimate relationships among themselves. Women, on the other hand, have learned to wait rather than to take initiative with each other. In a pastoral relationship, women-to-women intimacies may present a problem as women struggle to develop truly mutual relationships. In either case, a "win-lose" dynamic may become operative that fosters unhealthy competition for males and jealousy for females. How these dynamics affect and inform ministry is an important question for the supervisor.

Of course the same dynamic is at work in supervision. One's expectations (both conscious and unconscious) about relating and sharing in the supervisory relationship can hinder or enhance the process, depending on the person's awareness and openness regarding these gender issues surrounding authority. It is interesting to note how frequently men will present for

review cases involving women rather than men-to-men relationships. Women tend to bring in more male case presentations.
Underlying this imbalance in case reviews is an avoidance of
looking at same sex ministry. This indicates not only an uneasiness in same sex ministry but a less clear pastoral identity that
is being avoided.

Dody H. Donnelly follows the terminology of Jeanne Block of
the Institute of Human Development in suggesting a refocus of
male and female cultural identities that can be helpful to one's
movement from stereotypical models:

> A man should not be considered "feminine" when he is impul-
> sive, loving, sensitive and sympathetic, but rather a person high
> in "communion" characteristics. Nor should a woman be called
> "masculine" if she is ambitious, critical, dominating, rational,
> responsible, and practical. Rather she is high in "agency" charac-
> teristics.[7]

Spirituality and Gender

Our search for integration as human beings goes beyond the
body and the psyche. Growth of the spirit accompanies it. Our
spirituality matures with our psychosexual growth and vice
versa. Integration is constantly taking place at the level of the
body (male, female), the psyche ("feminine," "masculine"), and
the spirit (core of being).

Mature personal integration for the minister takes place at all
these levels. S. Chavez-Garcia and D. A. Helminiak describe this
integration: "It represents the availability of our whole being to
respond to reality as felt, understood, known, or desired.
Human wholeness entails willingness to respond with as much
of our totality as we are able."[8]

Spirituality is fashioned out of who God is for the individual
and for all of humanity. Spirituality involves getting in touch
with ourselves and others as created in God's image and as
revelation of God through embodied persons. Growth in a relationship with God is fostered by an openness to the many and
varied ways God reveals God's self in and through all peoples
as we experience them. Being stuck in stereotypical identities or
in a limited revelation of ourselves or others limits the ways we
come to know who God is and how God continues to be present
in the ongoing building of the kingdom. Growth in spirituality
is growth in the awareness of the truth and honesty of our
relationship with the other. It is growth in the awareness of the
truth about ourselves as a male or a female.

How one prays with another in a one-to-one relationship or as a leader of communal worship is sometimes a clue to where we are in this process. Our prayer language has shaped our perceptions and our perceptions have shaped our language. In private prayer, the one who prays articulates what is meant and felt on a personal level. In public prayer, the participants reach out to receive the meaning of the prayer for themselves. In its language it incorporates the leader's awareness of his or her relationships to self, others, and God. If public prayer is exclusive by its language, the one excluded cannot find meaning as a communal participant. The leader projects a concept of the other as not in the relationship. An exclusive prayer style arises from this person's lack of awareness and incorporation of the diversity and the uniqueness of all those present. The leader who prays for "all men" effectively excludes the women congregants who reach out to receive the meaning of God's action in the world.

Conclusion

Parker Palmer writes, "To teach is to create a space in which obedience to truth is practiced."[9] To learn is to be obedient. To be obedient is to listen—to ourselves and to others. A key to ministry is, indeed, to learn to listen. Listening involves creating a space for others as they present their unique selves. Listening involves creating a space for our own uniqueness as persons and the uniqueness of the others, male and female. Listening demands attention to the learning problems and the problems about learning related to gender and sexuality, problems expressed in perceptions, feelings, and interpersonal relationships.

To learn is to listen to the truth of the images of God. "God created them male and female. In God's image were they created—male and female" (Gen. 1:27, paraphrased).

APPENDIX: EXERCISES

There are several good experiential exercises to get in touch with one's gender perceptions. They are best done with a group of peers.

1. Write a descriptive paragraph about yourself and set it aside. Then write a paragraph about yourself assuming that you are the opposite sex. Now set that aside. As a group, list the qualities and characteristics that each was taught about the same and the opposite sex. Make two columns on a blackboard. One

column is for male responses; one is for female responses. Under male responses list characteristics that males were taught about themselves and about women. Do the same under female responses for the characteristics that women were taught about themselves and about men.

Take some time to look for patterns that may emerge from the way women and men were taught to perceive the opposite or the same sex. Examine as a group the similarities and the differences associated with how women perceive themselves and how men perceive them. Do the same for male perceptions. Ask some questions regarding ministry. For example, suppose as a male you are perceived as a protector. You have accepted this identity as who you are as a male. How might you go about ministering to a female or enter into a collegial relationship with a woman? What effect will this protector identity have on your being with a male? Will it set up competitiveness or mutuality, uneasiness and distance or warmth and closeness?

After spending time with this exercise, go back and review your descriptive paragraphs. How do you see yourself and the opposite sex in relation to the list of characteristics on the board? Could you and your opposite sex minister to and with each other? Now ask your peers to share with you five qualities or characteristics they have experienced in you. Do the same for each of them. Compare the similarities and differences that you hear of others' experience of you and of your own feminine or masculine self identified in your paragraph. What have you learned about your gender identity and how might this inform your ministry? As a woman who sees herself as a caretaker, do you take on the pain and difficulties of others? As a man, do you tend to give "be tough" sermonettes because you perceive yourself as one who is not to show emotions?

Though this exercise is best done with a group of five or six, it can be adapted to personal and supervisory reflection. In either case, it is good to follow the exercise with reflection on ministry and collegial relationships. Spend some supervisory time discussing your perceptions of the same or opposite sex relationships. How might you be different in these relationships? What about your use of supervision?

2. A healthy exercise for persons in ministry is to reflect on the developmental process and to ask, "Where am I really?" How does your concept of the opposite sex involve a "not me" that fears losing control or fears the experience of a sexual attraction? How do you feel about discussing with a woman the effect of her mastectomy on her sexual identity and sexual relationships? How do you feel about discussing with a man the

effect of his orchectomy on his sexual identity and sexual relationships?

One way of answering these questions is that of picturing yourself in relationship with the other. Picture yourself through drawing the relationship, using colors to position each of you in dialogue; make a collage that speaks of how it might be for you. Ask yourself what your picture implies in terms of your feelings and in terms of your understanding of ministry. Is there anything getting in the way of effective ministry? How does your picture affect the full use of yourself in the supervisory relationship: for example, the manner in which you are supervised?

3. An exercise to assist you in expanding the awareness of your perceptions of the relationship of God to men and women is that of examining your public prayers. What is the language used? Is the language true to the meaning that is meant to be conveyed? Is the language consistent with the reality of the theology of faith tradition? Is it exclusive not only in intent but in actuality of the language used? How do the men and women congregants hear the prayer? What does the prayer as prayer say about one's concept of God? Is it a concept that can be received and lived by men and women? Is there a healing that is needed in your concept of God which is being limited by perceptions of yourself as a man or a woman, or by your perceptions of and feelings about the opposite sex? Is the image of God as expressed in prayer open to both male and female imagery, with a diversity of masculine and feminine characteristics? These are not easy questions. Our history makers have led us to fall into certain patterned ways of conceptualizing God among us. Yet, for our spiritual growth to move toward completion these questions must be honestly asked and answered.

NOTES

1. M. Cavanaugh, "The Impact of Psychosexual Growth on Marriage and Religious Life," *Human Development* 4(3):16–17 (1983).

2. E. H. Erikson, *Identity and the Life Cycle* (New York: W. W. Norton & Co., 1980), pp. 51–107.

3. L. Kohlberg, *The Philosophy of Moral Development: Essays in Moral Development* (San Francisco: Harper & Row, 1981), vol. 1, pp. 409–412.

4. C. Gilligan, *In a Different Voice: Psychological Theory and Women's Development* (Cambridge: Harvard University Press, 1982).

5. J. D. Whitehead and E. E. Whitehead, *Seasons of Strength: New Visions of Adult Christian Maturing* (Garden City, N.Y.: Doubleday & Co., Image Books, 1984).

6. Ibid., p. 194.

7. D. H. Donnelly, *Radical Love: An Approach to Sexual Spirituality* (Minneapolis: Winston Press, 1984), p. 18.

8. S. Chavez-Garcia and D. A. Helminiak, "Sexuality and Spirituality: Friends Not Foes," *Journal of Pastoral Care* 39(2):156 (1985).

9. P. J. Palmer, *To Know as We Are Known: A Spirituality of Education* (San Francisco: Harper & Row, 1983), p. 88.

15

The Supervision
of Church Volunteers
in the Local Congregation

Grayson L. Tucker, Jr.

While greeting the last few worshipers at the close of the September 20 worship service, Pastor Davis noticed that the chairperson of the stewardship committee had been waiting as though wanting to talk after the others left. The minister continued casual conversations but at the same time thought about the work of this committee.

It had met back in the spring and decided on a different approach for eliciting members' pledges for the budget of the church. For as long as anyone could remember, a letter had gone to the members of the congregation setting forth financial needs and asking them to use the enclosed pledge card to indicate what they would give for the coming year. The committee had decided in the spring that they needed to do something different. Members would be visited in their homes by teams of trained visitors. Following conversation about church programs and mission, pledges would be secured. The proposed budget called for pledges averaging about one percent more of estimated household income than had been received by the church before.

The last worshiper now gone, the stewardship committee chairperson approached and Pastor Davis asked, "How are the committee plans going?" The group had had its first fall meeting just two weeks ago. Seventy-two possible visitors for the campaign had been selected and divided among the committee members for contact—eight calls for each of the nine members. The committee was scheduled to meet again tomorrow night, Monday the twenty-first, and make final plans for the visitor-training session to be held the week after that on the twenty-eighth.

Davis knew the committee chairperson was a reliable worker who could be counted on to complete a task, and thus no conversation had been held between them since the earlier meeting, now almost two weeks ago. The following transpired at the sanctuary door:

1. Pastor: How are the committee plans going?
2. Stewardship Chair: Gee, not very well, Pastor.
3. P: Not very well? What seems to be the problem?
4. S: Well, we're just real lethargic. I think we're in serious trouble trying to get all the people we need lined up for the campaign.
5. P: I see. Do you have time now to talk about this and share some problems and concerns?
6. S: I guess we have to, because there's no way we're gonna be ready for tomorrow night's meeting.
7. P: Why don't we go into my office and take a look at what's happening?

    (*The two move into the pastor's office to continue the conversation. After a couple of minutes, five-year-old Johnny, the pastor's son, interrupts.*)

8. S: I'm beginning to get the feeling that our committee and maybe most of the church just don't like this change in plans for making the budget.
9. Johnny: Daddy! Mama's waiting, and we need to go home!
10. P: Johnny, what have I told you? When the door is closed—
11. J: But I knocked. It's time to go.
12. P: Does your mother want to go?
13. J: Sure she wants to go. Lunch is ready, and it's gonna burn!
14. P: Okay. You and Mother go on home and eat. Tell her I'll warm mine in the microwave. I need to stay and talk about the stewardship campaign.
15. J: About the *what?*
16. P: Tell her it's about money.
17. J: Okay. (*Johnny leaves. The real scene is a seminary classroom with the pastor and stewardship chairperson in role play. Omitted from this transcript of the taped experience is the hilarious laughter that emerges from time to time, particularly when the professor surprises both players by becoming a new and unexpected participant in the scenario—little Johnny. Where and under what circumstances does one carry on pastoral consultation? The shift from the term "supervision" to "consultation" will be explained below.*)
18. P. Let's see . . . where were we? Oh, yes, you were just saying that some members may be having second thoughts

about the new pattern of doing home visits for the stewardship program.

19. S: Well, you could draw that conclusion based on the response we're getting from the people on the committee. I know that, in my own case, of the eight people I was to contact to make visits I've only got two affirmative responses. Three people said no outright, and I haven't been able—had time to contact the other three yet.

    I ran into Sarah between Sunday school and church today, and she's only contacted three of her people in the two weeks since we met last. She said she thought the rest of them could be contacted in time for our meeting tomorrow night, but I wonder if she's gonna have that kind of enthusiasm if she hasn't gotten the job done by now. She's just waiting till the last minute.

20. P: Right. *(Subdued)*

21. S: And then I got the real distressing news that Bill Brown is resigning from our committee, because he doesn't believe in the approach we're using. He says we're going too hard-sell. So we're behind in our quota of people we should get, and I don't see how we can make it.

22. P: And for the meeting tomorrow night they have to have all their contacts made.

23. S: That's right. We have to mail out reminders to all the visitors about the training session a week from tomorrow.

24. P: So the real problem you're dealing with right now is the committee members making all their contacts, not so much the responses.

25. S: Well, uh, we had hoped we would hear yes from about two thirds of the members asked to visit so each team would have only four homes to contact. As near as I can tell, we're not coming anywhere close to that. Now, uh, if we wanted to go ahead with this process, each team's gonna have to make eight to ten visits, and a lot of them are gonna quit.

26. P: So what do you see that needs to be done?

27. S: I don't know. I'm just really discouraged. Uh, I'm out of suggestions. I have no idea what to do.

28. P: So you've talked to Sarah and Bill. She says she'll make her contacts, but Bill said he wouldn't do any at all.

29. S: Yeah, Bill's washed his hands of the whole thing, and knowing Bill the way I do, he's probably gonna start talking with others in the congregation about how bad things are and it's gonna be a real bad situation. I'm really frustrated with the whole business.

At this point, I interrupted the role play and invited the class to provide suggestions for the pastor. What should be done differently? Among the ideas offered were the following:

- Be more directive. What does the chairperson want the pastor to do?
- We need to find out if the chairperson really wants to continue with the campaign. Sounds as though he's had it.
- Bill Brown may be just the tip of an iceberg of problems in the church.
- The chairperson needs a pat on the back. It sounds as if he's about ready to break down and cry. The pastor needs to say, "I really appreciate the work you've done. Now what can we do to salvage it?" (*The chairperson had been programmed in the role play to sound somewhat depressed.*)
- What about the chairperson's lunch? The pastor didn't bother to check on that.
- The pastor may need to change the whole stewardship plan. In my experience of contacting recruits, two weeks isn't enough time to recruit eight persons.

At this point we assumed that the time has shifted to 4 P.M., so that both the pastor and the chairperson have had lunch. A student who herself is a parent took the pastor's role, and the conversation continued:

30. S: I'm just really discouraged about the whole thing. I don't see any chance of getting it done.
31. P: Are you saying we should change our plans?
32. S: I don't know what to think. There doesn't seem to be much support for the program or for me. I'm just—
33. P: Are you taking this personally?
34. S: Yeah, I feel really badly that things haven't gone well. I feel betrayed by many that they're not tackling the job and I'll be blamed for a program that hasn't got a chance to work.
35. P: Who'll blame you?
36. S: Everybody in the church, when it comes time to look at the budget!
37. P: You're really blaming yourself, then, aren't you?
38. S: Yeah, when the money's not there, a lot of fingers will be pointing at me.
39. P: Seems to me you've done your job very well and are taking the blame for what others haven't done. I think what we need to do now is see how we can pull things together.

Again, the role play was broken, and discussion followed. Next in the role of pastor was a student who had been a salesman. He tried to persuade the chairperson that things were not as bad as had been thought: "Let's get on the phone and see what results other members of the committee have had. After all, we've only heard from you and two others—that leaves six." The sales pitch did not work. The fourth person to role-play pastor had mentioned in the second break for discussion that maybe something else was going on with the stewardship chairperson. The following thus took place toward the end of the hour-and-a-half class:

40. P: I'd like to come up with some suggestions as to what can be done here. What do you think?
41. S: I don't know. I'm at my wits' end.
42. P: How long has this been bothering you?
43. S: The past two weeks. The last few weeks have been really bad.
44. P: The last few weeks have been hard? What's been bad about the last few weeks?
45. S: This just seems to be one of a whole lot of failures that have been happening lately. The company I work for has not been doing well financially, and they're having to lay people off and I may be let go. As if that wasn't enough, I haven't been able to make my contacts because my wife and I had another big fight the other day. We just haven't been talking the past few months.
46. P: Looks as though we have a lot to talk about besides this stewardship concern.

At this point the pastor broke out of role, as surprised as the rest of the class. Only the chairperson and I had known about the home and work situation, and the role required that these data not be mentioned unless one of those role-playing the pastor gave a word that opened this door to personal concerns.

The Value of the Supervisory Model

In this exercise, the attention of those in the role of the pastor and those in the group providing suggestions to the pastor is usually focused on ways to salvage the stewardship campaign. I have used this role play with eight different groups of seminary students and with two groups of experienced pastors. In only three of these experiences has the underlying agenda been identified.

The supervisory model presented in chapter 3 helps the minister escape this trap. The pastor in the left-hand circle in that diagram has been replaced here (Figure 15-1), by a parishioner, in this case the stewardship committee chairperson. The process of ministry is that of chairing the stewardship committee. The persons in the circle on the right are eight other members of the stewardship committee and the eight church members the chairperson was to recruit as visitors. The arrow protruding into the process of ministry from above representing administrative concerns has to do, in this particular parish setting, with a successful stewardship campaign. Finally, the arrow protruding from below pictures the relationship between the pastor and the stewardship chairperson.

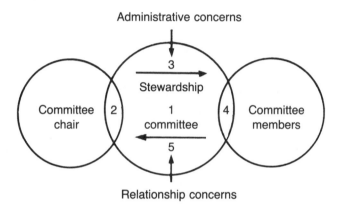

Figure 15-1. Pastoral Consultation in the Parish

Onc way of looking at the role play is to observe that, almost invariably, the pastors and their "coaches" in the class or training group give attention to the arrow of administrative concerns (3) protruding into the process of ministry. How do we salvage this program so crucial to the survival of the institution? What steps should be taken to prevent a major failure? The stewardship chairperson saw fingers of blame pointing to him from the official board and from members of the church in general. I edited the role play at item 17 where the pastor tells son Johnny how to explain to his mother the delay in lunch. The student in role actually said, "Well, tell her it's about money, and remind her of the red dress she wants!" Administrative concerns become a powerful trap.

Notice from the transcription of the tape presented above that meaningful conversation is almost completely diverted from the primary channel (1) on which one asks, "What went on in this process of ministry?" We learn from line 2 that things have not gone well. From lines 19 and 21 we pick up some facts about contacts the stewardship chairperson has made. There is no exploration, however, of details of conversation between the chairperson and the church members who declined; no details about dialogue between the chairperson and Bill Brown.

Conversations designed to help persons grow in their capacity to participate in ministry should focus precisely at this point. Given a less loaded situation, the pastor and the chairperson of the stewardship committee should give primary attention to details of the conversation with Bill Brown. In the informal setting of the parish, this attention may well begin with a reconstruction of the conversation with Bill. Given a picture of what went on in this dialogue, a host of questions may be addressed. For example:

- To what degree did the chairperson really "hear" what Bill was saying?
- Why was Bill silent when plans were being made back in the spring?
- What is the nature of the bad relationship between the chairperson and Bill as revealed in line 29 of the verbatim?
- What next steps should be followed in relation to Bill, and who should carry them out, the chairperson or the pastor? If the latter, how is the confidentiality issue handled in relation to the conversation between Bill and the chairperson?

A dimension completely ignored in the role play is represented by the intrusion of the arrow (5) which reminds us of dynamics in the relationship between the pastor and the stewardship chairperson. In consultation, as in supervision, attention is needed from time to time on this issue. The pastoral approach of the student who had been a salesman is not provided in detail above. It presented a prime illustration, however, of a case in which attention to area (5) is crucial. The chairperson became angry at the hard attempt to persuade him that things were not really as bad as they seemed. A sensitive salesperson could pick up on this and shift the focus by saying something like, "Let's put aside the stewardship issue for a moment and look at what's going on between us. I sense that you became angry when I pressed the point that things may not be so bad after all."

The major reason I designed the role play and have used it over the years is to drive home the importance of being pastoral in the processes of church administration. This seems simple enough, but the fact that overlap (2) is invariably neglected demonstrates the difficulty of implementing what seems obvious. Pastors frequently have a tough time being pastoral. They get "hooked" on the immediate task.

The depth of the difficulty is more clearly revealed when the context of the role play exercise is known. It follows (by about two weeks in the classroom, and almost immediately in a workshop with pastors) a presentation on balancing a concern for task accomplishment with concern for persons and their growth in ability to do ministry. A model developed by Robert Blake and Jane Mouton is helpful here (see Figure 15-2).[1]

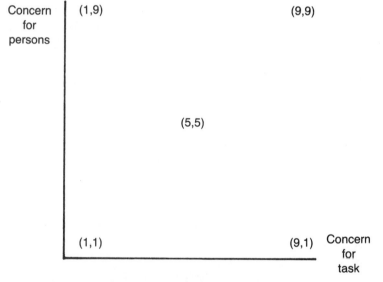

Figure 15-2. The Managerial Grid

The managerial grid developed by Blake and Mouton pictures five leadership styles. The ideal is to move toward the (9,9) pattern in which there is strong concern both for task and for persons. The (9,1) pattern of high concern for task and low concern for persons could be characterized as a dictatorial pattern. In contrast, the (1,9) pattern of low concern for task and high concern for persons is a country club style. In the middle (where many of us live) is the accommodating pattern of (5,5). The (1,1) pattern, low concern for both task and persons, represents the individual who has psychologically left the organization.

A variety of tests have been developed that provide a clue to understanding one's pattern of leadership in terms of this grid model. I have adapted one of these to the parish setting and it contains twenty items like the following:

> **When committee members get into open conflict, I:**
>
> a.___Let them work out their differences by themselves.
> b.___Smooth it over by pouring oil on troubled waters.
> c.___Get them together to "talk it through" to resolution.
> d.___Suppress it by dealing firmly with both. Conflicts can't be tolerated.
> e.___Talk to them one by one to understand the problem and yet to explain how fighting in the committee can cause everyone to lose.

Respondents enter a "1" by the item that is closest to what they would do, a "2" by the next most likely item, and so on, through a "5" for their least likely response. In the illustration, the number inserted for a is counted as a (1,1) response; b is the (1,9); c is (9,9); d, (9,1); and e is scored as (5,5). The pattern receiving the lowest sum for the twenty items is one's preferred leadership style.

Almost without exception, students find (9,9) to be their leadership style—high concern for both task and persons. Answers are heavily influenced by what one *thinks* is best, so that standardized scores become important. The point for our discussion here is that, with exposure to this way of looking at leadership, persons are all the more surprised by their degree of entrapment by concern for the task of getting the stewardship program back on track. Again, the supervisory model, adapted to the parish, better equips the minister to "cover all the bases" in a consultative conversation.

From Supervision to Consultation

I have shifted the terminology in this chapter from "supervision" to "consultation," and this move calls for an explanation. The rationale may be seen by contrasting what more typically takes place in the congregation with the definition of supervision presented in chapter 3. First, it is pointed out there that supervision is an extended conversation at regular intervals and not a one-shot affair, as consultation sometimes is. Such conversations in the parish setting occur most frequently in a trouble-shooting context, as in the role play above.

Second, the aim of supervision is clearly set in chapter 3 to be the personal development in the pastoral role of the one being supervised. In contrast, parish consultation most often has as its primary objective the resolution of some particular problem. Whether the pastor or a church member initiates the conversation, the understanding, at least implicit, is that some concern related to a church program can be worked through.

This does not mean that one ignores the personal growth of the member involved in consultation. To the contrary, this growth should be a strong secondary aim in parish consultation. A different view violates the understanding of Ephesians that the gifts of pastors are to equip the saints—church members—for the work of ministry (Eph. 4:11–12).

The first "volunteer pastor" apparently had this secondary objective in mind when, at line 26, the question was asked, "So what do you see that needs to be done?" Some analysis of the concern had been completed and the pastor could have come forth with a solution—"Here's what we can do." The growth of the stewardship chairperson is enhanced if one helps her or him find a solution.

There is yet a third major difference between supervision as seen in other chapters of this text and pastoral consultation being discussed here. Coupled with supervision in the educational setting is the supervisor's responsibility to evaluate the work of the person in training. Further, this evaluation can have an impact on the career of the supervisee, and each party in the relationship knows this.

In the relationship between pastor and church member, the evaluation is still there. It takes place, even if sometimes out of conscious focus, whenever two persons are involved in conversation. The life of the church member can be affected by the process. Pastors exert varying degrees of power when the church is deciding who will be on which committee, who will serve as officers, and so on. But in the parish setting, there is not an above-the-board understanding by each party that evaluation is going on and that it may make a difference.

From Consultation to Supervision

Having set forth the key differences between consultation in the church setting and supervision in the educational one, I want to argue now that ministry is enhanced when there is a movement from consultation toward supervision. This chapter has already pointed to the ways in which pastoral consultation can be strengthened by incorporating insights from clinical supervision. The ongoing task of troubleshooting, which no pastor can avoid, is carried out more effectively when the supervisory model is kept in mind.

But why must pastoral consultation await some critical issue to bring minister and lay leader together? A process very close to clinical supervision may be implemented as part of a church's leadership development. A pastor, or a skilled lay leader, can enter into covenant with those beginning new tasks to engage in regularly scheduled dialogue focused on specific acts of ministry of the leaders in training, with the articulated goal of enhancing the ability of these new leaders to engage in effective ministry.

Take, for example, persons who are doing visiting on behalf of the church. Regardless of whether the homes they are entering contain prospective, inactive, or troubled church members, the learning process is the same. The visitors plan to meet on a regular basis, and a part of the commitment is that they agree, in turn, to present summary or written verbatim reports of their work. The initial anxiety about this is decreased through a presentation of the supervisory model and through initial use of verbatim reports prepared by others. An example of this process and of such a verbatim may be found in the booklet *Person to Person Evangelism.* [2] If some laypersons do not want to do written homework as a part of leadership training, then a portion of a visit can be reconstructed through verbal report.

Another option is to use a video camera to record what happens in a church school classroom. The video tape will present the concrete processes of ministry for examination in individual supervision of the teacher or, perhaps even better, for a small-group supervisory process. The key here is that the relative importance of troubleshooting in the class and the personal growth of the teacher have been reversed to place primary weight on the latter. Consultation has shifted toward supervision.

One last illustration of this shift can be seen in the case of the stewardship chairperson. Imagine that the facts were different. Instead of being a seasoned and reliable worker, the chairperson had taken responsibility for a committee for the first time. The pastor could have contracted for some time after each meeting of the committee in which the two would share dialogue about what had taken place during the session. Prime time in this postmeeting conversation would be devoted, according to the initial agreement, to channel (1) in the circular supervisory model. What interventions did the chairperson make at strategic points in the meeting—exactly what was said? What could be assumed to have gone on within other members of the committee at these strategic points—channel (4)? What did the chairperson feel within herself at these points in the meeting—channel (2)? What is going on in the postmeeting conversation between the pastor and the chairperson—channel (5)? Somewhere in the conversation between these two, an agreement may well be made to shift the focus from the concrete acts of ministry of the chairperson, with focus on his growth in ability to do ministry (supervision), to problem solving about what needs to happen next, conversation in which the task is the primary goal (consultation).

A Point of Style for Consultation and Supervision

One important issue remains for an adequate analysis of the role play with which this chapter begins and for enhancement of the reader's ability to engage in either supervision or consultation. This issue has to do with the leadership style of the supervisor or consultant. The Blake-Mouton grid leadership model is correct in claiming that high concern both for task and for persons is ideal—(9,9) is the preferred model. For-profit organizations that incorporate this model through training become more profitable. Volunteer organizations become more effective.

The problem is that one can have high concern both for task and for personal growth, and thus know how one should *feel* in leading others, yet not know how to *act*, what to say, in differing leadership situations. For this reason it is helpful to augment the Blake-Mouton picture with one developed by Paul Hersey and Ken Blanchard in their text, *Management of Organizational Behavior.* [3]

These authors distinguish between task behavior and relationship behavior. In task behavior, the leader (consultant or supervisor) tells the other person or group what is to be done and how to do it. In relationship behavior, the leader engages in two-way conversation: listening, supporting, facilitating, and giving positive strokes. The mix of these sets of behavior provides four leadership styles.

A leadership pattern that is high on task behavior and low on relationship behavior is labeled a TELLING style by Hersey and Blanchard. A style that is high on both dimensions—task and relationship behavior—is called SELLING. The name given to the pattern that is high on relationship behavior but low on task behavior is PARTICIPATING. Finally, the leader who relates with low task and low relationship behavior is relating with a DELE-GATING style.

With these definitions in mind, the Hersey-Blanchard model claims that the consultant or supervisor should shift his or her pattern of relating to fit the maturity of the supervisee *in relation to the specific task at hand.* The latter is crucial. A church member or counselor in training may be quite skilled (mature) in many areas, yet be at the beginner's level in others. Maturity is viewed in this model as a two-dimensional concept. First is one's level of experience and ability in relation to the task at hand. Second is one's level of motivation, of willingness to assume responsibility in relation to the particular task. A person who does not know how to do a specific task and has no eagerness to do it is at the lowest level of maturity in relation to the task, and the Hersey-Blanchard model claims that a TELLING style is most effective. When the person knows the job as well as or better than the supervisor and is still highly motivated in relation to it, DELEGAT-ING is the style that is recommended. Levels of maturity in between call for the PARTICIPATING style for those toward the higher end of the maturity scale and for the SELLING pattern for those with less knowledge and experience.

Hersey and Blanchard recommend a developmental cycle whereby the leader begins with a style that fits the initial maturity level of the follower, then moves through successive stages whereby the follower's maturity is increased until finally the DELEGATING pattern is appropriate. They also remind us that the maturity level of a person may suddenly or gradually *decrease,* so that an abrupt shift from DELEGATING back to SELLING or TELLING may be required. This retrogression is not due to change in ability or experience. It stems from the psychological dimension of motivation and commitment.

This is precisely what has happened to the stewardship chairperson in the role play scenario. Recall that the pastor and the observers are aware that the chairperson "was a reliable worker who could be counted on to complete a task." The pastor had appropriately been using a DELEGATING pattern—leave the ball in the chairperson's hands, and things will be done well.

The point missed by the different pastors and observers is that the one responsible for the stewardship program had moved backward down the maturity scale to a point where a shift in style was called for. The first pastor shifted from DELEGATING to PARTICIPATING when he learned that the chairperson had a problem. Unfortunately, the first pastor became stuck here. The response at line 26, "So what do you see that needs to be done?" was appropriate. The ball was missed at point 28. The pastor's question had been answered with a very immature, helpless, "I don't know. I'm just really discouraged. Uh, I'm out of suggestions. I have no idea what to do."

Guided by Hersey and Blanchard, this response is seen to be out of character from one who, in the past, has been counted on in a delegating pattern to get things done. At line 28, the pastor remained stuck in the pattern of participation. What the chairperson had said in line 27 was ignored, and the pastor returned to problem analysis with, "So, you've talked to Sarah and Bill."

With an awareness that something out of the ordinary has probably happened to the chairperson, the pastor could check this out and open the door for the underlying and hidden role agenda. An alternate response for 28 could read, "You're discouraged and out of ideas. This doesn't sound like you. You'd ordinarily take a setback like this in stride. What's going on?"

Hersey and Blanchard thus provide a helpful guide whereby the supervisor or consultant can sense when a shift in style is needed. Their work also casts light for seeing what agenda items need attention in channel (1) of the supervisory circle. Specific instances of ministry should be sought in which the church member has a need for growth in understanding and skill. Other areas can be handled in a delegating pattern—"Let's deal with that only if you sense a need to talk."

My central purpose in this chapter has been to underscore the importance for the pastor to learn the process of supervision. This skill is not simply an art essential for those who teach professionals. It is crucial for the minister in developing the gifts of the laity. Further, just as insights from clinical training have informed the field of church administration, so too has administration provided helpful understandings to the field of clinical supervision.

NOTES

1. R. R. Blake and J. Mouton, *The Managerial Grid* (Houston: Gulf Publication Co., 1964).

2. G. L. Tucker, Jr., *Person to Person Evangelism* (New York: Presbyterian Church (U.S.A.), 1978).

3. P. Hersey and K. H. Blanchard, *Management of Organizational Behavior,* 2nd ed. (Englewood Cliffs, N.J.: Prentice-Hall, 1972); see particularly ch. 7.

16

Supervising Teachers in a Christian Education Program

Louis B. Weeks

"Here's a tentative agenda for us. Are there items we should add to it?" Lauren Cooper paused and looked around the table. She seemed nervous, and she fiddled with a pen as she talked. But her competence and her openness prevailed as the meeting got under way.

Lauren named three major topics for consideration by the Christian education committee: the need to begin a youth group, the selection of curriculum materials for the confirmation class, and the emergency recruitment of two teachers for the church school already under way.

As her supervisor in the congregation-based Christian education course at the seminary, I sat observing her work with the committee. Members of the group became quickly oblivious to my presence as they moved through the discussion and made decisions. I tried to sort out behavioral patterns of, and contributions by, Lauren Cooper the seminarian.

Which seemed to foster the work of the group? Which might impede decisions? Were topics opened freely? Did the organization of an agenda aid them? Was subsequent responsibility assigned? Did Ms. Cooper respond in assertive ways? broach the matter of process? support good ideas from others? Did she foster honesty and a sense of caring and purpose? How?

I took notes, plotted the energy level of the group, and marked major points along the way. When the meeting adjourned, I also listened to the comments of the participants in the midst of their departure. In my car, on the way home, I began to rehearse the upcoming supervisory meeting with Lauren Cooper.

She had wanted me to observe particularly concerning her "bringing order amid chaos" for the Christian education committee. That committee had not functioned regularly, and individuals in recent years had simply "run things on their own," according to resentful parents and the frustrated pastor.

As a student in the "congregation-based" program in Christian education, she considered that a well-functioning committee would be essential both for her own learning and for the vital Christian education program the congregation sought. I analyzed her "act of ministry" particularly from that perspective, but I also considered which issues to raise and how to focus the supervisory session that would follow.

The observation, the analysis, and the conference formed just a part of my work as a supervisor with Lauren Cooper. Typical of the range of supervisory responsibilities in a seminary, however, this particular occasion affords a look at some resources available in theological education and at some requisite skills on which to focus in the supervisory process.

The Range of Seminary Supervision

The preparation of ministers for their faithful witness in leading the people of God remains the awesome task of seminaries, and today this work seems to grow rather than to diminish. While most of the chapters in this book center on clinical settings for the teaching of pastoral care, that area is but one (albeit extremely important) element in the total work of the minister. The minister engages in all kinds of leadership in behalf of the Christian gospel, which defines the nature of the body of Christ. "You shall be my witnesses"; "Bear one another's burdens"; "They are in the world. . . . They are not of the world"; "Whoever gives . . . even a cup of cold water because he is a disciple"; "Worship the Lord in the beauty of holiness"—all of these and more definitions of personal and corporate Christian behavior also define particularly the nature of ministry and the goals of the minister in the instruction of God's people.

Supervision as the process of honing one's skills in teaching, preaching, caring, leading, and witnessing involves us in a distinctive enterprise; but theological education can use and has benefited from tools developed elsewhere. My purpose is to present just a couple and to suggest ways of applying them in supervision for seminarians especially.

When I came to Louisville Presbyterian Theological Seminary almost two decades ago, I discovered a definite pattern of thorough supervision in pastoral care already present. A "clinical program" in prophetic ministry also existed, seeking to equip students in that area. With colleagues, I helped develop and subsequently have taught in a program in Congregation-based Christian Education that offers equally inductive opportunities in that field. Subsequently, courses in evangelism and preaching have focused on supervision of "acts of ministry" and analysis of them for learning. We even employ supervision for the moderator of the Seminary Forum, our equivalent of a student body president, in order to have that become a focused, intentional learning situation. The tools and skills I describe are equally useful in all these areas of apprenticeship.

A Five-Stage Model

Out of his experience in supervising education students in their teaching, Robert Goldhammer has provided a tool that has proven very useful—a five-stage model for supervision itself.[1] Goldhammer names a preobservation conference, the observation itself, analysis and strategy, the supervisory conference, and a postconference analysis (or "postmortem"). Though this sequence, or "cycle" of supervision, has been offered for teachers in public schools in particular, I have found it equally useful, with some small modifications, for supervising theological students in Christian education and in other aspects of ministry as well.

Basically, the preobservation conference focuses with as much specificity as possible on the goals and objectives of the student in the activity to be observed. Goldhammer calls it the drawing of a supervisory "contract." To get the student to select important matters for concentration—to be able to name and describe them—takes the supervisory "cycle" from empty ritual to careful instruction. Though Goldhammer calls these "generally short-term affairs" and seems to envision most taking place immediately before the teaching event to be supervised, I think they are extremely important and should occur at least one day in advance of the act of ministry to be observed.

In the conference, I ask about anticipation of the event to come: "Why engage in this act of ministry?" "What is the purpose of this work in terms of the gospel?" "What are you seeking as you work?" "What may inhibit you?" "What will you do if . . . ?" The conversation bridges theology, the practice of ministry, preparation of the person in supervision, and many other topics. Most important, I ask about the role I can play as supervisor: "How can I help?" "What would you like for me to focus?" "What patterns of your behavior reinforce your goals?" "What patterns are you seeking to shed?" "Do you have ways I can tell about your sense of purpose and energy level during the event?"

At the occasion of ministry, I ask the students to introduce me as their supervisor. Then I promise to be unobtrusive and simply sit there watching, listening, and taking notes. After a number of years doing it, I feel confident I seldom impede the processes. If anything, I sometimes sense heightened involvement of most participants, a pattern of interaction probably not altogether the same as if I were absent, but not really artificial either. Occasionally a participant will remark on the level of participation or other factors during the session.

I record what I can of patterns of behavior, notes that will later remind me of concrete illustrations and significant moments. The observation provides a "reality testing" I have not found in presentation of verbatim recitations.

According to Goldhammer, the third stage consists in the supervisor's analysis of the issues for instruction and attention to strategy for the supervisory session. In addition, I have grown to ask the students to perform the same tasks in anticipation of the supervisory session, seeking to develop in them the analytical skills and goals for instruction that ministers need so badly. What relationships can be discerned among the data? In what ways do means and ends coincide or produce dissonance? (I ask this same question concerning my own efforts toward the supervisory session, by the way.) And since students are evolving styles of ministry and apprenticing themselves to others, I ask about those areas also.

In the fourth stage, the supervisory session itself, I use a pattern that I developed of asking most of the time for the student's perceptions and analysis first. This evident confidence in the students' ability to see themselves seems worthwhile, though it occasions frustration and even hostility in some.

In the postmortem, what Goldhammer terms the "conscience of the cycle," I try to remember our primary task—to foster growth for ministry. I seek to show that both of us can grow, at least when the cycle has been seriously undertaken by the student or students. Not only do we seek wisdom, which "cannot be told," we also seek consciousness of judgment, grace, providence, and understanding.

Images of the Cycle Components

In such a brief article, I cannot explain in detail the full dimensions of the five-stage cycle as employed. Goldhammer offers excellent discussions of techniques at each stage, together with responses to such questions as "What if the student reveals woefully inadequate preparation or a lack of gifts for analysis?" Other works on supervision offer supplemental aids. I can offer here some visual images of the cycle in relationship to the model presented in chapter 3.

Stage 1: The Preobservation Conference

The preobservation conference envisions and anticipates an act of ministry on the part of the student in behalf of others (or at least another; see Figure 16-1).Its task is to focus on the minister/teacher (student under supervision), the students (who are participating in the occasion), and the teaching/learning process itself. The conference may center on any of these three clinical poles. Usually elements of it will address all three. The supervisor and the minister/teacher achieve during the conference a kind of contract in behalf of the upcoming event.

The teaching/learning event will have limits, though the minister/teacher and perhaps the students as well may become totally involved. The preobservation conference allows me an opportunity to restrict my upcoming observations to certain elements: worldview conveyed, for example, or demonstrations of the theological virtues (faith, hope, and love). I also listen carefully to the minister/teacher, and I decide how vulnerable and defensive the minister/teacher might be in anticipation of the other stages in supervision.

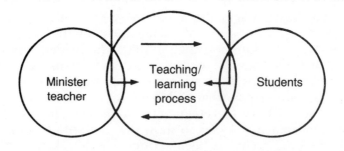

Figure 16-1. Anticipating Observation Focus

During the preobservation conference, I also choose how much to rehearse the upcoming event and how much to seek analysis by the minister/teacher in proleptic fashion. Goldhammer cautions nicely against the supervisor's embarking on a line of questions that might undermine the strategy or plans of the one being supervised. By the same token, I find it imperative to broach seriously the goals and plans, to rehearse in some fashion the upcoming event. Balance in behalf of sustaining self-esteem for the minister/teacher and encouraging anticipatory wisdom remains a goal for me.

Stage 2: Observation

The observation stage can be viewed as intentionally capturing a discrete act of ministry for analysis and reflection. Naturally, as human beings we cannot completely accomplish such a feat. With practice and with careful attention to significant matters, however, we can glean something of the patterns of behavior, the frames of reference, and the nature of the transactions among the minister/teacher and the students.

The supervisor, according to Goldhammer, should follow all the dialogue and note as much of it as possible, especially the speeches of the supervisee and the other major participants. The supervisor serves as a kind of stenographer/observer with open eyes, ears, and mind.

In theological education, it seems to me, the supervisor also looks for theological dimensions in the event and among the participants. Is it too dramatic to say I try to see powers and principalities at work? Instances of grace and those of judgment, occasions of sin and forgiveness, openings for community and for the work of the Spirit—all are potentially there, and part of the process means identifying them in humility and with questions. The discernment can be defective, or injurious, as well as helpful and instructive.

I find the image of the artist a useful one as I engage in observation. Out of the whole realm of experience and perception, I try to discern something coherent, perhaps even something aesthetically pleasing. I record the hints and sketch the outlines of a work of art in the making—pertinent patterns, body language, words, transactions, and other clues that might be of use in analyzing the event.

Stage 3: Analysis

This stage calls for separate reflection by the supervisor and the minister/teacher upon the completed act of ministry. Both prepare for supervision by anticipating their coming time together. I try to think about the needs and plans of the minister/teacher, the specific patterns of teaching I observed, the ways to present material and insight, and other such things.

The transition will be a significant one—the minister/teacher becomes again the student, and I become the minister/teacher for the supervisory conference. Particularly, I ask if there are ways to illustrate in the supervisory session my perceptions of patterns and habits observed previously. If I can embody the pattern or habit desired as I teach, I can better call the attention of the student to it and more confidently expect growth or change.

I work as Figure 16-2 indicates. The two of us will address the teaching/learning process. Together we will assess the response of students throughout the event. Together we will reflect upon the minister/teacher's use of self in helping others to learn. I am mindful now of the role reversal and my responsibility to model the minister/teacher role in supervision.

Stage 4: Supervisory Conference

Goldhammer says that no two conferences are exactly the same, so it remains a very difficult thing to characterize conferences. In general, though, I ask first for the analysis of the event by the student. Frequently that exposition will contain many of the same observations I have made.

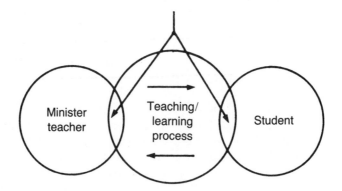

Figure 16-2. Focus on Supervision Analysis

I also try to keep from lecturing—a tough job! Can I ask questions instead of simply giving speeches? Sometimes. I keep in mind the wisdom of education experts who report the small percentage of learning on the part of students simply hearing things. If the student can voice the insight, chances are the learning can be solidified.

My dwelling on the student's analysis, on the insights of the student, and on letting the student talk more than I do will frequently produce some hostility on the student's part. "Tell me what was right and what was wrong!" one exclaimed in frustration. I do feel the obligation to tell what I observed, and I sense an obligation truthfully to describe my own feelings during the event (as elsewhere). But I am willing usually to take the hostility and the frustration as necessary elements in the learning process. They certainly are.

The conference mixes reports of observations with theological perceptions. I find students tempted, and I myself as well, to focus merely on the horizontal dimensions in the event. I seek ways to discuss the work of the Spirit, the community of the faithful, and the grace of God.

Stage 5: Postmortem

At the close of the conference, I ask the student especially to reflect upon the whole process, especially upon the supervisory conference. Have I been helpful? Has learning occurred? Have we preserved the primary task—to foster growth for ministry? If we need to set another time just for exploring what we open together during this postmortem, I try to set one just for the purpose.

Classroom Observation Form

Although Goldhammer encourages the supervisor simply to observe and record as much dialogue as possible together with some perceptions of the classroom environment, I have found that the use of a more disciplined "form" for observation helps immensely.

A colleague through the years, Garth Rosell, developed one such form that is superb for observing educational events. Several of us helped him in the process, and he returned the favor with permission to reproduce it. (See Figure 16-3.)Most of the spaces for recorded observations are self-explanatory. The energy chart to the left provides the scale for the supervisor to record estimates of the energy level present in the classroom over the entire period on a scale ranging from relaxed to intense. We began by using this chart for the supervision of case teachers, since many of us together have tried to bring inductive methods more fully into theological education. Supervision for other aspects of ministry would demand variations on the theme.

The form features two major ingredients—an energy chart and an interaction chart. Two other larger spaces allow record-

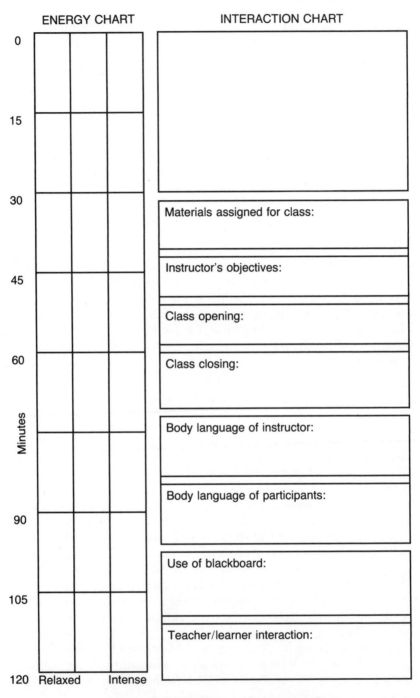

Figure 16-3. Classroom Observation Form

Prepared by Garth M. Rosell, Academic Dean and Professor of History, Gordon-Conwell Theological Seminary, South Hamilton, Massachusetts.

ing of body language, two more focus use of chalkboard and interaction among teacher and learners. Small spaces provide for recordings of assignments, objectives (listed from both preobservation conference and statements in class), opening, and closing.

The energy chart bears explanation. The atmosphere for learning includes, indeed may well center on, the heuristic power of the subject under consideration. Moreover, patterns emerge as one perceives energy levels. Actions and words by the participants may affect the energy levels of groups. The teacher who brings "enthusiasm" for the subject as well as mastery of it commands greater attention and perhaps evokes full learning. Good use of humor in teaching can raise energy levels enormously. Students bring energy to learning as well, and the gathering of a class makes its own atmosphere.

The matter remains complex indeed, for more energy does not necessarily yield more learning. Sometimes energy can produce anxiety and stifle learning, or high levels of humor can make for entertainment rather than learning. Garth and others of us perceive that a variety of energy levels during a classtime is preferable to the maintenance of a more constant one. Perhaps classes even come to have a rhythm, and varieties in the "melodies" of learning experiences can be discerned.

All the same, we are reluctant to evaluate and employ insights from this area of knowledge and experience. So in supervision, we carefully disclaim any scientific objectivity in the "measure" of energy. By focusing on it, we can relate other matters of dialogue and classroom presence to changes in the mood or energy level in the session.

Interaction charts are more common, but for supervisors to use them in theological education remains an infrequent practice. Even in pastoral care, where group dynamics become central for the discipline, interaction charts actually following transactions are relatively rare. And in our society, with its excessive emphasis on individuals, students in supervision seldom come to the process with mature perceptions of the centrality of transactions. The chart can show who sat where, and how interaction occurred. Of course, in case study such records become all the more important for analysis and learning from the experience. But even for lecture and discussion, or in administrative events such as the one noted above, interactions tell as much as the words employed, maybe more.

Several other elements in the form have been dealt with in others' chapters in this work. David Steere has pioneered in the study of body language, and supervisors reading his *Bodily Ex-*

pressions in Psychotherapy can note concrete examples of communication through images of the teacher and the students during the session.[2] The opening and closing times in supervision have their functional equivalent in the classroom.

Servants of Christ

The five-stage supervisory model offered by Goldhammer and the Classroom Observation Form are two good tools for supervising seminary students and others in preparation for ministry. They represent a whole range of tools that now exist in this area. I am convinced we need all the good tools we can obtain, but I also try to keep in perspective the relative value of such helps.

The supervisory process cannot be mastered in the mere acquisition of these or any other tools. Indeed, having supervised others for almost two decades, I find myself increasingly persuaded that supervision cannot ever be "mastered," in the general meaning of that word. Rather, I become increasingly convinced that God's gifts underlie growth in students and their acquisition of both skills and knowledge.

I consider this a wonderful yet troubling time for men and women who serve as ministers in congregations. Nowhere else in our North American society are people asked to enter into all of life with such a wide variety of other people—times of crisis and joy, occasions of growth and of tragedy. At the same time, demands on the minister multiply, and human resources do not suffice.

Appropriately, the Christian movement has proclaimed that we are not left primarily to human resources. The Bible is full of promises that God will not forsake those who trust him. In the one letter that Paul wrote to Christians at Corinth, he spoke of being a "servant of Christ." That passage, 1 Corinthians 4:1-5, also identifies the first mark of the "servant of Christ," being trustworthy. Faithful ministry, as trustworthy education, can best be served as a gift from God. Human criticism pales beside the Christian expectation of God's judgment; but according to Paul, servants of Christ will receive "commendation" from God.

We, and all who live as servants of Christ, depend upon God's judgment; but according to Paul, servants of Christ will receive "commendation" from God.

We, and all who live as servants of Christ, depend upon God's Spirit for sustenance, insight, and the theological virtues of faith, hope, and love. That is the perspective permitting us to engage in such a bold and thorough enterprise as supervision.

In that perspective, the creative use of good tools takes on its appropriate priority.

NOTES

1. R. Goldhammer, *Clinical Supervision: Special Methods for the Supervision of Teachers* (New York: Holt, Rinehart & Winston, 1969).

2. D. A. Steere, *Bodily Expressions in Psychotherapy* (New York: Brunner/Mazel, 1983).

17

An Experiment in Training Supervisors for Field Education

David A. Steere

The quality of supervision determines the effectiveness of seminary programs in field education. G. I. Hunter characterizes the late 1960s and most of the 1970s as a time when experiments in experience-based learning struggled to overcome old stigmas associated with programs of "apostolic works" and "field work" which were peripheral to the curriculum and exploited seminarians as "cheap help."[1] The emphasis shifted to what can be taught on the field and to training professional people to render effective supervision there. Yet surprisingly little has been done to develop and evaluate training programs for supervisors among the practical disciplines in theological education.

In this chapter we will examine an experiment in training supervisors for field education at Louisville Presbyterian Theological Seminary during 1967–68.[2] Our program placed students in diverse settings of ministry for fourteen to sixteen hours a week during the academic year. In each field, a pastor/supervisor was responsible for overseeing the seminarian's experience. Our experiment sought to determine whether a relatively brief period of training for these pastors could significantly upgrade the character of their supervision. We will consider (1) the adaptation of our model for supervision to this task, (2) the structure of training built upon it, and (3) the research conducted to evaluate the results.

The State of the Art

Field education has proven notoriously difficult to supervise. On the one hand, there is the need to develop competent supervision on the field among personnel of varied professional backgrounds and interests. On the other is the continual concern to integrate the content of the theological curriculum into the teaching/learning process so that students are encouraged to "think theologically" about what they do. The issues remain the same across the years, although the buzz words to describe them change from time to time. For example, the term "think theologically" was ours. More recently, the task may be one of doing "theological reflection," making a "pastoral diagnosis or assessment," constructing a "praxis-oriented theology," or undertaking "a hermeneutic of engagement."[3]

Three recurring issues are easily discerned. First, there is the matter of who actually does the supervision. It is exceedingly difficult to establish and maintain solid supervisory personnel throughout the diversity of settings in the normal field education program. Some have sought to solve the problem by resting the burden of supervision upon professional supervisors or teaching fellows who are trained members of the seminary staff.[4] At the time of our project, the Yale In-Parish Training Program had just discarded the interposed specialist approach because this threatened the centrality of the pastor as a model, committing themselves to train ministers on the field in the teaching/ supervisory role.[5] We followed suit, believing that a clinical model required supervisors who were engaged in the actual practice of what they were supervising.[6] I am still to witness a permanent and successful supervisory program conducted by external specialists who are not actively engaged in the same tasks of ministry as their supervisees.

The second issue is how the greater body of knowledge in the theological curriculum is integrated into the teaching/learning experience on the field. This has always been a poser. In effect, we are asking field education to accomplish something that is not achieved anywhere else in the seminary curriculum. At the time of our experiment, Union Seminary in New York was undertaking a promising program involving selected faculty members in regular supervision and integration of classroom work through a cooperative seminar of supervisory training with participating pastors of churches.[7] It was abandoned shortly thereafter, as was a similar seminar involving faculty and students at our own seminary a few years ago. The same goals were present in the Boston experiment in Theological Education and Urban Mission involving persons trained in particular disciplines like Old Testament, philosophical theology, or Christian ethics in "team teaching" on the field.[8] They report difficulties similar to those encountered in these other experiments. Academicians trained to teach in conventional ways often lack the aptitude or willingness to engage in an enterprise that requires so much planning and negotiation. The resulting confusion produces its fair share of resistance on the part of professors who are used to an educational model that operates systematically and in a more rational and orderly manner. We still await some final word on this matter of how to integrate our theological thinking with our practice on the field. Our experiment sought to vest the responsibility for making this happen in the supervisory relationship on the field, through the kind of clinical reflection our model requires.

A third issue is where we undertake field education. Recently, a great deal of emphasis has been placed on the context in which it is done.[9] The organizational system—the people who serve and are served in it, together with the surrounding environment—exerts a profound impact on shaping the student's view of mission and style of ministry. A tension emerges between training students in carefully selected experimental environments and placing them in more traditional settings of ministry where the quality of engagement may not be so intense. Those who argue for a contextual emphasis want to train students where new ideas emerge readily, for instance, where they may hammer out a "theology of urban mission" working with female and male, black and white, lay and ordained persons, theological professors and street people confronting the "crisis of the city."[10] Those who place students in more conventional expressions of church life point out the futility of adapting beginning ministers to costly forms of experimental ministry for which it is unlikely they will receive a call, at least in the immediate future. Better to wrestle realistically with the same issues in the traditional settings toward which most are bound.

At our school, as at most, we have never been faced with the choice. Economic necessity has always dictated a "both and" situation in which the lack of resources to go entirely experimental always requires conventional placements for a majority of students. The supervisors we trained were representative of the great diversity in background and settings of most field education programs. They ranged from pastors of suburban, inner-city, and small-town churches to an Episcopalian canon supervising students in an experimental lay ministry where they worked in "secular" jobs, a Catholic priest supervising a student in a coffeehouse ministry in a black community of the "west end," and a lay leader directing a neighborhood council project sponsoring a group of students working to restore a deteriorating downtown area just across the river.

The training program was conducted over a two-week period at the seminary and was followed by a period of six weeks of supervised supervision in which all supervisors submitted regular audio or video recordings of their work for individual attention. The staff of clinically trained supervisors who conducted the program included myself; Grayson Tucker, who was then professor of church administration and director of field education; George Bennett and James Faucette, who were CPE supervisors and adjunct professors at the seminary; and Carleton Riddick, who was a visiting administrator while completing his doctoral studies at the University of Louisville.

The Model Applied

Central to the experiment was an effort to make use of the conceptual tools of the theological curriculum in the supervisory process, so as to make the teaching/learning process on the field an integral part of our whole educational enterprise. This involved addressing the tasks of ministry that are encompassed by the "practical field" of theological studies. Our clinical model was easily adapted to the traditional "offices" or "roles" of ministry and we felt compelled to follow them, since they still dominated the organization of the "practical curriculum" in our school. Twenty years later, when I sent the article containing our original model to current professors in the practical field asking for suggestions to improve it, none were forthcoming. John McClure, who teaches preaching and worship, made the following candid observation:

> You could, of course, "slice" parish experience differently, seeing professional ministry not in terms of *roles* but in terms of "perspectives" (Hiltner), "fields" (or Nichols, via Victor Turner), etc. As progressive as other models may be, it is still true that our Seminary curriculum and local parish perception are organized along lines of "offices," "functions," or "roles." In Field Education, we are probably better off to limit our supervision to these things, rather than trying to supervise students' "perspectives" or interaction in various "fields," and so on.[11]

The adapted model for supervision of ministry is shown in Figure 17-1. It received unanimous acceptance among our professors in the practical field as a workable structure for theological reflection upon concrete patterns of ministry in their respective disciplines. The response by Hal Warheim, our professor of prophetic ministry, was representative:

I have read the article which you want to "revisit" and find it very useful and relevant to supervision of Prophetic Ministry as it stands. It presents a model which I want to encourage my supervisors to employ and adapt to the specific objectives which the PM program pursues. I have asked Dot to give me extra copies of this piece for the PM supervisors and plan to discuss it with them at a future meeting this spring. There are, of course, special "wrinkles" to supervising students in PM, but they can be comprehended by your model without discussing the specifics.[12]

This strengthens our original premise that good supervisory procedures hold their essential character from one discipline or perspective of ministry to another. (See Figure 17-1.)

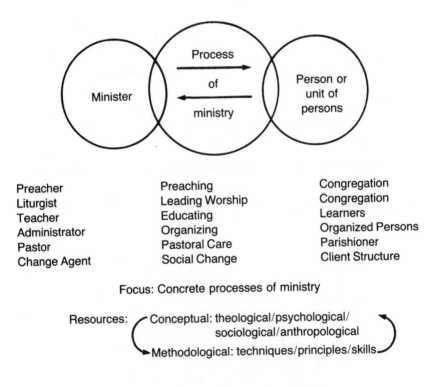

Preacher	Preaching	Congregation
Liturgist	Leading Worship	Congregation
Teacher	Educating	Learners
Administrator	Organizing	Organized Persons
Pastor	Pastoral Care	Parishioner
Change Agent	Social Change	Client Structure

Focus: Concrete processes of ministry

Resources: Conceptual: theological/psychological/ sociological/anthropological
Methodological: techniques/principles/skills

Figure 17-1. The Supervision of Ministry

Definition

As it has been defined in chapter 3, supervision is an extended conversation at regular intervals in which the student and a qualified supervisor commit themselves *to reflect upon the concrete processes of ministry* in which the student is engaged in an effort *to focus all available resources* on the student's *personal development in specific roles of ministry.* Its structure is depicted in Figure 17-1.

The larger circle at the center of the diagram depicts the focus of the supervisory conversation. Supervision has its inception in a detailed analysis of a particular process of ministry. The six areas of ministry shown in Figure 17-1 represent the major offices or functions of the parish minister around which practical teaching in the theological school is usually organized. Whether the minister is functioning as a preacher attempting to communicate the character of the Christian faith in the context of worship, as an administrator attempting to organize a particular phase of congregational ministry, or as a social change agent undertaking mission within a larger client structure within the surrounding community, the same fundamental structure of supervision may be exercised.

Essential Elements

There are a number of elements that are essential in order to make this supervisory model effective. At least five things are implied in its adoption.

1. The supervisee agrees to present the particular series of events that transpired in a *concrete process of ministry.* Various methods for doing this range from simple recall and reconstruction to the presentation of narrative accounts, process notes, case studies, or audio and video tape recordings of a given instance of ministry, such as teaching a class, conducting a meeting, or counseling with a person.

2. Supervision is a *reflective discipline.* It begins with a question: "What went on?" Through reconstructing the sequence of events in a given process of ministry, supervisees begin to re-think the character of their involvement with objectivity and distance. The supervisor functions somewhat like a mirror, re-flecting as accurately as possible the image of what is seen. Supervisors may spot possibilities, responses, attitudes, missed opportunities, blind spots, inconsistencies, and incongruencies which can be reflected with great benefit to the supervisee. In good supervision, supervisees strengthen their own capacity for self-evaluation in a way that will enable them to continue the process on their own. Its realistic value is measured in terms of what the supervisory conversation yields in the form of immediate alternatives, different approaches, and better operations of ministry in the present context.

3. Supervision is interested in *personal development* only with reference to a *specific role in ministry.* The diagram of our supervisory model depicts this by shading the elliptical area of overlap between the larger supervisory circle in the center designating the process of ministry, and the smaller circle at the left representing what is internal to the minister. Supervisory conversations are legitimately concerned with these concepts of the minister's personality that are operative and significant in understanding the given process of ministry at hand. The minister's own feelings, problems, strengths, attitudes, or inadequacies are a vital part of the data in any sequence of events. Growth and change are inevitably sought in this reflective process, as in all good educational procedures. But supervision is distinguished from counseling or psychotherapy by confining itself to seeking personal changes in the supervisee only as they enhance that person's performance in a specific role of ministry. Concerns with the origin and management of personal problems are to be worked through in a more appropriate context for therapy.

4. A similar focus is involved in considering the *person* or *unit of persons receiving ministry.* Supervision is concerned with the area of elliptical overlap into the central circle representing the process of ministry, not the remaining area of the circle to the right in the diagram. It studies persons and their needs for the expressed purpose of addressing a particular ministry to them. In an instance of teaching or pastoral care or social change, it is essential to know something of the psychological and sociological makeup of the recipients. These must be carefully considered in evaluating ministry, framing strategy, and understanding the processes of interactions involved. When we go beyond this to concentrate on the study of a number of persons or institutional units of persons per se, we are entering the domain of the psychology of religion or the sociology of the religion or some related discipline and departing from that of supervised field education.

5. This reflective process presupposes *conceptual tools* from the body of the *theological curriculum.* In a given instance of preaching, appropriate tools from biblical criticism, theology, hermeneutics, and philosophy may be coupled with a grasp of communication theory in assessing what went on. In an instance of pastoral care, a knowledge of what transpired may follow upon the use of appropriate tools from the theory of pastoral care, the psychodynamics of human relationships, developmental and systemic understandings of the human life cycle, and particular theological doctrines that emerge in the process. When some form of social action is under consideration, the

appropriate tools may be from the field of Christian social ethics and such sociological concepts as social class, economics, power, and change. If field education provides real clinical or laboratory dimensions to the resources taught in the classroom, the supervisor must be familiar with these resources. Supervision is incomplete until it has brought the full impact of one's theological resources to bear upon the situation at hand, affording the opportunity for *a genuine integration of belief, theory, concept, and action.*

The Training Program

Several considerations went into designing the supervisory training program upon this model. Foremost was a commitment that the method of training should be consonant with the teaching/learning process of supervision itself. In effect, this meant that our task as a seminary staff was to supervise supervisors in their supervision. All seminars took on the character of working sessions in group supervision, requiring teaching personnel to model their own materials. The conceptual presentations in these sessions were put into position papers and distributed for reading before the trainees arrived. This normally freed the group to spend a short period discussing the content and to use its time working with the actual process of a given supervisory conversation in order to test and apply it. All reflection upon the supervisory process itself was done through the use of audio and video recordings of segments of the trainees' own relationship with their students. While on campus, each supervisor was encouraged to make at least one videotape of a supervisory conversation for use in this way. Planned recording in various areas of ministry permitted us to select significant segments for illustration, application, and analysis in keeping with key seminar themes. Using current material from each participant's own supervision greatly heightened their involvement and afforded an immediate opportunity to make use of what was learned.

The conceptual materials given out to supervisors fell into three natural areas: (1) the supervisory relationship, which was described through the model and various "process tools" to assist everyone in understanding its implementation, such as different types of supervisory responses, the role of confrontation, recognizing resistance, and evaluation; (2) conceptual tools from the operation-centered disciplines—such as Christian education, church administration, pastoral care, prophetic ministries, and homiletics—which could be employed in supervision to comprehend a particular instance of ministry that had been brought for reflection; and (3) conceptual tools from the more "classical disciplines"—such as biblical theology, systematic theology, historical theology, and philosophy of religion—which formed the basic frame of reference out of which "theological thinking" takes shape for the minister.

The first two types of content fit well into the supervision seminars we have described. Various professors led the seminar in applying their conceptual materials to an appropriate segment of supervision recorded on videotape, dealing with ministry from their perspective. For example, the professor of worship and preaching set forth basic tools for analyzing communication patterns in public worship. The seminar visited the church where one of the students under supervision led worship, met afterward with a selected group of laypersons to ascertain their response to what happened, and then viewed the pastor/supervisor's work with the student on videotape, employing their conceptual tools together with the entire backlog of the experience. Repeatedly, we witnessed that the acquisition of such concepts as "sender and receiver," "encoding" and "decoding" messages, the "meeting of meanings," or even the "hermeneutic principle" depended upon the carefully timed discovery of their value in understanding what was going on. The entire design was to enable the pastor/supervisor on the field to employ the same conceptual apparatus used in the classroom to heighten concurrent learning in both settings.

The third type of content—conceptual tools from the classical disciplines—did not fit the supervision seminars so unambiguously. In one sense this content was omnipresent in all the operation-centered disciplines. But it was not present in the form and structure taught in the classroom. To design working seminars on the use of conceptual tools from biblical, theological, historical, and philosophical disciplines did not seem feasible for many reasons, not the least of which was the reluctance of faculty to undertake them. Instead, we employed the standard "Louisville Scholars Seminars" offered to visiting pastors for several years, designed to update persons in recent developments in a field. No effort to force correlation with current practices of supervision was made. The idea was to permit this to happen naturally when and where it would. To experiment in developing the use of theological constructs in supervision, we instituted a *unit of concentration* plan where supervisors were given four key books in any basic course elected by their students to read concurrently and search for natural emergence of the material within supervision. This plan remained in operation for a number of years and was one of the longer-lasting elements in the training program. Other than favorable comments made on it, we were never able to assess its value in terms of concrete theological integration for supervisor and student.

Integral to the entire program was the continuing focus on the actual relationships of participating supervisors to their students. Division of the trainees into groups of two or three under the supervision of a staff member permitted all participants to make a careful evaluation of their own work and to follow closely the recorded work of one or two others. The groups met two to three times each week when the supervisors were on campus and once a week for six weeks afterward. An interesting development came when one of this author's groups asked to include their students in what they were doing during the follow-up period. The give-and-take between three supervisors and their students regarding such things as who was evading what, where the conversation accelerated or broke down, and what was helpful and what was not proved to be of real value in cementing supervisory bonds and commitment.

Some Keys in the Teaching-Learning Process

Several key points in the teaching and learning of supervision emerged from this experience. Perhaps the most important thing is the extreme caution one must exercise in saying exactly how supervision should be carried out. This is not an appeal to some mystery in its processes but the frank recognition that no two persons are alike and that no two persons should be forced into the same mold in working with others. This accounts for much of the reticence to define supervision among the helping professions and the tendency to regard it as an "art" rather than a discipline. Beyond the general guidelines of our model, every effort was made to grant freedom to each supervisor to discover his or her own unique style for doing supervision.

Structure

From the beginning, it was evident that the way one structures supervision is crucial to implementing its mutual contract to give and receive help. A firm commitment to a regular period each week in an office or place of work proved essential. Moves toward informality and casual meetings inevitably represented an effort to evade the basic commitment of supervisees to present their work for examination by their supervisors. The three types of supervisory contracts advanced in chapter 3 provided the necessary framework:

1. *Administrative contracts* contained procedures mutually agreed upon for conducting regular supervision and evaluation. They also spelled out specific *performance goals* that had to do with accomplishing selected programs, purposes, phases of ministry and tasks, and so forth.

2. *Professional contracts* contained the personal goals that had to do with the supervisee's own development of professional competence in various areas of ministry. This included specific areas of personal growth and change these skills required in order to do more effective preaching or teaching or administrating.

3. *Psychological contracts* had to do with what each party needed from the other in order to establish and maintain the working alliance of supervision. We encouraged supervisors and students to reflect regularly upon the quality of their work together.

The final evaluation organized itself around an appraisal of the supervisee's progress in each of these three areas. Its value was found to stand in direct proportion to the clarity with which the initial contracting had been established and kept in focus throughout the training period. We also learned early on that the only way to teach effective contracting to supervisors was to engage in it effectively with them.

Process

Developing among supervisors the capacity to implement the reflective processes of supervision without harnessing them with wooden restrictions is a delicate task. One seminar was spent presenting five basic types of supervisory responses adapted from Elias Porter's categories.[13] These proved helpful in assessing the intent and appropriateness of a given response. Often supervisors could break out of a rut and become more flexible in accomplishing their conversational purpose through implementing their basic intent in language of their own choice. At least one supervision seminar was devoted to identifying them in a video-recorded conversation.

1. P—*Probing.* A response that indicates that the supervisor's intent is to seek further information, to provoke further discussion along a certain line, to query. He or she has in some way implied that the supervisee ought or might profitably develop or discuss a point further.

2. U—*Understanding.* A response that indicates that the supervisor's intention is to so respond as in effect to ask the

supervisee whether the supervisor understands correctly what the supervisee is "saying," how the supervisee "feels" about it, how it "strikes" the supervisee, how the supervisee "sees" it.

3. E—*Evaluative.* A response that indicates that the supervisor has made a judgment of relative goodness, appropriateness, effectiveness, and rightness. He or she has in some way implied what the supervisee might or ought to do, grossly or subtly.

4. I—*Interpretive.* A response that indicates that the supervisor's intent is to teach, to impart meaning to the supervisee, to show him or her. He or she has in some way implied what the supervisee might or ought to think, grossly or subtly.

5. S—*Supportive.* A response that indicates that the supervisor's intent is to reassure, to reduce the supervisee's intensity of feeling, to pacify. He or she has in some way implied that the supervisee need not feel as he or she does.

Other attempts have been made to classify supervisory interventions. One of the more helpful ones is advanced by C. Loganville, E. Hardy, and U. Delworth for supervision in clinical psychology.[14] Their list includes (1) facilitative interventions creating a supportive atmosphere, (2) confrontive interventions, (3) conceptual interventions, which offer theoretical understanding, (4) prescriptive interventions providing a plan of action, and (5) catalytic interventions, which seek to promote change in the supervisee. Contemporary presentations to supervisors in training may contain one or more of these models, but I would heartily recommend the retention of Porter's five categories for their simplicity and clarity.

The Use of Videotape Recordings

We found that videotape provides the most productive medium for supervisory reflection because of their added dimension of preserving bodily postures, expressions, and movements in a conversational relationship. Often we viewed tapes on a stop-start basis, permitting members of the seminar to interrupt and offer reflective comment on the process. This afforded the opportunity for immediate reaction to content or interaction ("Why did you pass that up? He wanted to tell you about it"; or "You're both leaning back, bored to death, avoiding each other"). The leader can introduce simple teaching procedures like *possibility* ("What other things could the supervisor have done here?"—"You might have 'probed' a little to find out what she meant by that," or "I think he needed some 'support' instead of your negative reaction; he knows it didn't come off"), or *prediction* ("How will this affect the interaction? What will happen next?"—"You are going to take his problem away from him again and solve it for him," or "You are going to change the subject and leave her hanging").

We also adopted the procedure of viewing segments of tape five to fifteen minutes in length and assigning trainees various listening roles. For example, one group could observe from the standpoint of the student, another the supervisor's responsiveness, another the nonverbal interaction, another the use of conceptual tools as resources, and so forth. It proved essential to allow two to three times as long for discussion as it takes to view the tape. In such a training program today, I would heartily recommend the addition of live supervision of supervision in the manner described in chapter 11.

The Therapeutic Dimension

The therapeutic dimension of supervision presented itself repeatedly through the necessity of dealing with personal impasses that emerge among students as they seek to develop skills in various areas of ministry. Learning problems similar to those discussed in chapter 2 were in evidence in the acquisition of skills throughout the whole range of pastoral tasks. Students followed inevitable tendencies to act and respond in ways that were determined not by the needs of the context of ministry but by characteristic and inappropriate patterns from their own past. Present were what Thomas Klink termed "characterologically cross-grained experiences," in which students were involved in relationships where their habitual mode of responding was inappropriate but an appropriate mode seemed to transgress deeply ingrained traits of character.[15] Similar patterns emerged around a recurrent theme throughout many areas of ministry in which the student functioned. For example, student A tended to be passive and avoided conflict. He evidenced a reluctance to assert himself in managing his youth group, an indecisiveness or timidity in conducting public worship, a tendency to avoid emotional involvement in his pastoral visits, and a reluctance to take initiative in the supervisory conversation itself. Supervision invariably became focused around student A's personal impasse as a recurring problem emerging in various phases of ministry. Seminar sessions were devoted to identifying, contracting, and working for change around such areas of personal growth that emerged in supervision. A frequent question among trainees when we presented the concept of personal impasses was: "Does everybody we supervise have to have a problem?" Our stock answer became: "Yes, unless they are perfect, in which case there is no need for supervision."

The Working Alliance of Supervision

A similar stance was taken in addressing resistance in supervision which necessitates the task of reflecting upon the dimension of its working alliance. Conceptual tools surrounding what we described in chapter 2 as *problems about learning* and the universality of parallel process were introduced. Our efforts were complicated by the fact that resistance to supervision was by no means a monopoly of students. Supervisors in training were found to respond just as evasively through a reluctance to exercise authority or to risk exposure or involvement or disapproval or inadequacy, and so forth.

We found the concept of supervisory games to be one of the more effective tools to address unwitting conspiracies between supervisors and students to resist the task at hand. We drew upon Eric Berne's concept of a psychological game as a series of ongoing complimentary transactions that progress to well-defined payoff that is predictable.[16] The payoff is a repetitive outcome in an interactional system between persons that is undeclared and undesirable. Berne's theory still forms a crisp description of what other systems theorists would call repetitive sequences, or tendencies toward patterns of recursion and redundancy in marital and family relationships.

In our seminars, a primitive anthology of supervisory games was developed to which each group of trainees managed to add. For example, "Fine" was a simple avoidance category game. The student consistently entered supervision saying in diverse ways that everything was going "fine." The problem lay in finding any problems with which to work. If the supervisor responded with some form of "good Joe" ("I like you—you like me—everything is fine"), or "friend" ("No, I wouldn't ruin our beautiful relationship by supervising you"), the supervision is firmly disestablished. Utimately both parties become resentful and disillusioned with the process. The antithesis lay in supervisors' identifying some of Fine's *learning problems* and if necessary assigning and receiving reports on some task they know will not go "fine."

An example of a game in the evasion category is "Sick." Here students manage to present so many personal problems with "the ministry" or their spouse or their "call" or their personal lives that the supervisor really cannot expect them to perform responsibly. One is "sick." If the supervisor responds as a nurturing parent, permitting the appraisal of performance consistently to go by the board in efforts to "help" or "support" the student, the two never quite get around to the task of supervision. The payoff for the student is release from the requirement to perform, accompanied by a lingering sense of adequacy. For the supervisor, the role of "Wonderful Counselor" can be claimed but with an underlying sense of uneasiness about its effectiveness. The antithesis for "Sick" is to refer the student to whatever counseling is necessary and get on with the job of supervision, terminating the relationship if the student is actually "too sick" to function.

Often naming the game was sufficient for the supervisor to identify some recurring block in the relationship and move it to a deeper level. No textbook games were imported into our proceedings. Each impasse in the working alliance of supervision received its own particular name. For example, "You're the Super" was a term coined to describe a manipulation-category game in which one student managed to manipulate his supervisor so as to remain dependent upon him and repeatedly get him to think for him. Inevitably his supervisor would get caught up in giving the answer, locating the resource, making the judgment, or offering the interpretation, in spite of himself assuming a role he characterized as "Big Daddy" ("Do as I say, my son, and all will be well with you"). This particular supervisor was able to spot seven such transactions in a recorded session of supervision. Through actively labeling the student's invitations to pontificate and his own responses, he was able to practice the antithesis during the next supervisory hour. He quit playing the role of "Big Daddy."

A common testimony among participants in our program was that the capacity to engage in confrontation is the most difficult thing to develop among untrained supervisors. Perhaps this roots in a rather pervasive need to please and be loved among pastors. Here the concept of supervisory games paid real dividends. It added a note of levity to the grim threat of actually confronting what is going on in the trainee's own relationships. The spirit of the supervisory group is a crucial factor. If it becomes one of a solemn hunt for inadequacy and weakness in one another, little is accomplished. We found the saving grace of humor to add a distance to the threat of exposure that reduces anxiety. Moreover, it furnishes an appropriate expression to the pleasurable discovery of insight.

Theological Reflection

The kind of theological reflection we sought to develop in supervision had one important difference from the kind of discussions common to most seminary settings. In the classroom or the bull session the exchange is usually of theological "positions" and profitably cast in some form of debate. In supervision we were concerned not with intellectual mastery but with concrete identification of beliefs operative in a given sequence of events. Very often one's formal "position" remained disastrously detached from the theology espoused in a sermon or in what was said to a rebellious teenager or in how one organized a community action group. The task of theological discussion in supervision was to relate belief and action, concept and concrete operation. This proved to be a delicate task. One common supervisory game was "Theology" in which a student and a supervisor permitted their relationship to be converted into a debate of theological positions unrelated to the given process of ministry at hand. Sometimes the student returned to declare that the pastor and the church were hopelessly rutted in institutional tradition, while the pastor wanted to know what we were teaching at seminary these days. Usually, something else entirely was at stake. It had to do with the threat of serious supervision or actually becoming responsible in what one believes and does.

The Effects of Supervisory Training

The effectiveness of our training program was measured by a Supervisory Assessment Questionnaire which we constructed in accord with our model. The questionnaire was designed to detect different perceptions of supervision in eight basic areas:

1. Structure: setting, definition of goals, etc.
2. Clarity of roles and contract
3. Content Area A: specific areas of ministry dealt with
4. Content Area B: theoretical-theological tools employed in process
5. Methodology: normal way of working at the reflective process
6. Attitude toward the relationship
7. Attitude toward the supervisor as a person
8. Conceptual understanding of the supervisory process

The instrument included fifty questions, ten in areas 4 and 5 because of their centrality to the model, five in each of the other areas. A forced choice was presented among four possible answers to each question rated in order of decreasing preference by five neutral judges. It should be emphasized that we were not attempting to measure the effects of supervision upon the functioning of the student but rather to assess different perceptions of the supervisory relationship by students engaged in it.

A sample question in area 5—methodology—is given below with the rating of the judges in order of preference. Answer 4 is more germane to the reflective process of our model and its stress upon developing the capacity to continue this on one's own.

When we are talking about what I should do in a given situation:

		Rating
1.	I can always find out what my supervisor would do by asking him.	3
2.	My supervisor will normally ask me to make up my own mind.	2
3.	My supervisor will usually tell me what to do.	4
4.	My supervisor will normally work toward getting out all the possibilities.	1

The instrument was administered to the students under three groups of supervisors. The students in Group I received supervision from accredited supervisors with the Association for Clinical Pastoral Education in a mental institution (Central State Hospital), a general hospital (Louisville Medical Center), and a correctional institution (Kentucky State Reformatory). Since our model was adapted from basic understandings of supervision in such clinical settings, we anticipated the highest measurement of supervision among students in this group. Group II consisted of students serving under pastor/supervisors who had gone through our supervisory training program at the seminary. Group III was a control group made up of students with pastor/supervisors who had not received training. Of students currently under supervision, eleven were selected at random from each group, making a total number of thirty-three subjects.

Scores were given each student in each of the eight areas of supervision. Carlton Riddick undertook their statistical analysis. The scores were standardized in terms of the percentage of optimal answers in each area. The statistical design took the form of a 3×8 factorial design, with subjects nested within groups and repeated measures on each subject in each area. No attempt was made to validate the questionnaire, which was a proper concern for future research.

An analysis of variance with planned comparisons of the three groups was made. Further tests were conducted concerning the interaction of the areas and groups. The variables entering the analysis involved the three groups (I—Clinical Supervisors, II—Trained Supervisors, and III—Untrained Supervisors) and the eight areas of supervision listed above. The differential effects on the student's perception of supervision by (1) groups, (2) areas, and (3) combination of groups and areas is shown in Table 17-1. There was a real difference between the groups (F=5.39, 2 and 30 df, p < .01). Further tests were made on the group means, using the Newman-Keuls procedure, shown in Table 17-2. The results indicated there was a statistical difference (p < .05) between Groups I and III and Groups II and III.

Table 17-1

Source	df	MS	F
Areas (A)	7	.1376	14.9565*
Groups (G)	2	.1690	6.3295*
A x G	14	.0236	2.5652*
A x subjects	210	.0092	. . .
Subjects within groups	30	.0267	. . .

*.01 level of significance

Table 17-2

	Group III	Group II	Group I
Group III		*	*
Group II			. . .

There was no significant difference between Groups I and II. The combination of particular areas within the groups also shows a significant effect (F=1.23, 14 and 210 df, p < .01). The differences are most easily seen in Figure 17-2. Group I measured highest, Group II next, and Group III lowest. The shaded section of the figure depicts the area of difference between the trained and untrained supervisors in field education.

Discussion

The results indicated significant differences between the type of supervision that students received from trained and untrained supervisors. As predicted, the questionnaire measured a generally higher quality of supervision, according to our model, for supervisors in Groups I (clinically trained) and II

Percentages

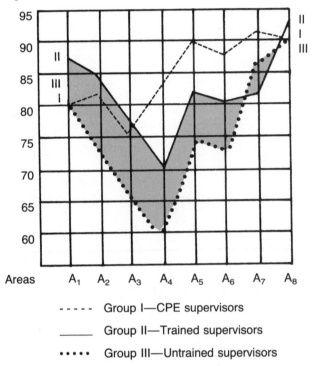

- - - - -   Group I—CPE supervisors

_____   Group II—Trained supervisors

• • • • •   Group III—Untrained supervisors

Figure 17-2. Differences Between Groups by Areas

(seminary trained) than for Group III (untrained). The results suggest that a supervisory training program such as we conducted can produce a distinct difference in the character of supervision that students receive within a relatively brief period of time.

Although the CPE supervisors tended to produce a slightly higher measurement overall, there was no significant statistical difference between them and the supervisors we trained. This could have been due to the insensitivity of our instrument in detecting certain dimensions of depth and interaction in supervision in the clinical setting. Since our instrument was designed to detect performance in accord with our model in the broader practice of supervision in field education, we probably omitted significant elements in CPE proper. The results do suggest, however, that field education supervisors may be trained in such a program to alter patterns of supervision significantly in the direction of the quality of supervision offered in clinical training.

Figure 17-2 presents the differences between the three groups in the areas the questionnaire measured. There was not much difference in the way people structured supervision (area 1). Whether trained or untrained, most met in an appropriate place with the same frequency and amount of time. Differences began to appear in area 2—clarity of roles and contract. This was the only operational area in which the seminary-trained supervisors measured substantially higher than those in CPE. Perhaps the particular attention given to this in our training program was responsible.

The most significant differences between trained and untrained groups appeared in areas 3, 4, 5, and 6. These measured the core of the supervisory process: the content of the conversation in terms of areas of ministry dealt with, the theoretical-theological tools employed, the basic methodology used in supervision, and the student's attitude toward the supervisory relationship. The training program was designed to effect changes precisely in these areas of concrete supervisory operations.

Of interest was the total lack of significant difference in area 8—the conceptual understanding of supervision. Every other area attempted to measure what the students perceived to be going on in supervision. Area 8 measured only what students understood intellectually about its function. The fact that all three groups scored approximately the same indicated that our process of orientation to field education inculcated an equal conceptional understanding of supervision in everyone. Whatever changes the training program effected lay in how supervision was implemented, not understood. This underlined the need for such training programs to integrate actual practice with intellectual understandings which, if left to themselves, prove inadequate to the task.

While not statistically significant, the scores in area 7 are worthy of note. This area measured students' attitudes toward the supervisor as a person. It could be said that students "liked" our untrained supervisors better than those we trained. One possible explanation may be found in the emphasis we placed on confrontation during the supervisory training program.

Since most persons prefer not to be confronted with their inadequacies, some resentment of the changing relationship may well have been registered by Group II students. If so, the rating could express a tribute to the developing security of the trained supervisors, who became less concerned about "being liked" and more concerned with doing a responsible job.

In Retrospect

This experiment demonstrated the possibility of effecting significant change toward a clinical model of supervision among relatively unskilled pastor/supervisors in field education. By implication, more effective supervision in many educational settings may be developed in comparably short periods of time. The seventy-two hours of presentations, seminars, and supervised supervision that we undertook over an eight-week period is probably minimal. As our own personnel changed, this investment in time became eroded. Training at the level we conceived of it initially was diluted and eventually reduced to a point beyond recognition.

If such a program is worth doing, it is worth doing well. In field education, this demands a solid commitment of time and energy on the part of its director and supporting colleagues across the years. Annual repetition is necessary as trained pastor/supervisors move and others take their place. Such an investment is not without a number of benefits for both seminary and church. Lasting ties were created across institutional boundaries that often separate us.

Those of us from the seminary who participated as professors and clinical supervisors invariably grew in our own teaching and grasp of concrete problems in the church and world around. Working pastors came to feel an integral part of theological education. And it did not come as a surprise when some of the supervisors we trained registered profound appreciation for the way the experience had changed their way of working in their own congregation. Some form of mutual supervision is the spark of life that sustains creativity among members of a multiple staff. And some form of supervision is the key to a professional minister's enabling a whole congregation to discover its mission through the diverse ministries of its people.

NOTES

1. G. I. Hunter, *Supervision and Education—Formation for Ministry* (Cambridge, Mass.: Episcopal Divinity School, 1982), p. 51.

2. These materials were originally presented in D. A. Steere, "An Experiment in Supervisory Training," *Journal of Pastoral Care,* Dec. 1969, pp. 202–217.

3. See Hunter, *Supervision and Education,* pp. 83–103; P. W. Preyser, *The Minister as Diagnostician* (Philadelphia: Westminster Press, 1976); W. J. Close, "What Does It Mean to Think Theologically," in *Theological Field Education: A Collection of Key Resources* (Association for Theological Field Education, Kansas City, Mo., II, Jan. 1979), pp. 78–81; and J. L. Seymour, "Placement Design: Defining the Context for Field Education," in *Theological Field Education: A Collection of Key Resources* (Association for Theological Field Education, Kansas City, Mo., III Jan. 1981), p. 218.

4. See J. Furnas, "A Search for Adequate Supervision," in "Seventh Biennial Consultation on Seminary Field Work" (Austin Presbyterian Theological School, Austin, Tex., Feb. 15–16, 1963, mimeographed), pp. 57–63; or C. H. Reid, "The Unstructured Group Approach to Field Work Evaluation at Union Theological Seminary, New York," in "Sixth Biennial Consultation on Seminary Field Work" (Vanderbilt University Divinity School, Nashville, Tenn., Jan. 20–21, 1961, mimeographed), pp. 39–51.

5. R. J. Becker, "The In-Parish Pastoral Studies Program at Yale: The Report of an Experiment 1960–66," in "Ninth Biennial Consultation on Seminary Field Education" (Christian Theological Seminary, Indianapolis, Ind., Jan. 19–21, 1967, mimeographed), pp. 37–38.

6. See T. W. Klink, "Supervision," *Theological Education* 3:176–217 (1966), who insisted on the same practitioner role for supervisors.

7. See R. T. Handy, "Involvement of Entire Faculty in Professional Education," in "Report of the Ninth Biennial Conference of the Association of Seminary Professors in the Practical Fields" (Wesley Theological Seminary, Washington, D.C., June 6–8, 1966, mimeographed), pp. 25–34.

8. See Hunter, *Supervision and Education,* pp. 57, 58.

9. See Seymour, "Placement Design," pp. 218–220; Hunter, *Supervision and Education,* pp. 51–66.

10. See Hunter, *Supervision and Education,* pp. 52–59.

11. J. McClure, personal memorandum dated March 15, 1988.

12. H. Warheim, personal memorandum dated March 7, 1988.

13. E. H. Porter, *An Introduction to Therapeutic Counseling* (Boston: Houghton Mifflin Co., 1950), p. 201.

14. C. Loganville, E. Hardy, and U. Delworth, "Supervision: A Conceptual Model," *The Counseling Psychologist* 10(1): 32–36 (1982).

15. T. W. Klink, "How Is Supervision Carried Out?" in *Clinical Education for the Pastoral Ministry,* ed. E. E. Bruder and M. L. Barb (Advisory Committee on Clinical Pastoral Education, 1958), p. 109.

16. See E. Berne, *Transactional Analysis in Psychotherapy* (New York: Grove Press, 1961), pp. 98–115.

Contributors

Clarence Barton retired in 1988 as Chief Chaplain at Central State Hospital in Louisville, where he had served for thirty-five years. Clarence has been a consultant to the Kentucky Department of Mental Health, an instructor in Clinical Pastoral Education at Louisville Presbyterian Theological Seminary, and an Adjunct Professor in the Department of Psychology and Religion at Southern Baptist Theological Seminary. He is the dean of CPE supervisors in the Louisville Cluster ACPE.

George F. Bennett died in January 1987 while serving as pastor of the First Presbyterian Church, Dayton, Kentucky. A CPE supervisor at Central State Hospital, George later became Dean of Students at Louisville Presbyterian Theological Seminary and an Adjunct Professor in Pastoral Care and Counseling. George was the author of *When the Mental Patient Comes Home* and *When They Ask for Bread.*

Kathleen Ogden Davis is a Chaplain Supervisor at Frazier Rehabilitation Center in Louisville and an Adjunct Professor in Pastoral Care and Counseling at Louisville Presbyterian Theological Seminary. In addition to being a Presbyterian minister, Kathleen holds a Doctor of Jurisprudence from the University of Louisville School of Law and is a member of the Kentucky Bar Association.

Nancy Fontenot is a Licensed Clinical Social Worker with a private practice in Louisville. An adjunct Professor at Louisville Presbyterian Theological Seminary in Pastoral Care and Counseling, she has directed training programs for the Kentucky Department of Human Resources and the Metropolitan Social Services Department in Louisville. Nancy is a Clinical Teaching Member in the International Transactional Analysis Association, a Member of the American Group Psychotherapy Association, and a ruling elder in the Presbyterian Church (U.S.A.).

Mark Jensen is Associate Director of the Department of Pastoral Care and Director of Pastoral Counseling for East Tennessee Baptist Hospital in Knoxville. He is a member of the American Association of Pastoral Counselors and an Associate Supervisor with the Association for Clinical Pastoral Education. He is currently working on a manuscript for Broadman Press on the discovery of our Christian identity through vocation.

John D. Lentz is Chief Chaplain at Kentucky Correctional Institution for Women at Pewee Valley, Kentucky, and an Adjunct Professor in Pastoral Care and Counseling at Louisville Presbyterian Theological Seminary. John is a Clinical Member of the American Association for Marriage and Family Therapy, a Member of the American Association of Pastoral Counselors, and president of the Kentucky Association for Specialists in Group Work. He is the author of *Effective Handling of Manipulative Persons.*

Carolyn Lindsey is a Marriage and Family Therapist at the Pastoral Counseling and Consultation Center in Louisville. She has a Master's degree in Child Development and Family Relations from Western Kentucky University and is an Adjunct Professor in Pastoral Care and Counseling at Louisville Presbyterian Theological Seminary. Carolyn is an Approved Supervisor in the American Association for Marriage and Family Therapy and is past president of the Kentucky Division of the AAMFT.

Amanda W. Ragland is a candidate for the Doctor of Ministry degree in Marriage and Family Therapy at Louisville Presbyterian Theological Seminary. Her undergraduate degree is in computer engineering at Auburn University, and she is a member of Tau Beta Pi, a national engineering honor society. She is currently a resident intern at Personal Counseling Services, Jeffersonville, Indiana.

Barbara A. Sheehan is a Chaplain Supervisor at St. Elizabeth Medical Center in Covington, Kentucky. A member of the Roman Catholic Sisters of Providence, she holds a Master of Arts in Theology from Xavier University. Before becoming a CPE Supervisor, Barbara taught chemistry, mathematics, religion, and English. She also worked as a medical technologist and in hospital administration. In 1972, she won the Kentucky State Medical Technologist Award for research on blood subtypes in the population of Lexington, Kentucky.

Bruce Skaggs is a Licensed Clinical Social Worker with a private practice in Jeffersonville, Indiana. He is an Adjunct Professor in Pastoral Care and Counseling at Louisville Presbyterian Theological Seminary. Bruce is a Clinical Member of the International Transactional Analysis Association and has served as Dean of Students at Spalding College and as consultant for the Hoosier Valley Economic Opportunity Council.

Alexa Smith is a candidate for the Doctor of Ministry degree in Marriage and Family Therapy at Louisville Presbyterian Theological Seminary. She graduated Magna Cum Laude from West Virginia University and has served as a reporter and editor for the *Times-West Virginian*. Alexa has developed family life education programs with Planned Parenthood of Louisville and is currently a resident intern at the Methodist Counseling Center in Louisville.

David A. Steere is professor of Pastoral Care and Counseling at Louisville Presbyterian Theological Seminary. He is a Certified Supervisor with the Association for Clinical Pastoral Education, a Diplomate with the American Association of Pastoral Counselors, an Approved Supervisor for the American Association for Marriage and Family Therapy, and a Clinical Teaching Member in the International Transactional Analysis Association. He is the author of *Bodily Expressions in Psychotherapy.*

Darryl J. Tiller is staff CPE Supervisor at HCA Presbyterian Hospital in Oklahoma City, Oklahoma. Before going to Oklahoma, he was Chief Chaplain and Director of Clinical Pastoral Education at Luther Luckett Correctional Complex in La-Grange, Kentucky, where he served as a Field Education supervisor at Louisville Presbyterian Theological Seminary. Darryl is a Certified Supervisor with the Association for Clinical Pastoral Education and a member of the American Association of Pastoral Counselors.

Grayson L. Tucker, Jr., is Professor Emeritus of Church Administration and Evangelism at Louisville Presbyterian Theological Seminary. A former dean at that institution, he is a Diplomate in the American Association of Pastoral Counselors and currently serves as a consultant to the Stated Clerk of the General Assembly of the Presbyterian Church (U.S.A.). He is the author of *A Church Planning Questionnaire* and has consulted with congregations of various denominations in its use.

Louis B. Weeks is dean of Louisville Presbyterian Theological Seminary and the Paul Tudor Jones Professor of Church History. He has taught workshops and seminars in educational methodology in more than fifty colleges and seminaries. He is the author and editor of fifteen books, including *Case Studies on Christ and Salvation, Kentucky Presbyterians, To Be a Presbyterian,* and *Making Ethical Decisions.*